ECO-EFFICIENCY
&
GLOBAL JUSTICE

ECO-SUFFICIENCY
&
GLOBAL JUSTICE

WOMEN WRITE POLITICAL ECOLOGY

EDITED BY
ARIEL SALLEH

PLUTO PRESS
www.plutobooks.com

and

First published 2009 by Pluto Press
345 Archway Road, London N6 5AA and
175 Fifth Avenue, New York, NY 10010
www.plutobooks.com

and

Spinifex Press, PO Box 212 (504 Queensberry St)
North Melbourne Vic 3051 Australia
www.spinifexpress.com.au

Distributed in the United States of America exclusively by
Palgrave Macmillan, a division of St. Martin's Press LLC,
175 Fifth Avenue, New York, NY 10010

British Library Cataloguing in Publication Data
A catalogue record for this book is available from the British Library

ISBN   978 0 7453 2864 5   Hardback
ISBN   978 0 7453 2863 8   Paperback (Pluto Press)
ISBN   978 1 876756 71 0   Paperback (Spinifex Press)

Library of Congress Cataloging in Publication Data applied for

This book is printed on paper suitable for recycling and made from fully
managed and sustained forest sources. Logging, pulping and manufacturing
processes are expected to conform to the environmental standards of the
country of origin. The paper may contain up to 70 per cent post consumer
waste.

10   9   8   7   6   5   4   3   2   1

Designed and produced for Pluto Press by
Chase Publishing Services Ltd, Sidmouth, England
Typeset from disk by Stanford DTP Services, Northampton, England
Printed and bound in the European Union by
CPI Antony Rowe, Chippenham and Eastbourne

CONTENTS

PREFACE AND ACKNOWLEDGEMENTS

As I write this, sunlight glistens through morning rain and *casuarinas* bow to a soft north east breeze. Who ever would guess that life on earth is falling into precarity – threatened by global free trade, militarism, climate change, sexual violence, genetic and nano technologies. For this reason, these essays are a call to people who care: community leaders, researchers, students of political ecology, ecological economics, environmental ethics, global studies, movement politics, or critical geography. Others know the call already: activists in the World Social Forum, Via Campesina, Seattle to Brussels Network, or Ecological Debt campaign. The arguments will resonate too, with supporters of *The Commoner* project; with *Green Left Weekly*; with Women in Black, Code Pink, Women and Life on Earth, the World March of Women; and with friends who try to keep big NGOs and party politicians on track. The anthology has its roots in my earlier book *Ecofeminism as Politics*, part of an ongoing project to rethink humanity–nature relations with an embodied materialist epistemology. Here, a group of authors exposes the costs of 'othering' bodies and ecosystems. They show how capitalist globalisation carries forward cultural dualisms, which in turn, sustain primal forms of patriarchal power. Even climate change is gendered and racialised in its causes, effects, and solutions. But gender and ethnicity are not just descriptors of victimhood; far from it, ecological feminists recognise 'difference' as a source of innovative leadership for global alternatives.

Today, as the classic texts in political economy are giving way to political ecology, many scholars are unsure how to turn their human-centred study into a wider nature-oriented one. New conceptual tools are needed for describing the humanity–nature interface, working constructs such as – embodied debt – meta-industrial labour – eco-sufficiency – and metabolic value. At the same time, the transdiscipline of ecological economics – often appropriated as a tool of governance (read social control) – demands special attention. A hybrid of economics and sustainability science, ecological economics was until recently a rather *ad hoc* field, with little epistemological depth or socio-political reflexivity. Nevertheless, some of its leading practitioners are now responding to globalisation and its crises by boldly linking their research to NGO work. This anthology enjoins that transformative agenda, counter-balancing deconstructive critique with reconstructive remedies. It is inspired by life at the peripheries of power, where autonomous and ecologically sound models of economic provisioning are practised. And its authors are convinced that an inclusive definition of global justice will depend on internal capacity building and structural adjustment in the global North. However, a gender literate political ecology requires a broader understanding of human labour than the Marxist paradigm allowed for. That is realised here, in the notion of a meta-industrial class made up of household caregivers, peasants, and indigenous labour. This broad labour focus is necessary, both for analytical purposes, and for building a synergistic strategy within the movement for 'another globalisation'.

Part of my life belongs to the global South, and this, along with the experience of the Earth Summit at Rio in 1992, informs the case being made for postcolonial justice. The chance to participate in the UNCED Prepcom where Agenda 21 was worked out, and eventually in the Brazil meeting itself, turned out to be an incomparable education. This, and grassroots struggles against corporate globalisation in my own neighbourhood, have helped me integrate ecology with women's and indigenous claims for a voice. Other aspects of this book were born during a consultancy to the EU Thematic Network on Sustainability Strategy based in Berlin; others again, through networking with contributors, some of whom are co-editors of the journal *Capitalism Nature Socialism*. Students have been an important stimulus too, especially in Environmental Studies at York University, Canada; in Social Ecology at the University of Western Sydney, Australia; and at the Institute for Women's Studies in the Philippines. In addition,

I am indebted to several institutions for support and recognition through visiting professorships, research and travel grants; in particular, the Humanities and Social Science Council of Taiwan; Linköping University, Sweden; and the Lyman Briggs School of Science at Michigan State University, USA.

Over the past decade, too much of what is called transnational feminism has been dominated by North American writing, and – constrained by the requirements of academia – it has lost political saliency and penetration. Thus, the plan for celebrating a global spectrum of voices ran fast forward when a multi-cultural group of women scholars and activists came together for the symposium on Ecological Feminist Economics at the Ninth Biennial Conference of the International Society for Ecological Economics in New Delhi, December 2006. The enthusiasm of ISEE President Joan Martinez-Alier of the Autonomous University of Barcelona, was critical to the realisation of that special event. A parallel meeting was made possible by Professor Robert Chapman, Director of the Pace Institute for Environmental and Regional Studies, and host of the United States Society for Ecological Economics Conference held in New York, June 2007. Warm thanks are due to both.

Several chapters in this book grew out of these international gatherings; others were invited. And I am grateful to – Autonomedia, *DAWN Informs*, *Gender and Development*, and Inanna, for permission to adapt the following essays to the anthology:

Silvia Federici, 'The Devaluation of Women's Labour': adapted from *Caliban and the Witch: Women, the Body, and Primitive Accumulation*, New York: Autonomedia, 2004.

Gigi Francisco, 'Mainstreaming Trade and Millennium Development Goals' and Peggy Antrobus, 'Mainstreaming Trade and Millennium Development Goals': each adapted from *DAWN Informs*, September 2003.

Marilyn Waring, 'Policy and the Measure of Woman': adapted from 'Counting for Something', *Gender and Development*, 2003, Vol. 11, No. 1, 35–43. Reprinted by permission of the publisher Taylor and Francis Ltd; <www.informaworld.com>.

xii ECO-SUFFICIENCY AND GLOBAL JUSTICE

Ana Isla, 'Who Pays for Kyoto Protocol: Selling Oxygen and Selling Sex?': adapted from 'The Tragedy of the Enclosures' in Genevieve Vaughan (ed.), *Women and the Gift Economy: A Radically Different Worldview is Possible*, Toronto: Inanna, 2007.

Against the grain of conventional wisdom, this anthology puts environmental and social justice questions under the lens of a sex/gendered political ecology, and in doing so, opens up a conversation with political and ecological economists, and even eco-socialists, about hidden levels of meaning in their analyses. The embodied materialist lens is used as an interpretive frame for the book, but I do not want to imply that all authors necessarily subscribe to my own approach. The essays speak for themselves. Together, the authors make a foundational contribution to political ecology, and they certainly challenge the parameters of sustainability science. I value the commitment of those who have given freely of their time to write chapters. And this acknowledgement extends also to Chaone Mallory, Veronika Bennholdt-Thomsen, Maria Mies, Carolyn Merchant, Hilkka Pietila, Vandana Shiva, and our late sister Teresa Brennan – all of whose voices are a presence in this book.

Ariel Salleh
Broken Bay, New South Wales
September 2008

1

ECOLOGICAL DEBT: EMBODIED DEBT

Ariel Salleh

From the World Social Forum in Caracas and Nairobi, to G8 meetings in Gleneagles and Heiligendamm, the call is 'cancel the debt'. For it is now widely understood how World Bank lending policies impoverish communities in the global South by demanding interest repayments many times greater than the sum they have borrowed. The global North recognises that cancelling unpaid interest on so called development loans, removes opportunities for easy capital accumulation; and so, some metropolitan powers are looking for new ways of doing business with the clean, resource rich, non-industrial periphery.[1] But peasants, indigenes, and autonomous grassroots women, are watching them. These diverse groupings formed a loose political alliance at the 1992 Rio Earth Summit, when a new dimension entered international conversations about foreign debt. Corporate leaders and politicians were becoming aware of nature's cycles of purification and renewal through sunshine, soil bacteria, streams, and plant life. To the commercial eye, these free 'environmental services' were potentially valuable; not only in sustaining the very possibility of production and consumption, but as tradeable commodities in themselves. So at the Earth Summit, the global North offered the South a new 'win/win' solution to their foreign debt crisis – 'debt for nature swaps'. The rationale was this: developing countries might be low on cash, but have ample biodiversity for DNA harvesting, and forests for converting carbon waste from industrial regions into breathable oxygen again. At the time, it seemed an appealing idea for big states in the North and small states in the South to negotiate these debt for nature trade offs. The idea soon entered the jargon of international relations and appears in the UN Framework Convention on Climate Change as a Clean Development Mechanism (CDM).

However, activists in the global South, particularly women environmentalists in Ecuador, saw things differently. They turned the North's functionalist analysis of the earth as 'a physical system in equilibrium' into an historical diagnosis of the earth as a social system in dis-equilibrium. For the truth is, that a 500 year long colonisation of South American land and appropriation of natural goods like silver, timber, or potato seed by the merchants of Europe, has left the global North far more heavily in debt to the South, than vice versa.[2] If a notional monetary value is imputed for extracted resources and ecosystem damage, the affluent world's ecological debt to the global South far exceeds the latter's unpaid World Bank loans. Corporate patenting of traditional knowledge from the global South – as intellectual property of the North, is another facet of ecological debt. In fact, the injustices of modernisation are multiple, as confirmed by scientists and ecological economists in a recent publication of the US National Academy of Sciences:

> ... we make a conservative estimate of the environmental costs of human activities over 1961–2000 in six major categories (climate change, stratospheric ozone depletion, agricultural intensification and expansion, deforestation, over fishing, and mangrove conversion), qualitatively connecting costs borne by poor, middle income, and rich nations to specific activities by each of these groups. Adjusting impact valuation for different standards of living across the groups as commonly practiced, we find striking imbalances ... Indeed, through disproportionate emissions of greenhouse gases alone, the rich group may have imposed climate changes on the poor group greater than the latter's foreign debt.[3]

The post-Rio debt for nature logic only adds to what the global North owes to former colonial regions. Of course, the actual calculation of ecological debt in monetary terms would be an impossible computational exercise, but efforts such as the one above are good for political consciousness raising. The next step is to look into how the typical capitalist process of monetary valuation of nature as such, reinforces an epistemologically reductive reading of complex relational processes, by attempting to measure weblike metabolic relations of matter and energy along a single linear index. This said, the campaign for public recognition of ecological debt goes forward, and it is critical that people committed to global justice support it. At the same time, publics and decision makers must turn to the deeper questions, like: What is the character of these peculiar social relations of production that cause all kinds of debt?[4] Are there other ways by which humans can satisfy their material and cultural needs without debt? This book is intended as a small contribution to that learning.

Triangulating political ecology

This collection speaks to two interrelated contexts. The first is people's struggles for an alternative to globalisation, particularly the efforts of women, worker, peasant, indigenous, and ecological activists in the *alter-mondiale* movement. The second is the crisis of relevance affecting contemporary academic disciplines like political ecology, ecological economics, environmental ethics, and even women's studies. As they discuss the footprint of corporate expansion which compromises life on every continent, the authors make it clear just how capitalist economics is 'rationalised' by patriarchal 'mores' – militarism, the world's greatest polluter, not least of them.[5] Violence and calculated competition pervade the global economy, a system in which living habitat is sacrificed for a few; and so called 'minorities' of gender, race, and class, are unfairly used. However, sex/gender is the hardest of these discriminations to resolve, because it has the longest history.[6] Women's subjection is supported by an old belief that they are 'closer to nature' than men. No coincidence that in German, the word for mother, *Mutter*, is linguistically tied to words for mud, sludge, and swamp.[7] By colonial times, cultural allusions such as these gendered and racialised metaphors would come to be used interchangeably by ruling elites: just as women were unclean, so were natives; and the 'exotic oriental' man was invariably said to be 'feminine'. These deeply rooted attitudes have served to construct the inferiority of 'others' and to justify the exploitation of their bodies alongside the resourcing of nature at large.

Questions of exploitation and relations between one economic class and another are the classic terrain of political economy. But today, this discipline is being re-framed as political ecology in order to include the ecosystem that humans are embedded in. At the same time, in an era of feminist and postcolonial liberation, gender and race become integral to any such analysis. Conventional political economists explain where profit comes from, by identifying a 'theft' of labour time from the bodies of workers. As they point out in the labour theory of value, in manufacturing a commodity, the worker generates a 'surplus' for the entrepreneur but never receives back in wages as much value as he or she puts in. However, as political economy is transformed into political ecology, additional concepts are needed. This essay begins with the readily understood activist notion of ecological debt to describe how the very means of production itself in non-industrial communities is still being stripped away by colonisation. Ecological debt involves a debt beyond the extraction of value from waged labour; it involves an appropriation of people's livelihood resources. However, there is yet a third dimension to take account of, for the means of production as such is regenerated by reproductive workers, whose synergistic holding labours maintain the very conditions of its existence. One of the most important of these conditions is the intergenerational supply of new labour-power. Thus, political ecologists, ecological economists, ethicists, and others, might look towards a model that integrates these three kinds of subsumption:

- the *social debt* owed by capitalist employers for surplus value extracted from the labouring bodies and minds of industrial, service, and enslaved workers (the focus of socialism);
- the *ecological debt* owed by the global North to the South for direct extraction of the natural means of production or

livelihood of non-industrial peoples (the focus of postcolonial and of ecological politics);

- the *embodied debt* owed North and South to unpaid reproductive workers who provide use values and regenerate the conditions of production, including the future labour force of capitalism (the focus of feminism).

The 'movement of movements', which includes workers, women, indigenes, peasants, and environmentalists, may also find it useful to think about their respective *alter-mondiale* struggles as interlocking forms of debt, labour, and value, in a worldwide system of capital accumulation. Significantly, all four movements converge in the irreducible metabolic space where humanity and nature materially flow into each other.

If political ecology moves beyond the anthropocentric focus of political economy, an 'engendered' political ecology will open up the meanings of exploitation and accumulation even further, by exposing internal relations normally kept inside the patriarchal black box. For instance, when ecological economists speak of land and labour as 'embodied' in exports, they pass over the need to make a gender literate distinction between productive and reproductive labour and the different kinds of value that these generate. As part of that knowledge making, this anthology applies an 'embodied materialist' epistemology.[8] It engages with discourses from socialism, women's studies, and postcolonial theory, but simultaneously defies their limited ecological understanding. Equally, an embodied materialist perspective challenges professionals in environmental ethics or ecological economics for a limited grasp of global justice questions. The project involves multiple levels of argument and cannot be treated systematically in a book of readings such as this, but my own chapters and several others discuss aspects of it. To help articulate this all but taboo margin between the human and the natural, some new working constructs are introduced: – *embodied debt – meta-industrial labour – eco-sufficiency – metabolic value – and fit*. The harmonious material process by which humans take from nature, digest, and give back in return is known as the humanity–nature metabolism. Capitalist industrialisation and the rise of cities created a 'metabolic rift' in this thermodynamic reciprocity, with environmental degradation the result.[9] However, beyond the circuits of capitalist exchange, in the home and in the field, this metabolism mostly remains intact and the value that it creates is preserved by people doing 'meta-industrial labour'. The non monetary but regenerative activities of this hitherto nameless class are entirely necessary for the global economy to function. Meta-industrials include householders, peasants, indigenes and the unique rationality of their labour is a capacity for provisioning 'eco-sufficiently' – without leaving behind ecological or embodied debt. Where 'development' has not consumed local resources, the labour of peasants or indigenous gatherers in the South demonstrates a good metabolic fit between human needs and biological growth. It preserves and generates metabolic value. In the North, the meta-industrial labour of mothers and other human care givers is also attuned to natural cycles. These reproductive labour forms give rise to a distinct set of economic skills and values – at once material and ethical.[10]

In an era of post-Kuhnian scholarship, where feminist and postcolonial understandings are widely acknowledged, an embodied materialist understanding is indispensable to the transdiscipline of political ecology.[11] US philosopher and activist Chaone Mallory describes the approach as 'prefigurative', and identifies it in the vital citizenship politics of ecological feminism, which

> ... originated in direct action movements, such as the peace movement, anti-toxics movement, and mothers' movements, and then moved into the academy explicitly to use its tools and epistemological resources to better effect change in intra- and trans-human ecosocial relations. Ecofeminism has been called 'engaged theory' and asserts that theory and praxis are mutually reinforcing. Theory is made more relevant, accurate, and compelling when it incorporates the perspectives, knowledges, and voices of those who are struggling for change 'on the ground' ...[12]

To be sure, an ecological feminist perspective emerges from *praxis* – action learning – and has nothing to do with some special 'virtue' of 'the fairier sex and weaker vessel'. The global majority of women – being mothers and care givers – are culturally positioned as labour right at the point where humanity and nature interact. Likewise, men 'outside of' capital, such as small farmers and forest dwellers, undertake regenerative or meta-industrial labour. Unlike factory work, or academic work, the labour of these socially diverse groupings oversees biological flows and sustains matter/energy exchanges in nature.[13] It is certainly no exaggeration to say that the entire machinery of global capital rests on the material transactions of this reproductive labour force. Embodied debt is accrued by the global North when it denies forms of value generated by this gendered and racialised labour. But over and above any notional calculations, these agents of complexity are practising both an alternative economics and an alternative epistemology.

In related vein, Philippines sociologist Walden Bello writes of the environmental movement in the global South as 'The Pivotal Agent in the Fight Against Global Warming'. Australian academic and AidWatch activist James Goodman considers that the South now has 'political leverage' on the international stage, as does South African political economist Patrick Bond.[14] Each scholar argues from a social justice perspective, pointing to how the ecological footprint of the South is far less than that of the North. But the case for leadership by the South is stronger than any moral position based on a 'we are not the polluters' argument. Many of these communities have invented models of economics that protect ecological sustainability. A 2007 posting by the international peasant movement Via Campesina implies this when it claims: 'Small Scale Sustainable Farmers are Cooling Down the Earth'.[15] What is at stake here is an intellectual knowledge base honed in meta-industrial labour; an 'epistemology of the South', to borrow Boaventura de Sousa Santos' phrase.[16]

The counter-entropic logic of regeneration contrasts sharply with the corporate push for a Knowledge-Based-Bio-Economy (KBBE) being sponsored by the European Commission.[17] Here the additive processes of molecular biology are to become the driver of 'productivity and competitiveness'; but a bio-economy in the true sense of the word is only found at the periphery, where meta-industrial provisioning is eco-sufficient. The bearers of ecological and embodied debt are thus not simply victims of capitalist patriarchal institutions, they are leaders, and their people's science is one for the global North to emulate. The bearers of debt are also innovative political strategists in the struggle for global justice. For example, in August 2007, grassroots movements in Ecuador established a Commission for the Integral Audit of Public Credit (CAIC), to examine the legitimacy of foreign debt claimed by predatory financial institutions in the North. The Quito Statement announces the formation of a Social-Ecological Debt Creditors Alliance among nations of the South who have been exploited by global financial institutions, and it supports withdrawal from the International Center for the Settlement of Investment Disputes (ICSID). The Quito Statement also demands the removal of para-military squads sent by the global North into 'developing countries' to protect corporate activities. It demands full citizenship rights for displaced military-economic refugees to the North; and reparations from governments of the North as conditional to any future trade agreements. Peasant and indigenous communities in Ecuador are taking legal action against Chevron-Texaco, and their government has resolved to respond to global warming by keeping its crude oil in the ground to protect the integrity of Yasuni National Park.[18]

Models of eco-sufficiency imply local autonomy and resource sovereignty – and by these means, global justice. But because the capitalist system is at the same time a patriarchal system, the delivery of justice must be sex/gendered. Advocates of social change will need techniques like gender literacy, ideology critique, and personal reflexivity, before old social institutions and economic relations can be deconstructed and new ones put in their place. The Quito Statement speaks of ecological debt but not of embodied debt. The closest it comes to the latter is 'social debt' – a catch-all phrase that essentialises labour as a single process disguising the multiple forms of material reproductivity that are specific to women's work. But the failure of gender awareness has been equally apparent at the World Social Forum, cutting edge of the global movement of movements, whose Manifesto of Porto

Alegre 2005 was drafted by 18 white men and 1 African woman.[19] Reflecting on this, Santos suggests that the way forward is through acknowledgement, voluntary self-criticism, and putting measures in place to see that it does not happen again.

Many academics, activists, and policy makers, have difficulties integrating sex/gender issues in their environmental analysis. This is not at all surprising, because in the dominant global culture, the ontological condition of humans as part of nature is obscured by old gender myths. One time-honoured ideological stricture divides a 'masculine gendered' man from matter, positioning him 'over and above' raw material nature. A related stricture divides this man from 'woman', positioning her 'down in' with nature. Elsewhere, I have speculated on the source of this collective denial of women as full social agents – as the ancients had it: man is 'mind', while woman is 'body'.[20] But patriarchal origins not withstanding, women's fertility is soon enough captured as an economic resource for capitalism – much as the corporate world now realises that it can commodify life-giving environmental 'goods and services' like water, air, and forests. In this anthology, Ewa Charkiewicz spells out the process, by tracing the genealogy of women's juridico-political subjection in economic texts from classical Greece and onwards to the Chicago School. Silvia Federici's essay backs up that analysis by explaining how in the emergence of mercantilist Europe, the unvalued regenerative labours of women, and later slaves, were, and are still today, the indispensable force behind global capital accumulation. Susan Hawthorne examines how the discourse of mastery promotes social control by reducing biological complexity, then covering its tracks, by deleting history. The synchronic statistical correlations of ecological economics might be a case in point.

Sublimated or subconsciously displaced sex/gender attitudes are an integral factor in how the economy functions. In fact, gendered power relations have infused every field of human endeavour – from pig farming to positivist science, from religious imagery to economic logic. But the social construction of gender difference has been achieved by recourse to a highly abstract 'symbolic nature', one that mystifies its materiality, and our own human embodiment in that. The master discourse operates through two supposedy natural and complementary ideal-types – masculinity and femininity – deleting the fact of men's and women's shared material identity. Under the eurocentric canon, masculinity is treated as part of civilisation – on the human side of the humanity–nature dualism – while femininity is treated as 'closer to nature'. The notion of 'citizenship' replicates this mantra, so that today, women who would be emancipated face many contradictions. Women, deprived of the vote for centuries, are now expected to adopt the behavioural gendering of 'universal man' in order to prove themselves worthy of it. Similarly, indigenous people who now enjoy the privilege of sitting on deliberative committees are expected to obey ostensibly universal – but really eurocentric – terms of reference. To question such terms is to commit a gaffe. On the other side of the coin, the association of femininity (and indigeneity) with the 'lower order of nature', explains why it is considered humiliating in many quarters, to draw attention to a man's 'feminine' side.

When deeply personal and libidinally charged cultural attitudes go unexamined, they can lead philosophers, political theorists, and economists into falsely essentialised thinking. Thus some researchers overlook the fact that people who are differently sex/gendered do not have the same access to resources, do not get the same pay for the same work, and most importantly – do not get to use matter/energy with the same outcomes for the ecosystem. Economists have no trouble acknowledging differences with respect to variation in the consumption levels of regions, and they often communicate that with the ecological footprint metaphor. This brilliant – albeit ahistorical – indicator was devised by Canadian biologist Bill Rees and his colleague Mathias Wackernagel to measure 'how much nature we have, how much nature we use, and who uses what'. The ecological footprint 'represents the area of biologically productive land and water a population requires to provide the resources it consumes and to absorb its waste, using prevailing technology'.[21] International footprint comparisons show clearly the ecological debt that the industrialised global North owes to the South with its pristine forest stands and fishing grounds. The ecological footprint is also used by the environmental justice movement to show how the living areas of lower class or racialised communities are targeted as landfill sites by the beneficiaries of capitalist consumerism. But to this point, the ecological footprint has been applied in an essentialist way, aggregating humanity as a unity, and failing to differentiate between socially ascribed masculine and feminine consumption behaviours. On the other hand, if the measure were used in a gender literate way, it might help deconstruct injustices of 'the body economic' by demonstrating the markedly lower ecological footprint or ecological debt generated by women compared to men globally speaking.[22] Here, Meike Spitzner's chapter on global warming as gendered in its causes, effects, solutions, and policies, makes a significant contribution. And she asks why it is that the United Nations' concessional principle of 'common but differentiated responsibilities' applies between small and big nations, but not to women vis-à-vis men.[23]

Could the ecological footprint as a measure of geographic or exosomatic energy use be adapted to communicate the invisible but systemic debt born by women? Embodied debt concerns the harnessing of physiological or endosomatic energy in the context of unjust power relations. Perhaps embodied debt and meta-industrial labour is better expressed not by spatial analogies as ecological debt is, but by the vector of time? For example, research for the European Parliament records that it is mainly unwaged women who run or wait for public transport, and the trade off is that while they may save nature by this free (or enforced) choice, it adds to their own time poverty.[24] Again, the timing of reproductive labour tasks is slower than the speeded up pace of capitalist working time, because regenerative work is bound to preserving, not interrupting natural processes. This responsiveness to the needs of plants or human bodies is what makes meta-industrial labour appear to be achieving very little, while in fact, it is achieving the highest goal of balancing economic provisioning with intergenerational sustainability. All this goes to show how monetary value as conceived in the masculinist economic framework is a badly skewed tool. To echo the veteran socialist feminist Selma James: by the logic of men's 'exchange value', he who bombs a forest with dioxin is considered to generate worth and is highly paid accordingly, whereas the woman who builds her hut of hand-cut wattle and daub, then births a new life within, creates only 'use value', is not considered to be working or 'adding value' and remains unpaid.[25]

An acknowledgement of how notions like exchange value are profoundly sexualised is essential to achieve lasting change. But such a claim looms like a Galilean heresy in the face of modernist reason. The political Left and Right have each resisted what ecological feminist scholars and activists have had to say, but the humanity–nature relation is a problematic construct for some feminists too – at least for those who identify with core values of the global North.[26] Quite early on, the ecocentric lens was rejected by some educated women, uncomfortable at being associated with 'the swamp of material nature' in any way. They noted too, that connecting all women with 'nature' might blur important sociological differences. As the technologised urban lifestyle now transcended earthiness, re-kindling any such association was thought to be a politically backward move. However, the global majority of women do labour hands-on with nature and cope with the matter/energy transformations of their own gestational bodies. In this respect, academic attempts to silence womanist voices sound rather like class denial on the part of serviced, time free, and often childfree, middle class feminists.[27]

Some liberal feminists, and men who follow their line, have incorrectly judged ecological feminism to be conservative theory, because it opposes the gender neutrality of mainstreaming policy. Ecofeminists argue that mainstreaming suits masculinist governments, because it saves them dealing with women's specific materially embodied needs. The problem here is that mainstream feminists conflate what ecofeminists say, with what ancient woman-nature mythologies say – that women have a fixed, innate, identity or essence, which is 'closer to nature' than the essence of men is. In fact, materialist ecofeminists emphasise that both men and women are made of nature, while yet socially, geographi- cally, historically, constructing their lives. Liberal feminists thus fall into the error of making an idealist or culturalist reading of a materialist literature, failing to observe how myth and ideology operate in the service of economic power.[28] The objection that ecofeminist theory propagates old essentialisms is thus epistemologically shallow. It remains locked into a literal acceptance of masculinist universalism, and often evolutionist attitudes about progress as well. As such, liberal feminism itself is essentialising, ideological, and conservative. But more importantly, when it censors ecofeminism, it becomes a 'wedge politics' hindering broad *alter-mondiale* alliances for social and environmental change.

The concept of embodied debt helps explain why both the sex and gender of people's bodies remains relevant even in an era of transgender emancipation.[29] In fact, the statistical record of violence on women should register as embodied debt, because in a capitalist patriarchal system, this violence is not simply sexual but economic. Women's International League for Peace and Freedom (WILPF) notes that in Russia, 14,000 women die annually as a result of violence in the home. In the Sudan, systematic rape is used as a weapon of war. Social disruption stemming from rapid economic change, land reform, or harsh IMF imposed structural adjustment measures, also leads some men to thrash out in frustration. In the USA today, a woman is raped every four minutes. In Colombia, where 3.5 million people are displaced, most are women with children. Worldwide, women make up 80 per cent of those living in refugee camps.[30] Sex/gender violence, intimidation, and harassment is 'economic' because it ensures women's compliance in handing over resources like land, or working for meagre wages, or reproducing the next generation of labour with no compensation to their own lost 'opportunity costs' – biological, economic, and social costs. Since women globally are differently implicated in the use and nurture of natural resources, attention to this violence is central to research into – and action for – global justice and ecological sustainability. But WILPF reports that progress is very slow:

> Since 1995 substantial work has been done to implement the Beijing *Declaration* and *Platform for Action* arising from the 4th UN World

Conference on Women; 185 countries – more than 90 per cent of the UN member states – have now ratified the 1979 *Convention on the Elimination of All Forms of Discrimination Against Women* (CEDAW); and, United Nations Security Council adopted Resolution 1325 on *Women, Peace and Security* in 2000 … Despite this recognition, violence against women is a reality that cuts across borders, wealth, race, religion and culture.[31]

The meta-industrial labour class

In a recent book on the global North/South divide, Paul Collier, former head of development research at the World Bank and now Professor of Economics at Oxford, speaks about the failures of small nation states, eliding the fact that they may well be historical creditors of the North.[32] And right now, the material flow from South to North looks like being exacerbated by policies like the EU's 'Global Europe: Competing in the World' programme. In a statement of opposition to this aggressive neoliberalism, the Seattle to Brussels (S2B) Network names those targeted for bi-lateral trade agreements and growth by deregulation as India, South Korea, the ASEAN states, Central America and the Andean Region, Russia, MERCOSUR countries, and the Gulf Cooperation Council. The Network sees the object of 'Global Europe' as access to natural resources, particularly energy reserves, as well as geo-political influence on former colonies. In the opinion of the Network, Economic Partnership Agreements (EPAs) for trade deals in African, Caribbean, and Pacific (ACP) countries, will destabilise the livelihoods of millions of people in the global South.

Global Europe poses a serious threat to social justice, gender equality and sustainable development, not only outside the EU, but also within. The erosion of workers' rights, the worsening of the quality of jobs within the EU, the destruction of a sustainable model of farming are also intrinsically linked to the external EU trade agenda … EU policies based on so-called 'competitiveness' and increasingly open and deregulated markets … have led to more insecurity, precarity, deteriorating salaries and working conditions, deepening inequalities between countries, regions and between women and men. This strategy also puts under threat environmental and health regulations ... Farmers, and particularly small-scale women farmers, who simply cannot compete with powerful European agribusinesses, will be driven off their land.[33]

The S2B Network adds that trade ministers, whose decisions reinforce unsustainable forms of production, are directly responsible for climate change.

The 'Global Europe' programme illustrates the old axiom that economics is war by other means. And indeed, the Seattle to Brussels Network goes on to expose the EU's 'externalization of borders policy' and its preoccupation with detention and deportation.[34] So it is disappointing to encounter influential UN adviser Jeffrey Sachs, Director of the Earth Institute at Columbia University, by-passing this *realpolitik*. His BBC *Reith Lectures* promote further eurocentric expansionism, and when he talks of 'technology' as the foundation of economic development, the implication is distinctly Darwinist. For Sachs, the solution to the global crisis is not 'a massive cutback of our consumption levels or our living standards', but 'smarter living ... to find a way for the rest of the world ... to raise their own material conditions as well ...'[35] Sachs' vision is buoyed up by innovation in the business and professional sectors, thus:

In early February [2008], the United States National Academy of Engineering released a report on 'Grand Challenges for Engineering in the 21st Century.' ... The report, like the Gates Foundation's similar list of 'Grand Challenges' in global health, highlights a new global priority: promoting advanced technologies for sustainable development.[36]

But this missionary zeal fails to factor in all the cradle to grave operations of mining, smelting, transport, waste disposal, and their entropic costs. Scholars of social metabolism and material flow analysis like Alf Hornborg or sociologists like Eugene Rosa demonstrate such ecological modernist expectations to be quite short sighted in a thermodynamic sense.[37] Beyond this, of course, an embodied debt remains to be registered.

Sachs certainly appreciates that there are environmental and social problems associated with provisioning by means of modern technologies, but is confident that genuinely dematerialising and foolproof solutions will be found. However, once the engineering is solved, a second set of complexities rolls in: the sociological dilemma of how to steer the juggernaut of unregulated economic growth.

> We can harness safe nuclear energy, lower the cost of solar power, or capture and safely store the CO2 produced from burning fossil fuels. Yet the technologies are not yet ready, and we can't simply wait for the market to deliver them, because they require complex changes in public policy to ensure that they are safe, reliable, and acceptable to the broad public. Moreover, there are no market incentives in place to induce private businesses to invest adequately in developing them.[38]

Is technological optimism, managerial flair, and business-as-usual enough to save the earth? If the standard of living of the global North was extended worldwide, and its economic externalities fully acknowledged, the notional calculation of ecological debt from the degradation of soils and streams, or loss of plant and animal life, would be a phenomenal sum. Consider the loss of metabolic fit as decomposing soil bacteria are killed off by depleted uranium in the Balkans and Middle East. Consider the loss of eco-sufficient pest control as ladybirds are killed off by factory emissions; each 'economic service' is worth millions of dollars. It is interesting to hear that UK economist Nicholas Stern, came forward at the Climate Change negotiations in Bali, 2007, with the message that rich countries must now make 'sharp domestic reductions' in consumption.[39] Stern is getting closer to the ecofeminist demand for 'capacity building and a reverse structural adjustment' in the consumerist North.

Plainly, there is still much to be learned from the late ecological economist Nicholas Georgescu-Roegen. And indeed, new work in ecological economics is now re-framing his original interest in social metabolism using a world-systems model. Hornborg et al.'s anthology *Rethinking Environmental History* examines impacts of imperialism and geopolitics, monocultural land use, global markets and material flows, structural asymmetries between core and periphery, externalisation of ecological burdens, distribution conflicts, and prospects for long term sustainability.[40] But this important historical approach to ecological economics is not yet articulating these problems with the sociology of gender in a way that explains how women are socially positioned at the humanity–nature interface, taking care of biological flows, catalysing matter/energy cycles.[41] Neither neoclassical economics, philosophy, nor socialism, has identified this counter-entropic work, let alone conceptualised its social context and value. This, despite the fact that global capital is thoroughly dependent on its regenerative metabolic transactions. Moreover, in the time-consuming daily negotiation of embodied livelihood, reproductive workers apply a life affirming economic rationality, demonstrating what professional economists and managers tend to abstract and glorify as 'complexity, multi-criteria valuation, and intergenerational modelling'. Such women, mothers especially, replace risk by precaution; they use a synergistic approach to needs; define development by health and sustainability; and they know that distribution and consumption actually stand closer to poverty than subsistence prosumption does. My own concluding essay in this book – 'From Eco-Sufficiency to Global Justice' – looks more closely at the features of this environmentally benign meta-industrial way of provisioning. The related themes of biological time and self reliance are taken up in Mary Mellor's chapter on communality versus monetary exchange; and Leo Podlashuc's essay prefigures another model of economic relations beyond alienation.[42] In fact, the work of both authors merits serious attention as capitalist institutions hover on the brink of global meltdown.

If the principle of eco-sufficiency is second nature to women's grassroots economic practices in many regions, it is all but absent in the master discourse. In 2006, the Sustainable Europe Research Institute (SERI), Finland Futures Research Centre, and other consultants, reported to the European Union that eco-sufficiency is the approach least often considered by experts.[43] The more popular policy measures include – 'ecological footprint, cradle-to-cradle assessment, dematerialisation, and transition management'. As a sustainability science, ecological economics is usually about quantitative efficiency rather than qualitative eco-sufficiency. The focus is on how to optimise land use, or the productivity of material and energy throughput. The practice of eco-sufficiency departs from this functionalist closed-system reasoning and challenges corporate and government assumptions that 'more' of the same, must be 'better'. Eco-sufficiency bypasses consumerism and energy wasting international markets. It rests on the logic of permanently reproducing the humanity–nature relation; it is a permaculture, to echo Australian ecologist Bill Mollison's practical vision.[44]

'What is missing from the ecological modernisation agenda is a concern with sustainable consumption' says John Barry, an outspoken critic of the emphasis on 'resource efficiency'.[45] SERI et al. illustrate this by citing the differential rates of consumption between global North and South as 10 to 1 respectively. They note too, that a policy based on eco-sufficiency would require a commitment to annual reductions in resource use by industrialised nations. In saying this, SERI et al. anticipate a move towards global justice through structural adjustments in the North's consumption pattern. The benefit of such a policy for protecting the integrity of the global ecosystem is obvious, as is its reduction of ecological and embodied debts owed on women's labour and to peoples of the South. But eco-sufficiency might also benefit the North – and humans as much as nature. For high GDP is not consistently correlated with human satisfaction and health. The release of labour time following lowered material production might even enhance daily life in the North by reducing sex/gender frustration and violence. SERI et al. add that an economics of eco-sufficiency might be adopted, 'To create a socially inclusive society by taking into account solidarity within and between generations and to secure and increase the quality of life of citizens as a precondition for lasting well-being.'[46] Eco-sufficiency is a strong sustainability, because it involves both metabolic fit with nature and transformations that reach down into the cultural fabric of socio-economic life. As ecological economists, SERI et al. do not interrogate core social relations of production; but moves towards eco-suficiency and cultural autonomy would certainly destabilise injustices of the market.

Indeed, the European neglect of eco-sufficiency in sustainability science very likely reflects the fact that it threatens the neoliberal growth economy. But factory workers and professionals are just as locked into productivism as the business class is. There is also an unspoken sex/gender dimension in the commitment to mega-projects. The gatekeepers of economics are protective of the competitive masculinist rhetoric which graces the discourse of the nation-state and international financial institutions. They are protective too of the dissociated instrumental rationality that fuels this top-down economic managerialism. The tools of this life abandoning dissociation are generally mathematical formulae based on physical indicators like – input/output models – complex systems – probability distributions – decision theory – ecological services – green accounting – millennium assessments – risk monitoring and uncertainty reduction. Sabine O'Hara's chapter in this book remarks on the tacitly gendered division of labour in economics – so entrenched, that few practitioners can recognise the social and ethical implications of their methodologies. Introducing concrete examples of this problem, Marilyn Waring explains just how measures like the UNSNA and ISEW are corrupted by the gendered power relations that shaped their formulation. Gigi Francisco and Peggy Antrobus observe this blindness in international policy mainstreaming and in the Millennium Development Goals promoted by United Nations agencies.[47]

As Derek Wall of the UK Green Party writes: 'Economics is, in many ways, the dominant discourse of modern and postmodern societies.'[48] This collection of essays endorses that insight, highlighting both the masculinist and eurocentric aspects of economics. The hegemonic role of the discipline is exposed in apartheid like statements about human interaction 'with' nature – as if the ecosystem were a distinct 'other'. For the word 'with', implies that nature is a separate entity from 'man' – discontinuous from 'his' embodied human condition. This separation has a certain plausibility, since women over the centuries have been co-opted to mediate nature for men in so many societies, and in this way, they express a consciousness of natural processes that most men have become alienated from. Thus, the first premise and deconstructive insight of an embodied materialism is that humans are themselves 'within' nature, and that social institutions and knowledges need to be reconstituted around that holistic reality. Too many ecological economists, environmental philosophers and sociologists, and even feminists, are hesitant to give up the old dividing line that represents relations between humanity versus nature reductively – as a dualism.[49] In fact, very few self-respecting scholars will dare blend humanity into its bio-geographic mix – as ecocentric deep ecologists have tried to do, for instance. Yet even then, deep ecologists opted for a safe, idealised subjectivity in nature – one that floats above the practical burdens that women and other colonised peoples carry on behalf of white male privilege.

Even in the journal of *Environmental Ethics* and the eco-socialist quarterly *Capitalism Nature Socialism*, most authors still deal with the humanity–nature transaction in a conventional two-sided way. But in reconstituting the Left and Greens as part of a globally inclusive movement, the materiality of embodied debt needs to become a central organising plank.

> More than two-thirds of the world's unpaid work is done by women, the equivalent of $11 trillion (approximately half of the world's GDP); Women make up 70 per cent of the world's poor and 67 per cent of the world's illiterate people – women still own just one per cent of assets worldwide ...[50]

There is no doubt that after horsepower, women have been the cheapest form of energy for harnessing – and certainly easier to marshall than oil supplies. The material and energetic exhaustion of women under global capitalism ranges from sex slaves to paid prostitutes, to wives and mothers, to cash cropping farmers and piece workers, to domestic help, to factory and service workers. In the tradition of political economy, socialists and liberal feminists have pushed for a monetised solution – the equal inclusion of women in the formal or paid labour force.[51] This remains an essential station on the road to global justice, but it is not our terminus. The focus of an embodied materialist analysis is to create awareness of a hitherto neglected sphere of metabolic labour

ascribed to 'women and natives as part of nature'. This epistemological critique reframes an androcentric political economy as
a gender literate political ecology, and spells out a new direction
in movement struggles for global justice.

The monetisation of labour and of nature is embedded in
corrupt relations of production, and for this reason, the present
discussion of debt should not be confused with the nature
accounting of the 'natural capital' school. The approach of
Paul Hawken or Robert Costanza, for example, bypasses social
relations and perpetuates capitalist patriarchal mythologies
by describing nature as 'capital'.[52] True, Marx used the term
'variable capital' to describe human labour, but in doing this, he
intended to demonstrate how the entrepreneur reasons. Today,
when ecological economists speak about manipulating varieties of
capital, it is clear that the object is to remedy, if not upgrade, the
international market system. Costanza also favours government
appointed trusts to 'manage the commons' – a notion that too
comfortably assumes that governments can be trusted to be
independent of business. His managed commons would include
'assets' such as – the atmosphere, water, airwaves, social networks,
and cultures. This totalising technocratic vision collides headlong
with the political meaning of autonomous people's commoning,
a model drawn from places in the global South where earth, air,
fire, and water, plant and animal life, are still ungoverned and
freely shared.[53]

Existing eco-socialist theory also has a rather limited relevance
for sex/gendered and racialised labour trapped in a system of
rampant commodification, but eco-socialists certainly do better
than the liberals' 'natural capital' approach when it comes to
alter-mondiale strategy. For one thing, an analysis of capital as
a system of global accumulation helps people understand why
they so often find themselves pitted against each other as separate
political interest groups. Waged working men in the North are
made obsolescent by the introduction of new technology or
fixed capital, or by offshore transfer of their jobs to dollar a day
workers in the global South. Hence, capital divides and rules
international labour, setting geographic and racialised fractions of

the working class against each other. Again, some wage labourers lose their employment to women casual workers, or have their own jobs flexibilised. The components of production are varied expeditiously by corporate capital from one situation to another. The neoliberal economist may regard such choices as innocent substitutions of human for natural capital, but reading capitalist patriarchal production with an ecological feminist lens keeps the displacement of embodied debt in focus. Thus, according to Nalini Nayak's essay, the mechanisation of fisheries in Kerala has benefited local village men, while causing women to lose their livelihood. Likewise, Ana Isla's chapter demonstrates how the establishment of environmental conservation zones can result in displaced rural women turning to prostitution for survival. On the other hand, Leigh Brownhill and Terisa Turner show that Nigerian women's loss of food growing land to Big Oil, has led them to become eco-warriors.

In the diverse matrix of social and natural relations, economic externalities evolve into political struggles between competing movements. Thus indigenous peoples whose foraging land is enclosed by a CDM order establishing it as an 'oxygen sink' for the global North, blame environmentalists for their loss. Middle class feminist animal right activists are attacked as myopic, by mothers in poor racialised communities fighting to oust a toxic dump from their neighbourhood. But these tensions are simply by-products of an irrational system of accumulation where people and their surrounds are pulled in or thrown off at the convenience of a privileged elite. The engineering efficiency and legislated solutions advanced by some green thinkers and ecological economists, will not resolve such 'distribution conflicts'.

A number of ecological economists attend to the social contra-dictions of globalisation; and indeed, the assessment of Richard Norgaard's detailed and discerning study *Development Betrayed*, is that modernity is 'a shambles'. He might have added too, that modernity is gendered masculine, for he is aware of and agrees with ecological feminist views on the contemporary crisis. Others who draw their profession closer to the insight that its proper study is the social relations of production include – Manfred Max-

Neef, Serge Latouche, Martin O'Connor, Joan Martinez-Alier, Ramachandra Guha, and John Gowdy.[54] Eco-socialist economists like Elmar Altvater, Roger Keil, and Paul Burkett, have also helped to historicise this very unselfconscious field of study.[55] But for the most part, practitioners of ecological economics and eco-socialism are yet to acknowledge the value of reproductive labours, let alone the ideas of women scholars. Only once these contributions are brought into ecological economic reasoning will old taken for granted constructs be exposed as inadequate.

In building an inclusive political ecology, there is much ideological debris to clear away. This externalist critique is carried forward by both 'feminist' and by 'ecological feminist' economists, several of them contributors to this book. Feminist economists tend to pursue the political economic objective of establishing 'equality', for women in theory, methodology, and problem iden-tification.[56] Conversely, ecofeminist economists are situated within political ecology. They dig down into the epistemological role of sex/gender and 'the principle of difference' as it constitutes the humanity–nature metabolism. Feminist economists will tend to stand on the anthropocentric side of the humanity–nature dualism, while materialist ecofeminists will be more ecocentric, concerned to explain how economic activities should fit inside an ecological frame.[57] This ideal-typical distinction in feminist theory is rather like the one drawn between 'environmental economics' and 'ecological economics'. Environmental economics, resting on the ontological separation of humanity versus nature, is about repairing capitalism, while ecological economics attempts (albeit still weakly) to transcend the *ad hoc* humanity versus nature divide. Of course, such polarisations are not hard and fast: individual thinkers can modify their attitudes over time. An example would be the path breaking feminist economist Julie Nelson, a consistent critic of de-contextualised thinking in her discipline, whose recent comments on climate change policy move her closer to an ecofeminist position.[58]

Despite the degradation of land, water, biodiversity, and concomitant poverty in local communities, the application of ecological economics in policy rarely encourages eco-sufficiency or tackles the interlocking problems of ecological and embodied debt. The professional mainstream seeks the 'scientific status' of positivism with its cool detached 'rigour' and avoids contact with grassroots NGOs and their university of the earth.[59] Yet judging from the statements of leading thinkers at the 9th International Society of Ecological Economics (ISEE) conference in Delhi, it is clear that ecological economics is not monolithic but reflects all the conflicts of a complex global society. Several of these thoughtful comments invite serious consideration. For instance, Robert Costanza urges colleagues to take a longer perspective on 'the human dimension' and 'the humanity-nature relationship'. John McNeill asks ecological economists to draw on 'history'

The (Subliminal) Meta-Industrial Economy

Economic discourse	'Man – productive sector'
Class agency	entrepreneurs, wage labour
Epistemology	reductionist, linear, stock focus
Benefit	exchange and use value – for a few
Cost = entropy × 3	
social debt	exploitation of worker's surplus
embodied debt	exhaustion of reproductive labour
ecological debt	degradation of natural metabolism
Remedial action	reflexive capacity, structural change
Subliminal discourse	*'woman/native – reproductive sector'*
Class agency	*meta-industrial carers, peasant, indigenes*
Epistemology	*relational, cyclic, flow focus*
Benefit	*use and metabolic value, bio-complexity*
Cost	*minimal*
Remedial action	*cultural autonomy, sex/gender justice*
Ecological discourse	'Nature – thermodynamic sector'
Agency	matter/energy trans via plants, animals
Process	relational, cyclic, flow, regenerative
Benefit	metabolic value, organic reproduction
Cost	nil
Remedial action	commoning, fit, and eco-sufficiency

in order to 'think more concretely, be grounded'. Arild Vatn talks about 'the socio-political embeddedness of the economy' and looks toward a 'social rationality' with 'inclusive-integrative institutions'. As Kanchan Chopra puts it, 'technological efficiency is not enough, we need a new development paradigm'. Helmut Haberl goes further, proposing 'a totally different type of societal organisation, a radical qualitative change'. And Jacqueline McGlade challenges her colleagues with: 'how do we bring it down to people's everyday life?'[60]

A womanist perspective has much to offer these heartfelt misgivings, for no ISEE plenary speaker conceded the fundamentally sex/gendered character of their disciplinary constructs, methods, and problems.[61] Against neoclassical economics or even Marxian class analysis, an embodied materialist lens reveals a third party – bridging the economic and the ecological. Thus, a new generation of textbooks might be organised around the heuristic schema shown in the table 'The (Subliminal) Meta-Industrial Economy'.

The triangulation is called for because by eurocentric reason, the condition of being human is always already differentiated along gendered 'productive' versus 'reproductive' lines. Stephen Bunker began to map this intricate conceptual terrain when he wrote:

> To understand the world economy as a whole and uneven development within it, we must generate models of natural production that allow us to trace the multiple interacting effects of natural and social systems. In other words, we must accord to the production of use-values a theoretical elaboration equal to that which Marx and others have developed for the production of exchange values. Only then can we understand the full complexity, interaction, and interdependence of both kinds of value. It bears repeating however, that such an endeavour can never yield the unidimensional standard of value that is assumed in labor-based theories of unequal exchange.[62]

Bunker was not addressing gender matters here, but his perceptive comment is very helpful in drawing attention to the relative autonomy of the reproductive labour sphere. For when economists simply proceed as if humanity is a unity in its dealings with habitat and material bodies, they write essentialist theory and make regressive politics. The consequence of blindness to the bridging functions of the meta-industrial sector is externalisation – downward cost shifting and debt on to women, peasants, indigenous peoples; in short, the squandering of metabolic value.

The move from an acknowledgement of sex/gender difference in political and ecological economics to a reconceptualisation of analytic terms and procedures, begs an intervening dialogue with materialist ecofeminist colleagues and comrades. This conversation is open to environmental ethicists, World Social Forum activists, feminists, whoever agrees that the imposts of capitalist patriarchal accumulation are unacceptable. Such a conversation can aerate the familiar premises of political ecology by examining how it is that

- the crisis of democracy and sustainability originates in an unconscious sex/gendered politicisation of the human relation to nature, which becomes institutionalised by capitalist patriarchal economic practices;
- globally dominant economic and social institutions are built on the extraction of surplus value from workers, use value from colonised and bridled bodies, and metabolic value from nature at large;
- political ideologies and professional disciplines preserve this status quo in constructs and methodologies that are gendered to the core;
- a reflexive political ecology and ecological economics will examine the origin of all forms of debt – foreign, ecological, and embodied;
- the object of economic, political, social, and cultural transformation is a regenerative humanity–nature metabolism without social externalities.

These propositions might inform an ecofeminist manifesto or a gender aware eco-socialist manifesto, or vice versa, a deep ecological manifesto grounded in a materialist analysis. In the first instance, it might guide professionals hoping to build a more comprehensive foundation for *ad hoc* and exclusionary disciplines. Academic researchers, political leaders, and movement activists need to work hand in hand with women North and South – prefiguratively – to learn about how eco-sufficiency and justice fit together. This is a necessary, though not sufficient, preparation for structural change on a global scale.

The recognition of embodied debt is justified by the fact that without regenerative labours – biological, economic, social – humanity could not exist. In the global South, most meta-industrial communities subsist graciously as well designed networks of prosumption; but this sustainable work needs an intact habitat, a means of production that is undisturbed by 'development' or 'conservation zones'. In the North, where livelihood is mediated by marketed commodities and services, landscapes and bodies are assaulted by intensive technological fall out. The medical burden of coping with electro-magnetic radiation, or heavy metals in water, is another facet of embodied debt. These externalities of capitalist patriarchal economics are generally left for care givers in the home to pick up in their own unwaged hours. In her discussion of neoliberalism, Ewa Charkiewicz describes *homo sacer* and *femina sacra*, the unspoken category of humans who may be sacrificed with impunity for the sake of profit. We see them waiting at the bus stop, Meike Spitzner's single mothers with baby trolleys and plastic shopping bags. For Zohl dé Ishtar, they are the Marshallese grandmothers who nurse children through cancer, while the US tests its nuclear arsenal on their island home. For Andrea Moraes and Patricia Perkins, use value and embodied debt is registered each time a Brazilian washerwoman carries buckets of water uphill to the *favela*.

By some quirk of reason, women are treated as equally culpable for climate change, though as 75 per cent of the world's poor, they may have no electricity, few consumer goods, and little time or money to spend on energy guzzling leisure pursuits. As global citizens they are indeed mainstreamed out of mind. The policy analyses in chapters by Francisco, Antrobus, Waring, O'Hara, Moraes and Perkins, offer immanent critiques of this status quo. Some readers may call their positions reformist, but the issues each author raises have profound theoretical implications for ecological economics, and beyond that political ecology. Antrobus' account of Millennium Development Goals amplifies Federici's argument on the patriarchal control of women's fertility as an economic imperative. Waring's cost-benefit analysis of 'embodied resources' such as mothers' milk, is a major conceptual challenge to an economics founded on the false categorical distinction between humans versus nature.[63] A phenomenon like climate change must be tackled at the level of epistemology: and as noted, analytic constructs and methods are gendered. Beyond this, as geographers Lise Newton and Joni Seager remind us, attention to 'the body' is central:

> The body is the touchstone of feminist theory ... a concept that disrupts naturalised dichotomies and embraces a multiplicity of material and symbolic sites, ones located at the interstices of power exercised under various guises ... [F]eminist theory draws on understandings of embodied experience to fundamentally challenge [the] bedrocks of Western social and political thought.[64]

When Jacqueline McGlade asks how to 'bring' ecological economics 'down to people's everyday life', an ecological feminist response is that it is already down there. And more, that everyday people know what they are doing. Nevertheless, in a world where social structures are corrupted by derogatory mythologies of gender, race, and class difference, one should ask – in order to avoid the essentialism of bureaucratic management – 'Which people's everyday life exactly?' The global division of labour is such that professionals, middle class men or women, often become enclosed in a virtual world of abstract indicators and formulaic decision criteria. This material de-skilling has dangerous consequences and it leads ecological feminists to insist on the protection of cultural autonomy as prerequisite to the protection of biodiversity.[65] In the global North, G8 and World Bank circles, grassroots expertise is too readily 'consulted' then brokered out to corporations for economic gain.[66] Indigenous creativity then becomes the thin end of the economic wedge for many communities. But even Left leaning political economists and socialist feminists operating by the principle of equality, have been keen to pull meta-industrial labour into the circuits of capital, a kind of eurocentrism that sells development as 'a human right'. The case for recognition of embodied debt spirals away from this monoculture. It is not an argument for reproductive labours to be waged, just as the case for ecological debt is not literally about monetising the whole of nature's 'services' across the globe. Commodifying strategies such as these, like climate change solutions based on carbon trading, merely band aid an incoherent civilisation.

Increasingly, activists North and South demand that land, property, and resources be held as commons and that market excess and polluting trade give way to local production and exchange in reciprocity. These inspiring projects are found in uncommon places; for example, the new utopian communities of Ireland; the Nayakrishi Andolon of Bangladesh; the Dominican Green Sisters of New Jersey; the organic growers network of Lombardy; the Lesbian farm collectives of Oregon.[67] The grassroots coalition Climate Justice Now! celebrates this shift from global to local provisioning. It observes how the global warming solutions put forward by financial institutions, corporations, governments, and development agencies, are yet further opportunities to profit by commodifying nature. In place of carbon offsets and agrofuels, the Coalition demands less consumption, redirected military spending, and debt cancellation. Like others in the movement of movements, Climate Justice Now! argues that justice for the global majority inheres in land rights and peoples' sovereignty over energy, land, food, and water.[68]

An embodied materialist politics seeks global justice via the principle of difference rather than the principle of equality. Beyond simplistic evolutionist notions of forward and backward, progress and regress, meta-industrial labour models cultural autonomy and an alternative scientific knowledge base. The UN Human Development Index therefore, should be re-geared to the concept of provisioning by 'metabolic fit' as the criterion of 'developed' capacity. Postcolonial reparations by the global North may be an economic response to ecological debt but is not an environmental one, because exchange value and metabolic value are entirely incompatible with each other. One helpful global justice strategy could be meta-industrial 'capacity building' for the North, with the South assisting dysfunctional capitalist states to reset their economies on an eco-sufficient course. This 'epistemology of the South' can give direction and hope to teachers, researchers, and decision makers, trying to make sense of the 'shambles' of modernisation. Perhaps too, the *alter-mondiale* movement of worker, women, postcolonial, and ecological activists, will find a new political synergy through its common ground in meta-industrial labour?

The anthology takes a dialectical tack through five interlocking themes: – Histories – Matter – Governance – Energy – Movement. The authors are united by a conviction that histories are many, and that the dominant narrative of global governance is failing because its first premise is internally contradictory. That is to say: the denial of human embodiment in nature makes no sense.

Notes

1. Shalmali Guttal, 'Corporate Power and Influence in the World Bank', *Focus on Trade*, 2007, No. 13, Online Available HTTP: <www.focusweb.org> (accessed 5 November 2007). For a classic statement on the economics of international debt: Susan George, *The Debt Boomerang*, London: Pluto Press, 1992.

2. Aurora Donoso, 'We are not Debtors, we are Creditors' in E. Bravo and I. Yánez (eds), *No More Looting and Destruction! We the Peoples of the South are Ecological Creditors*, Quito: SPEDCA, 2003. Local campaign reports Online Available HTTP: <www.deudaecologica.org> and international reports by Leida Rijnhout, coordinator of the Flemish Platform on Sustainable Development, Online Available HTTP: <www.vodo.be> (both sites accessed 1 September 2007). For a useful commentary, Gert Goeminne and Erik Paredis, 'The Concept of Ecological Debt: An Environmental Justice Approach to Sustainability', paper presented at the 7th Global Conference on Environmental Justice and Global Citizenship, Mansfield College, Oxford, July 2008.

3. U. Thata Srinivasan et al., 'The Debt of Nations and the Distribution of Ecological Impacts from Human Activities', *The National Academy of Sciences of the USA*, 2008, p. 1, Online Available

HTTP: <www.pnas.org/cgi/doi/10.1073/pnas.0709562104> (accessed 10 February 2008).

4. For a Marxist elaboration of this problem, see: Paul Burkett, *Marxism and Ecological Economics*, Leiden: Brill, 2006. Burkett is right to say that ecological economists tend to treat the market as a 'black box', failing to unpack the core relations of production which give rise to how nature is turned into social 'exchange value'. Nevertheless, Marxists seem to have another 'black box' when it comes to how these core relations of production are interlinked with the exploitation of regenerative reproductive labours.

5. While it was the late President Eisenhower who first raised concern over the military-industrial complex, its sex/gendering is amplified by the Women's International League for Peace and Freedom. To quote: 'We can have one combat ship for the same cost of sending 6.8 million children to school in Afghanistan for 9 years ... 26,000 nuclear weapons, "conventional" bombs, guns, cluster bombs and landmines, will not deter or remove the threat of a Tsunami, a hurricane, a flood, a virus, climate change or water shortage, the real security threats of our lives'. Felicity Hill, 'International Women's Day Disarmament Seminar, 5–6 March 2008', Online posting: <wilpf-news@wilpf.ch> (accessed 12 March 2008); also the Stockholm International Peace Research Institute, *SIPRI Yearbook 2007: Armaments, Disarmament, and International Security*, Oxford University Press, 2007; and on women's resistance to militarism, Cynthia Cockburn, *From Where We Stand*, London: Zed Books, 2007.

6. So it is that women still do 65 per cent of the world's work for less than 10 per cent of world wages. Anup Shah (2007), Global Issues website, Online Available HTTP: <www.globalissues.org/HumanRights/WomensRights> (accessed 25 November 2007). Biological sex is one thing, cultural gender is another, but the two interact in everyday life, and it is gender that politicises people's opportunities. Gender is like race and class in being '... a social construct that ascribes different qualities and rights to women and men regardless of individual competence or wishes'. Gerd Johnsson-Latham, *Initial Study of Lifestyles, Consumption Patterns, Sustainable Development and Gender*, Stockholm: Swedish Ministry of Sustainable Development, 2006, p. 6.

7. Michela Zucca (2000), 'Mothers and Madonnas of the Mountains', *Matriarchy and the Mountains III: Convention Proceedings*, Trento: *Centro di Ecologia Alpina*, 2008, Report No. 23, p. 45. This 'labelling' might be read as an early form of 'biopower'; manifest today as modern states enact sanitary, sexual, and penal control over bodies and over the movement of populations. See also the

chapters by Federici, and Charkiewicz, in Part II below. For a survey of common psychological approaches to this psychodynamic: Ariel Salleh, 'Body Logic: 1/0 Culture' in *Ecofeminism as Politics: Nature, Marx, and the Postmodern*, London: Zed Books, 1997.

8. On embodied materialism: Salleh, *Ecofeminism as Politics*, pp. 164–6 and 175–8. This interrogation of 'labour' set out to find a political common denominator for the key activist movements of our time – ecological, worker, womanist, and postcolonial struggles. Also Ariel Salleh, 'Globalisation and the Meta-industrial Alternative' in Robert Albritton et al. (eds), *New Socialisms: Futures Beyond Globalization*, London: Routledge, 2004.

9. In using the word 'fit', I am inspired by Jessie Wirrpa, one of the Australian Aboriginal mentors of anthropologist Deborah Bird Rose, author of 'Fitting into Country', *Capitalism Nature Socialism*, 2008, Vol. 19, No. 3, 117–21. At the same time, the idea of 'metabolic fit' speaks to Marx's observation of the 'metabolic rift' between town and country; an insight elaborated by John Bellamy Foster, *Marx's Ecology*, New York: Monthly Review, 2000. On the alienated sensibility that results from this rift, see: Peter Dickens, *Reconstructing Nature*, London: Routledge, 1995.

10. The interlinked notions of embodied debt, meta-industrial labour, eco-sufficiency, metabolic value, capacity building and reverse structural adjustment, should be treated as strategic categories, whose status remains to be debated. A good arena for exploration of these constructs is the joint meeting of the Marxist Theory and Environment sections at the American Sociological Association. At the Boston 2008 ASA, salient papers were delivered by J. Timmons Roberts, 'Ecologically-Unequal Exchange, Ecological Debt, and Climate Justice', Brett Clark, 'The Metabolic Rift and Unequal Exchange', and Kirk Lawrence, 'Toward the Thermodynamics of Ecological Degradation in the World-System'. The next step is to triangulate these two sections with the Class, Race, and Gender section of ASA.

11. For critical perspectives post-Kuhn, see: Sandra Harding, *Is Science Multicultural?*, Bloomington: Indiana University Press, 1998; Raewyn Connell, 'Northern Theory: The Political Geography of General Social Theory', *Theory and Society*, 2006, Vol. 35, No. 2, 237–64.

12. Chaone Mallory, 'Ecofeminism and Forest Defense in Cascadia', *Capitalism Nature Socialism*, 2006, Vol. 17, No. 1, 35–7. For a paradigmatic early statement of ecofeminist economics, see: Veronika Bennholdt-Thomsen and Maria Mies, *The Subsistence Perspective*, London: Zed Books, 1999.

13. The meta-industrial labour thesis aligns with the dynamics of imperialism outlined by Rosa Luxemburg, *The Accumulation of Capital*, New York: Monthly Review, 1968. But the epistemological framing of my argument is also materialist in an embodied sense.

14. Walden Bello, 'The Environmental Movement in the Global South: The Pivotal Agent in the Fight Against Global Warming', *International Viewpoint*, 2007, No. IV394, Online Available HTTP: <www.internationalviewpoint.org> (accessed 5 November 2007); James Goodman, 'Climate change, development, aid and trade', Sydney: AidWatch Discussion Paper, 2007; Patrick Bond, 'The Third World in the Movement for Global Justice' in *Against Global Apartheid*, London: Zed Books, 2003.

15. Via Campesina, 'Small Scale Sustainable Farmers are Cooling Down the Earth', 5 November 2007, Online Posting: <via-info-en@googlegroups.com> (accessed 5 November 2007).

16. Boaventura de Sousa Santos, *The Rise of the Global Left*, London: Zed Books, 2006.

17. Information on the European Commission's Knowledge-Based-Bio-Economy (KBBE) is Online Available HTTP: <www.europa.eu.int/comm/research/biosociety> (accessed 20 January 2008). See also Georgia Miller, 'Is Nanotechnology Rushing into a Repeat of the Biotechnology Backlash?', Online Available HTTP: <www.newMatilda.com> (accessed 20 September 2006). The sale of nano commodities worth US$32 billion in 2005 is expected to grow to US$1 trillion by 2011. Nano-engineering of synthetic body organs, fuel cells, stain repellent fabrics, smart robotic drugs, and even foods, remakes matter at a sub-atomic level with unknown implications for human and ecosystem health.

18. South Peoples' Historical, Social-Ecological Debt Creditors' Alliance, *Quito Statement*, 22 August 2007, Online Posting: <ieetm@accionecologica.org> (accessed 5 November 2007).

19. Ana Elena Obando, 'Sexism in the World Social Forum: Is Another World Possible', WHRnet, 2005, Online Available HTTP: <www.iiav.nl/ezines/web/whrnet/2005/february/pdf> (accessed 6 November 2007). For an effort to overcome this problem, see: Onyango Oloo, 'Gendering WSF Nairobi 2007', Online Available HTTP: <www.Forumsocialmundial.org.br/noticias_textos.php?cd_news=327> (accessed 8 January 2007). There were also few women in the first definitive appraisal of the WSF phenomenon, Tom Mertes (ed.), *A Movement of Movements*, London: Verso, 2004. The balance is rectified in Judith Blau and Marina Karides (eds), *A Better World is Possible, Necessary: The World and US Forums*, Leiden: Brill, 2008.

20. Salleh, *Ecofeminism as Politics*, pp. 35–52. To reinforce the point: biological sex should not be understood dualistically; it covers a range of body types, not all of which are sexually reproductive. However, culturally imposed gender templates are dualistic. The labels 'masculine and feminine' indicate learned gender styles. Women may be dominated through both physical sex and by gender role, which is why the term sex/gender is used in this text.

21. The original statement was Mathias Wackernagel and William Rees, *Our Ecological Footprint: Reducing Human Impact on the Earth*, Gabriola Island, BC: New Society, 1996. The quote is Online Available HTTP: <www.footprintnetwork.org> (accessed 20 April 2007).

22. Johnsson-Latham (in *Initial Study of Lifestyles, Consumption Patterns, Sustainable Development and Gender*) points out that even in the global North, women have a remarkably lower ecological footprint than men. Whereas men tend to shop for durable assets like computers, houses, or boats, women mainly shop for weekly necessities, nature's perishables. The difference is even more striking when it is appreciated that women's consumption is mostly made on behalf of others, that is, family members.

23. The United Nations Framework Convention on Climate Change, 1994, Article 3, Online Available HTTP: <www.unfccc.int/resource/docs/convkp/conveng.pdf> (accessed 10 May 2007).

24. To rectify this, the European Union commissioned a comprehensive transnational report see: European Parliament, *Women and Transport in Europe*, Brussels, 2006, Online Available HTTP: <www.europarl.europa.eu/EST/download.do?file=9558> (accessed 10 May 2007).

25. Selma James founded the Wages for Housework campaign in the 1970s and today it is particularly strong in Venezuela, Online Available HTTP: <www.globalwomenstrike.net> (accessed 1 September 2007). A global women's strike is a valuable consciouness raising tactic. For socialist feminists, it is as a step towards getting women's reproductive labours waged. From an ecofeminist perspective, its exposure of embodied debt points to the need for a profound reformulation of humanity–nature relations, a shift from thinking in terms of exchange value and use value, to metabolic value.

26. For responses to critics see Salleh in note 49 below.

27. For a refutation of liberal feminist objections, see: Phoebe Godfrey, 'Dianne Wilson vs Union Carbide: Ecofeminism and the Elitist Charge of "Essentialism"', *Capitalism Nature Socialism*, 2005, Vol. 16, No. 4, 37–66.

28. Liberal feminists occasionally converge with conservative economists who refer to women's reproductive labour as 'social capital', for instance, Robert Putnam (ed.), *Democracies in Flux: The End of Social Capital in Contemporary Society*, Oxford University Press, 2002. Putnam examines society as a functional machine, with women neatly accorded a 'moral role' within the system. Liberal feminists object to the moral role aspect, but have often embraced the notion of women's 'social capital'.

29. Some activists in the Lesbian-Gay-Bi-Transgender (LGBT) movement have criticised ecological feminists on the basis that the old dualist sex/gender model is passé. In terms of contemporary lifestyle options, this may be so, at least for some individuals, but traditional gender assumptions remain firmly embedded in social structures and in economic concepts. Consider the United Nations System of National Accounts, which deems biologically and socially reproductive activities to be 'non-labour'. A materialist ecological feminism is not about 'identity politics' but about the economic effects of historically reified gender structures and positions that limit people's life opportunities. Old fashioned words like 'men' and 'women' cannot be avoided in the process of deconstructing corrupt global institutions.

30. Women's International League for Peace and Freedom, 'WILPF Statement on the International Day for the Elimination of Violence Against Women', Online Available HTTP: <www.wilpf.int.ch> (accessed 25 November 2007).

31. Ibid.

32. Paul Collier, *The Bottom Billion: Why Poor Countries are Failing and What Can Be Done About It*, Oxford University Press, 2007.

33. Seattle to Brussels Network, 'No to Corporate Europe – Yes to Global Justice: Statement for the World Social Forum's Global Day of Action, 26 January 2008', Online Available HTTP: <www.s2bnetwork.org> (accessed 1 February 2008).

34. Ibid. Seattle to Brussels Network members include: Actionaid International, Action Solidarité Tiers Monde, Africa-Europe Faith and Justice Network, Anti-Globalisation Network UK, Attac, Berne Declaration, Both Ends, Campagna per la Riforma Della Banca Mondiale, Christian Aid, Coordination Paysanne Européenne, La Via Campesina, Corporate Europe Observatory, Ecologistas en Acción, Fédération Syndicale, Food and Water Watch Europe, For Velferdsstaten, Friends of the Earth, Global Roots, Greenpeace International, Institut pour la Relocalisation de l'Economie, Institute for Agriculture and Trade Policy, Initiative Colibri, Nature Trust Malta, New Economics Foundation, Norsk Bonde-Og Smabrukarlag, Oxfam Solidarity, People & Planet, ¡Prou OMC!, Rete Lilliput,

Center For Research on Multinational Corporations, Terra Nuova, The Corner House, Third World Network, Transnational Institute, Protect the Future, Vredeseilanden, War On Want, WEED, WIDE – Women In Development Europe, WILPF, Working Group against the MAI.

35. Jeffrey Sachs, 'Lecture I: Bursting at the Seams', 11 April 2007, BBC *Reith Lectures*, Online Available HTTP: <www.bbc.co.uk> (accessed 20 April 2007).

36. Jeffrey Sachs, 'Technology Cooperation', *Project Syndicate*, 2008, Online Available HTTP: <www.project-syndicate.org> (accessed 6 March 2008).

37. Joan Martinez-Alier, 'Marxism, Social Metabolism, and International Trade' in Alf Hornborg, J.R. McNeill, and Joan Martinez-Alier (eds), *Rethinking Environmental History*, Lanham MD: Altramira, 2007. For Vienna Sozial Oekologie accounting: Helmut Haberl, M. Fisher-Kowalski, F. Krausmann, H. Weisz, and V. Winiwarter, 'Progress Towards Sustainability: What the Conceptual Framework of Material and Energy Flow Accounting (MEFA) Can Offer?', *Land Use Policy*, 2004, Vol. 21, No. 3, 199–213. Some in the latter group contest the theory of unequal exchange favoured by dependency theorists.

38. Sachs, 'Technology Cooperation'.

39. Tom Athanasiou, 'Where Do We Go From Here? The Bali Meeting and the Lessons Learned', *Focus on Trade*, 2007, No. 135, December, Online Posting: focus-on-trade@lists.riseup.net (accessed 30 January 2008). Another cautionary tale is offered by Bello, 'The Environmental Movement in the Global South'. In capitalist China, a new 'user pays' high tech medical system has resulted in the resurgence of diseases like tuberculosis. Whereas in Cuba, whose health care delivery is based on the sufficiency of the 'barefoot doctor' concept, TB is eradicated.

40. Hornborg et al. (eds), *Rethinking Environmental History*.

41. Nicholas Georgescu-Roegen, *The Entropy Law and The Economic Process*, Cambridge, MA: Harvard University Press, 1971. See also Kolya Abramsky, 'Energy and Labor in the World-Economy', *The Commoner*, forthcoming, which offers a political economy analysis of energy circuits under capitalism. For a more top-down perspective, see: Christopher Chase-Dunn, 'Ecological Degradation and the Evolution of World Systems', *Journal of World-Systems Research*, 1997, Online Available HTTP: <www.jwsr.ucr.edu>.

42. Community based challenges to growth economics have a proud history, see: Molly Scott Cato and Miriam Kennett (eds), *Green Economics: Beyond Supply and Demand*, Aberystwyth: Green Audit, 1999; another route is via the North American Left Biocentrism

network of David Orton and friends, Online Available HTTP: <www. home.ca.inter.net/~greenweb/> (accessed 1 September 2007). See also Bill McKibben, *Deep Economy*, New York: Holt, 2007.

43. Report by the Sustainable Europe Research Institute (SERI), UN University, and Finland Futures Research Centre, *Environment and Innovation*, Vienna: Tender No. IP/A/ENV1/ST/2005-84, 2006. Sustainability science has 'hard and soft' versions. The present eco-sufficiency argument endorses the Friibergh position. Online Available HTTP: <www.earthethics.com/sustainability%20science. htm> (accessed 21 January 2007).

44. Bill Mollison, *Permaculture: A Designers' Manual*, Tyalgum, NSW: Tagari Publications, 1988.

45. John Barry, 'Towards a Concrete Utopian Model of Green Political Economy', *Post-Autistic Economics Review*, 2006, No. 36, 1–18, Online Available HTTP: <www.paecon.net> (accessed 21 January 2007).

46. SERI et al., *Environment and Innovation*. In addition: Frieder Otto Wolf, Pia Paust-Lassen, and Joachim Spangenberg, *Sustainability Politics and the EU SDS: A Synthesis Model*. TNW: *Improvement of Sustainability Strategy Elaboration for Economic, Environmental and Social Policy Integration in Europe*, Berlin: HPSE/CT/2002/50019-1, 2006. See also the refreshing stance of IUCN Resolution 3.075: 'Applying the Precautionary Principle in Environmental Decision Making and Management', World Conservation Congress, Bangkok, 2004. Here the precautionary principle is interlinked with three others – public participation in decision making, intra and intergenerational equity, common but differentiated responsibility. Online Available HTTP: <www.iucn. org> (accessed 8 January 2008).

47. For instance, UNDP, *Human Development Report*, New York: United Nations, 2001. On how the Millennium Development Goals help preserve capitalist patriarchal economics: George Caffentzis, 'Dr. Jeffrey Sachs' *The End of Poverty*: A Political Review', *The Commoner*, 2005, No. 10, Online Available HTTP: <www. thecommoner.org> (accessed 31 October 2006).

48. Derek Wall, 'Green Economics: An Introduction and Research Agenda', *International Journal of Green Economics*, 2006, Vol. 1, No. 2, 201–13, p. 202.

49. See Ariel Salleh, 'Deeper than Deep Ecology' in Baird Callicott and Clare Palmer (eds), *Environmental Philosophy* Vols. 1–5, London: Routledge, 2005; Ariel Salleh, 'Social Ecology and The Man Question' in Piers Stephens, John Barry, and Andrew Dobson (eds), *Contemporary Environmental Politics: From Margins to Mainstream*, London: Routledge, 2006; and the symposium, Ariel

Salleh (ed.), 'Ecosocialist-Ecofeminist Dialogues', *Capitalism Nature Socialism*, 2006, Vol. 17, No. 4, 32–124.

50. WILPF, Women and Human Rights seminar, Online Available HTTP: <www.wilpf.int.ch/events/2008IWDseminar.html> (accessed 23 January 2008). For an excellent account of new developments in embodied debt, see: Barbara Ehrenreich and Arlie Hochschild, *Global Woman: Nannies, Maids, and Sex Workers in the New Economy*, New York: Holt, 2002.

51. For a solid socialist position on justice for women, specifically exploited migrant labour: Jerry Mead-Lucero, 'Domestic Workers Emerge as a New Front in the "Non-Traditional" Labor Movement', *Labor Notes*, October 2007, 3–4. But this article begs the question of where unpaid housewives fit into the socialist picture or women traded internationally as sex slaves. On the latter, see: Nancy Holmstrom (ed.), *The Socialist Feminist Project: A Contemporary Reader in Theory and Politics*, New York: Monthly Review, 2002; Mary John Mananzan, *The Woman Question in the Philippines*, Manila: Institute of Women's Studies, 1997.

52. Paul Hawken, Amory and Hunter Lovins, *Natural Capital*, New York: Little, Brown, 1999; Robert Costanza, 'Review of Peter Barnes' *Capitalism 3.0*', *Nature*, 2007, No. 446, 613–14. Compare the critique of eco-managerialism by Tim Luke, 'The System of Sustainable Degradation', *Capitalism Nature Socialism*, 2006, Vol. 17, No. 1, 99–112.

53. On the commons, see: Massimo de Angelis, 'Neoliberal Governance, Reproduction and Accumulation', *The Commoner*, 2003, No. 7; Ariel Salleh, 'Sustainability and Meta-industrial Labour: Building a Synergistic Politics', *The Commoner*, 2004, No. 9, Online Available HTTP: <www.thecommoner.org> (both accessed 31 October 2006).

54. Richard Norgaard, *Development Betrayed*, New York: Routledge, 1994; Manfred Max-Neef et al., *Human Scale Development*, New York: Apex, 1991; Serge Latouche, *In the Wake of the Affluent Society*, M. O'Connor and R. Arnoux (trans.), London: Zed Books, 1993; Joan Martinez-Alier and Ramachandra Guha, *Varieties of Environmentalism*, London: Earthscan, 1997; John Gowdy (ed.), *Limited Wants, Unlimited Needs*, Washington, DC: Island Press, 1998.

55. Elmar Altvater, 'Global Order and Nature' in Roger Keil et al. (eds), *Political Ecology: Global and Local*, London: Routledge, 1998; Richard Westra, 'Green Marxism and the Institutional Structure of a Socialist Future' in Robert Albritton et al. (eds), *Political Economy and Global Capitalism*, London: Anthem Press, 2007; Burkett, *Marxism and Ecological Economics*. See also Joel Kovel

and Michael Lowy, 'An Ecosocialist Manifesto', *Capitalism Nature Socialism*, 2002, Vol. 13, No. 1, 1–2, 155–7; and Joel Kovel, *The Enemy of Nature*, London: Zed Books, 2002, which acknowledges the political relevance of ecological feminist analysis.

56. For a brief overview: Geoff Schneider and Jean Shackelford, 'Ten Principles of Feminist Economics: A Modestly Proposed Antidote', Online Available HTTP: <www.paecon.net> (accessed 5 November 2007); and for a gentle, nuanced feminist critique: Julie Nelson, *Economics for Humans*, University of Chicago Press, 2006.

57. For instance, Dianne Rocheleau et al. (eds), *Feminist Political Ecology: Global Issues and Local Experiences*, New York: Routledge, 1996, adopts a Left liberal or socialist feminist framework rather than an ecocentric one. Likewise, Luciana Ricciutelli et al. (eds), *Feminist Politics, Activism and Vision: Local and Global Challenges*, London: Zed Books, 2004, takes an anthropocentric gender and justice focus, without going into the cultural epistemology of women–nature linkages. This same distinction needs to be held in mind while reading the postmodern community economics approach developed by J.K. Gibson-Graham, *A Postcapitalist Politics*, Minneapolis: University of Minnesota Press, 2006.

58. Julie Nelson, 'Economists, Value Judgements, and Climate Change', Global Development and Environment Institute, 2007, Working Paper No: 07-03, Tufts University, Medford, MA.

59. An exception here is Joan Martinez-Alier, who as Chair of the International Society of Ecological Economics, has been proactively bridging ISEE and global NGOs.

60. Anna Chiesura, 'Ecological Economics for What?', *International Society of Ecological Economics Newsletter*, 2007, January, 9–11, Online Available HTTP: <www.ecoeco.org> (accessed 21 January 2007).

61. After writing this, I came across Wendy Harcourt, *Feminist Perspectives on Sustainable Development*, London: Zed Books, 1994, and it is disturbing that so few practitioners of ecological economics have heard what she pointed out years ago.

62. Stephen Bunker, 'Natural Values and the Physical Inevitability of Uneven Development under Capitalism' in Hornborg et al. (eds), *Rethinking Environmental History*, p. 253.

63. Some ecological feminists are researching alternatives to the capitalist patriarchal model in existing matriarchal societies, see: Heide Göttner-Abendroth, *Das Matriarchat I: Geschichte seiner Erforschung*, Stuttgart: Kohlhammer, 1988; Genevieve Vaughan (ed.), *Women and the Gift Economy: A Radically Different Worldview is Possible*, Toronto: Inanna, 2007.

64. Lise Nelson and Joni Seager (eds), *A Companion to Feminist Geography*, Oxford: Blackwell, 2005, p. 2.
65. Beyond the reasons offered here, eloquent arguments for a culturally autonomous economics are made by Gustavo Esteva and Madhu Suri Prakash, *Grassroots Postmodernism*, London: Zed Books, 1998; Patrick Cuninghame, 'Reinventing An/Other Anti-capitalism in Mexico' in Werner Bonefeld (ed.), *Subverting the Present, Imagining the Future: Insurrection, Movement, Commons*, New York: Autonomedia, 2007.
66. The medicinal Neem tree is a case in point, although this particular corporate patent on indigenous knowledge was reversed after an internationally organised people's court challenge, see: Vandana Shiva, *Earth Democracy*, Boston: South End, 2006.
67. Liam Leonard, 'Sustaining Ecotopias: Identity, Activism and Place', *Ecopolitics*, 2008, Vol. 1, No. 1, 105–55, Online Available HTTP: <www.ecopoliticsonline.com> (accessed 7 February 2008); Farida Akhter, 'Resisting Technology and Defending Subsistence in Bangladesh' in Veronika Bennholdt-Thomsen, Nicholas Faraclas, and Claudia von Werlhof (eds), *There Is An Alternative: Subsistence and Worldwide Resistance to Corporate Globalization*, London: Zed Books, 2001; Sarah McFarland Taylor, *Green Sisters: A Spiritual Ecology*, Cambridge, MA: Harvard University Press, 2007; *Associazione Donne in Campo cia Lombardia*, Piazza Caiazzo, Milan; Rachel Stein (ed.), *New Perspectives on Environmental Justice: Gender, Sexuality and Activism*, New Brunswick: Rutgers University Press, 2004.
68. Climate Justice Now! Media Release: 'What's Missing from the Climate Talks? Justice!', Bali, 14 December 2007, Online Posting: focus-on-trade@lists.riseup.net (accessed 30 January 2008). Members of this coalition include: Biofuelwatch, Carbon Trade Watch, Transnational Institute, Center for Environmental Concerns, Focus on the Global South, Freedom from Debt Coalition Philippines, Friends of the Earth International, Gendercc – Women for Climate Justice, Global Forest Coalition, Global Justice Ecology Project, International Forum on Globalization, Kalikasan-Peoples Network for the Environment, La Via Campesina, Durban Group for Climate Justice, Oilwatch, Pacific Indigenous Peoples Environment Coalition, Aotearoa, Sustainable Energy and Economy Network, The Indigenous Environmental Network, Third World Network, *WALHI* Indonesia, World Rainforest Movement.

Part I

Histories

It is usually assumed that progress is a linear, evolutionary process starting from a 'primitive', 'backward' stage and, driven by the development of science and technology, or in Marxist terms of 'productive forces', moving up and up in unlimited progression. In this Promethean project, however, the limits of this globe, of time, of space, of our human existence, are not respected. Within a limited world, aims like 'unlimited growth' can be realised only at the expense of others ...

Rosa Luxemburg has shown that capital accumulation presupposes the exploitation of ever more 'non-capitalist' milieux for the appropriation of more labour, more raw materials and more markets ... We call these milieux colonies ...

But as we had lived in Third World countries for a long time, we immediately saw that women's unpaid housework and caring work was not the only component of this invisible base of our economy; it also included the work of small peasants and artisans in still-existing subsistence economies in the South, the work of millions of small producers who produce for local needs.

Veronika Bennholdt-Thomsen and Maria Mies,
The Subsistence Perspective,
London: Zed Books, 1999, pp. 29–32.

2

THE DEVALUATION OF WOMEN'S LABOUR

Silvia Federici

Within less than a century from the landing of Columbus on the American continent, the colonisers' dream of an infinite supply of labour (echoing the explorers' estimate of an 'infinite number of trees' in the forests of the Americas) was dashed. Europeans had brought death to America. Estimates of the population collapse, which affected the region in the wake of the colonial invasion, vary, but scholars almost unanimously liken its effects to an 'American Holocaust'. In the century after the Conquest of America, the population declined by 75 million across South America, representing 95 per cent of its inhabitants.[1] By the 1580s, population began to decline also in Western Europe, and continued to do so into the seventeenth century, reaching a peak in Germany where one third of the population was lost. With the exception of the Black Death (1345–48), this was a population crisis without precedent, and statistics tell only part of the story. Death struck at 'the poor'. It was not the rich, for the most part, who perished when the plague or the smallpox swept the towns, but craftsmen, day-labourers and vagabonds.[2] They died in such numbers that their bodies paved the streets, and the authorities denounced the existence of a conspiracy, instigating a hunt for the malefactors.

But the population decline was also blamed on low natality rates and the reluctance of the poor to reproduce themselves. To what extent this charge was justified is difficult to tell, since demographic recording, before the seventeenth century, was uneven. But by the end of the sixteenth century, the age of marriage was increasing in all social classes, and in the same period, the number of abandoned children – a new phenomenon – started to grow. Ministers complained from the pulpit that youth were not marrying, in order not to bring more mouths into the world than they could feed. The peak of the demographic and economic crisis was the 1620s and 1630s. In Europe, as in the colonies, markets shrank, trade stopped, unemployment became widespread, and for a while there was the possibility that the developing capitalist economy might crash. For the integration of colonial and European economies had reached a point where the reciprocal impact of the crisis rapidly accelerated its course. This was the first international economic crisis of capitalism. It was a 'General Crisis', as economic historians have called it.[3]

Population and the disciplining of women

It is in this context that the question of the relation between labour, population, and the accumulation of wealth came to the foreground of political debate and strategy to produce the first elements of a population policy – in Michel Foucault's words a 'bio-power regime'.[4] The concepts applied were crude, often confusing 'populousness' with 'population', and the means by which the state began to punish any behaviour obstructing population growth, were brutal.[5] But it is my contention against Foucault, that it was this population crisis of the sixteenth and seventeenth centuries, not the end of famine in Europe in the eighteenth century, that turned reproduction and population growth into state matters and primary objects of intellectual discourse.[6]

I further argue that intensification of the persecution of 'witches', and the new disciplinary methods that the state adopted in this period to regulate procreation and break women's control over reproduction, are also to be traced to this crisis. However, other factors also contributed to the European ruling class' determination to control women's reproductive function. Among them were the increasing privatisation of property and economic relations that generated a new anxiety within the bourgeoisie concerning the question of paternity and the conduct of women. Similarly, the charge that witches sacrificed children to the devil – a key theme in the 'great witch-hunt' of the sixteenth and seventeenth centuries – reveals a preoccupation with population decline, but also fear of the propertied classes with regard to their subordinates, particularly low-class women who, as servants, beggars, or healers, might enter their employers' houses and cause them harm. It cannot be pure coincidence, that at the very moment when population was declining, and an ideology was forming that stressed the centrality of labour in economic life, severe penalties were introduced in the legal codes of Europe to punish women guilty of reproductive crimes.

The concomitant development of a population crisis, an expansionist population theory, and the introduction of policies promoting population growth is well-documented. By the mid-sixteenth century, the idea that the number of citizens determines a nation's wealth had become a social axiom. The French political thinker and demonologist Jean Bodin insisted that the strength of the commonwealth consists in men. The sixteenth century Italian economist Giovanni Botero had a more sophisticated approach recognising the need for a balance between the number of people and the means of subsistence. Still, he declared that 'the greatness of a city' did not depend on its physical size so much as on the number of its residents.[7] Henry IV's conviction that the strength and wealth of a king was the number and opulence of his citizens, sums up the demographic thought of the age. Concern with population growth is detectable also in the programme of the Protestant Reformation. Dismissing the traditional Christian exaltation of chastity, the Reformers valorised marriage, sexuality, and even women because of their reproductive capacity. Woman is 'needed to bring about the increase of the human race', Luther conceded, reflecting that 'whatever their weaknesses, women possess one virtue that cancels them all: they have a womb and they can give birth'.[8]

All this climaxed with the rise of mercantilism, which made the presence of a large population the key to prosperity and power of a nation. Often, mercantilism has been dismissed by economists as a crude system of thought, because of its assumption that the wealth of nations is proportional to the quantity of labourers and money available. The mercantilist's hunger for labour and the means applied in order to force people to work, contributed to this disrepute, as most economists wish to maintain the illusion that capitalism fosters freedom rather than coercion. It was a mercantilist class that invented the workhouses, hunted down vagabonds, 'transported' criminals to the colonies, and invested in the slave trade, all the while asserting the 'utility of poverty' and declaring 'idleness' a social plague. Mercantilist theory and practice is a direct expression of the requirements of primitive accumulation and the first capitalist policy explicitly addressing the problem of the reproduction of the workforce. This policy had an 'intensive' side consisting in the imposition of a totalitarian regime using every means to extract the maximum of work from every individual, regardless of age and condition. But it also had an 'extensive' side, consisting in the effort to expand the size of population, and thereby the size of the army and the workforce.[9]

A new concept of human beings also took hold, picturing them as mere raw materials, workers and breeders for the state. But even prior to the heyday of mercantile theory, in France and England the state adopted a set of pro-natalist measures that, combined with Public Relief, formed the embryo of a capitalist reproductive policy. Laws were passed that put a premium on marriage and penalised celibacy, modelled on those adopted by the late Roman Empire for this purpose. The family was given a new importance as the key institution providing for the transmission of property and the reproduction of the workforce. Simultaneously, we have the beginning of demographic recording and the intervention of the state in the supervision of sexuality, procreation, and family life. But the main initiative that the state took to restore the desired population ratio was the launching of a true war against women clearly aimed at breaking the control they had exercised over their bodies and reproduction. Starting in the mid-sixteenth century, while Portuguese ships were returning from Africa with their first human cargoes, all the European governments began to impose the severest penalties against contraception, abortion and infanticide. This last practice had been treated with some leniency in the Middle Ages, at least in the case of poor women; but now it was turned into a capital crime, and punished more harshly than the majority of men's crimes. In sixteenth century Nuremberg, the penalty for maternal infanticide was drowning; in 1580, the year in which the severed heads of three women convicted of maternal infanticide were nailed to the scaffold for public contemplation, the penalty was changed to beheading.[10]

Reproductive labour is natural and historical

New forms of surveillance were also adopted to ensure that pregnant women did not terminate their pregnancies. In France, a royal edict of 1556 required women to register every pregnancy, and sentenced to death those whose infants died before baptism after a concealed delivery, whether or not proven guilty of any wrongdoing. Similar statutes were passed in England and Scotland in 1624 and 1690. A system of spies was also created to surveil unwed mothers and deprive them of any support. Even hosting an unmarried pregnant woman was made illegal for fear that she might escape public scrutiny; while those who befriended her were exposed to public criticism.[11] As a consequence, women began to be prosecuted in large numbers, and more were executed for infanticide in sixteenth and seventeenth century Europe than for any other crime, except for witchcraft, a charge that also centred on the killing of children and other violations of reproductive norms. Significantly, in the case of both infanticide and witchcraft, the statutes limiting women's legal responsibility were lifted. Thus, women walked, for the first time, into the courtrooms of Europe, in their own name as legal adults, under charge of being witches and child murderers. Also the suspicion under which midwives came in this period – leading to the entrance of the male doctor into the delivery room – stemmed more from the authorities' fear of infanticide than from any concern with the midwives' alleged medical incompetence.

With marginalisation of the midwife, women lost control over procreation, and were reduced to a passive role in child delivery, while male doctors came to be seen as the true 'givers of life' (as in the alchemical dreams of the Renaissance magicians). With this shift, a new medical practice prevailed, prioritising the life of the foetus over that of the mother. For this to happen, the community of women that gathered around the bed of a future mother had to be expelled from the delivery room, and midwives placed under surveillance of the doctor. Midwives were also recruited for policing women. In France and Germany, midwives had to become spies for the state, if they wanted to continue their practice. They were expected to report all new births, discover the fathers of children born out of wedlock, and examine the women suspected of having secretly given birth. They also had to examine suspected local women for any sign of lactation when foundlings were discovered on the Church's steps.[12] The same type of collaboration was demanded of relatives and neighbours. In Protestant countries and towns, neighbours were supposed to spy on women and report all relevant sexual details: for example, if a woman received a man when her husband was away, or if she entered a house with a man and shut the door behind her.[13] In Germany, the pro-natalist crusade reached such a point that women were punished if they did not make enough of an effort during child delivery or showed little enthusiasm for their offspring.[14] The outcome of these policies – women were still being executed in Europe for infanticide at the end of the eighteenth century – was the enslavement of women to procreation.

While in the Middle Ages women had been able to use various forms of contraceptives, and had exercised an undisputed control over the birthing process, from now on their wombs became public property, the common territory of men and the state, as procreation was placed at the service of capitalist accumulation. In this sense, the destiny of Western European women, in the period of primitive accumulation, was similar to that of women slaves in the American colonial plantations who, especially after the end of the slave-trade in 1807, were forced by their masters to become breeders of new workers. The comparison has obviously serious limits. European women were not openly delivered to sexual assaults – though proletarian women, raped with impunity, were themselves punished for it. So too, European women suffered the agony of seeing their children taken away and sold on the auction block. The economic profit derived from their imposed births was far more concealed. In this sense, it is the condition of the enslaved woman that most explicitly reveals the truth and the logic of capitalist accumulation. But despite the differences, in both cases, the female body was turned into an instrument for the reproduction of labour and the expansion of the workforce, treated as a natural breeding-machine, functioning according to rhythms outside of women's control.

This aspect of primitive accumulation is absent in Karl Marx's analysis. Except for his remarks in the *Communist Manifesto* on the use of women within the bourgeois family – as producers of heirs guaranteeing the transmission of family property – Marx never acknowledged that procreation could become a terrain of exploitation and by the same token a terrain of resistance. He never imagined that women could refuse to reproduce, or that such a refusal could become part of class struggle. In the *Grundrisse*, he argued that capitalist development proceeds irrespective of population numbers because, by virtue of the increasing productivity of labour, the labour that capital exploits constantly diminishes in relation to 'constant capital' (that is, the capital invested in machinery and other production assets), with the consequent determination of a 'surplus population'.[15] But this dynamic, which Marx defines as the 'law of population typical of the capitalist mode of production', could only prevail if procreation were a purely biological process, or an activity responding automatically to economic change, and if capital and the state did not need to worry about 'women going on strike against child making'.[16] This, in fact, is what Marx assumed. He acknowledged that capitalist development was accompanied by an increase in population, and he occasionally discussed the causes. But, like Adam Smith before him, he saw this increase as a 'natural effect' of economic development, and in *Capital*

Volume 1 he repeatedly contrasted the determination of a 'surplus population' with 'natural increase'.

Why procreation should be 'a fact of nature' rather than a social, historically determined activity, invested by diverse interests and power relations, is a question Marx did not ask. Nor did he imagine that men and women might have different interests with respect to child making, an activity which he treated as a gender-neutral, undifferentiated process. In reality, procreation and population changes are so far from being automatic or 'natural' that, in all phases of capitalist development, the state has had to resort to regulation and coercion to expand or reduce the workforce. This was especially true at the time of the capitalist take-off, when the muscles and bones of workers were the primary means of production. But even later – down to the present – the state has spared no efforts in its attempt to wrench from women's hands the control over reproduction, and to determine which children should be born, where, when, or in what numbers. Consequently, women have often been forced to procreate against their will, and have experienced an alienation from their bodies, their 'labour', and even their children, deeper than that experienced by any other workers.[17] In fact, no one can describe the anguish and desperation suffered by a woman seeing her body turn against herself, as must occur in the case of an unwanted pregnancy. This is particularly true in those situations in which out-of-wedlock pregnancies are penalised, and when having a child makes a woman vulnerable to social ostracism or even death. By denying women control over their bodies, the state deprived them of the most fundamental condition for physical and psychological integrity and degraded maternity to the status of forced labour.

Women's productive labour as 'non-work'

A complementary historical process was the definition of women as non-workers, a phenomenon much studied by feminists. Women began losing ground even with respect to jobs that had been their prerogative. Proletarian women in particular found it difficult to obtain any job other than those carrying the lowest status: domestic servants, farm-hands, spinners, knitters, embroiderers, hawkers, wet nurses. As Merry Wiesner writes, the assumption was gaining ground (in the law, in the tax records, in the ordinances of the guilds) that women should not work outside the home, and should engage in 'production' only to help their husbands. Work that women did at home was treated as non-work and worthless – even when done for the market.[18] Thus, if a woman sewed clothes it was 'domestic work' or 'housekeeping', even if the clothes were not for the family, whereas when a man did the same task it was considered 'productive'. Such was the devaluation of women's labour that city governments told the guilds to overlook the production women (especially widows) did in their homes, because it was not real work, and because the women needed it not to fall on public relief. Wiesner adds that women accepted this fiction and even apologised when pleading for work.[19] Soon all female work, if done in the home, was defined as 'housekeeping' and even outside the home it was paid less than men's work – never enough for women to be able to live by it. Marriage was now seen as a woman's true career, and women's inability to support themselves was taken so much for granted, that if a single woman tried to settle in a village, she was driven away even if she earned a wage.

Combined with land dispossession, this loss of power with regard to wage employment led to the massification of prostitution. Le Roy Ladurie notes that prostitutes in France were visible everywhere, and by 1594 their 'shameful traffic' flourished as never before.[20] The situation was similar in English cities where every day, poor women arrived from the countryside, and even the wives of craftsmen rounded out the family income with this work. A proclamation issued by the political authorities in Madrid, in 1631, denounced the problem, complaining that many vagabond women were now wandering among the city streets, alleys, and taverns, enticing men to sin with them.[21] But no sooner had prostitution become the main form of female subsistence than institutional attitudes changed. Whereas in the late Middle Ages it had been officially accepted as a necessary evil, in the sixteenth century the situation reversed. In a climate of intense misogyny, characterised by the Protestant Reformation and by witch-hunting, prostitution was first subjected to restrictions, then criminalised. Everywhere, between 1530 and 1560, town brothels were closed and streetwalkers were banished, flogged, or met other cruel forms of chastisement. Among them was 'the ducking stool' or *acabussade*, whereby victims were tied up, sometimes forced into a cage, and then repeatedly immersed in rivers or ponds, till they almost drowned.[22] Meanwhile, in sixteenth century France, rape of a prostitute ceased to be a crime.[23] In Madrid, as well, it was decided that female vagabonds and prostitutes should not be allowed to stay and sleep in the streets and under the porticos of the town, and if caught should be given a hundred lashes, then banned from the city for six years, in addition to having their heads and eyebrows shaved.

We can connect the banning of prostitution and the expulsion of women from the organised workplace with the creation of 'the housewife' and reconstruction of the family as locus for the production of labour-power. An important factor in the devaluation of women's labour was the campaign that craft workers mounted, starting in the late fifteenth century, to exclude women from their work-shops, presumably to protect themselves from capitalist merchants employing women at cheaper rates. The craftsmen's efforts have left an abundant trail of evidence.[24] Whether in Italy, France, or Germany, journeymen petitioned authorities not to allow women to compete with them, went on strike when the ban was not observed, and refused to work with men who worked with women. The craftsmen were also interested in limiting women to domestic work because, given their economic difficulties, 'the prudent household management on the part of a wife' was an indispensable condition for their avoiding bankruptcy and for keeping an independent shop. Sigrid Brauner speaks of the importance accorded by German artisans to this social rule.[25] Women tried to resist this onslaught, but – faced with the intimidating tactics male workers used against them – they failed. Those who dared to work out of the home, in a public space and for the market, were portrayed as sexually aggressive shrews or even as 'whores' and 'witches'.[26] Indeed, there is evidence of a wave of misogyny in late fifteenth century European cities – reflected in men's obsession with the 'battle for the breeches' and with the character of the disobedient wife, pictured in the popular literature in the act of beating her husband or riding on his back.

The displacement of women from craft industry provided the necessary basis for their fixation in reproductive labour and utilisation as low-waged workers in cottage industry. From this alliance between craftsmen and urban authorities, along with the continuing privatisation of land, a new sexual division of labour, or in Carole Pateman's words, a new 'sexual contract' was forged. This defined women in terms – mothers, wives, daughters, widows – hiding their status as workers, while giving men free access to their bodies and labour, and the bodies and labour of their children.[27] According to this new social-sexual contract, proletarian women became for male workers a substitute for land lost in the enclosures – the basic means of reproduction – and a communal good that anyone could appropriate at will. Echoes of this 'primitive appropriation' can be heard in the concept of the 'common woman', which in the sixteenth century qualified those who prostituted themselves.[28] But in the new organisation of work every woman (other than those privatised by bourgeois men) became a communal good, for once women's activities were defined as non-work, women's labour began to appear as a 'natural resource', no less than the air we breathe or the water we drink. Poverty became feminised, and a new patriarchal order was constructed, reducing women to a double dependence: on employers and on men in general. In pre-capitalist Europe women's subordination had been tempered by the fact that they had access to common land and other communal assets, while in the new capitalist regime, women themselves became the commons, as their work was defined as a natural resource, lying outside of the sphere of market relations.

In the new bourgeois family, the husband became the representative of the state, charged with disciplining and supervising the 'subordinate classes', a category that for sixteenth and seventeenth century political theorists like Bodin included the man's wife and his children.[29] Thus occurred the identification of the family as a micro-state or a micro-church, and the demand by authorities that single workers live under the roof and rule of a master. Within the bourgeois family the woman lost much of her power, being generally excluded from the family business and confined to supervision of the household. While in the bourgeois family, property gave husbands power over their wives, a similar power was granted to working-class men over women by means of women's exclusion from the wage. Exemplary of this trend was the family of cottage workers in the putting-out system. Far from shunning marriage and family-making, male cottage workers depended on it, for a wife could 'help' them with the work they would do for the merchants, while caring for their physical needs, and providing them with children, who from an early age could be employed at the loom or in some subsidiary occupation. What stands out in this type of arrangement is that though the wife worked side-by-side with her husband, she too producing for the market, it was the husband who now received her wage.

It is in this sense that I speak of 'the patriarchy of the wage' and the concept of 'wage slavery'. If it is true that male workers only become formally free under the new wage-labour regime, the group of workers who, in the transition to capitalism, most approached the condition of slaves was working-class women. At the same time – given the wretched conditions in which waged workers lived – the housework that women performed to reproduce their families was necessarily limited. Married or not, proletarian women needed to earn some money, which they did by holding multiple jobs. Housework, moreover, requires some reproductive capital: furniture, utensils, clothing, and money for food. But waged workers lived poorly, 'slaving away by day and night' (as an artisan from Nuremberg denounced in 1524), just to stave off hunger and feed their wives and children.[30] Most barely had a roof over their heads, living in huts where other families and animals also resided, and where hygiene was totally lacking; their clothes were rags, their diet at best consisted of bread, cheese and some vegetables. Thus, we do not find yet, among the working class, the classic full-time housewife consumer.

The invention of 'femininity' and the 'housewife'

It was only in the late nineteenth century that the modern family, based upon the full-time housewife's unpaid reproductive labour, was generalised in the working class. Its development – following the passage of Factory Acts limiting the employment of women and children in the factories, reflected the first long-term investment the capitalist class made in the reproduction of the workforce beyond numerical expansion. It was a trade-off, forged under threat of insurrection, between the granting of higher wages, capable of supporting a 'non-working' wife, and a more intensive rate of exploitation. Marx spoke of it as a shift from 'absolute' to 'relative surplus', that is, a shift from a type of exploitation based upon the lengthening of the working day to a maximum and the reduction of the wage to a minimum, to a regime where higher wages and shorter hours would be compensated with an increase in the productivity of work and the pace of production. From the capitalist perspective, it was a social revolution, over-riding a long held commitment to low wages. It resulted from a new deal between workers and employers, again founded on the patriarchal exclusion of women from the wage – putting an end to their recruitment in the early phases of the Industrial Revolution. It was also the mark of a new capitalist affluence, the product of two centuries of exploitation of slave labour, soon to be boosted by a new phase of colonial expansion.

In the sixteenth and seventeenth centuries, by contrast, despite an obsessive concern with the size of population and the number of 'working poor', the actual investment in reproduction of the workforce had been extremely low. Consequently, the bulk of the reproductive labour done by proletarian women was not for their families, but for the families of their employers or for the market. One third of the female population, on average, in England, Spain, France, and Italy, worked as maids. Thus, in the proletariat, the tendency was towards the postponement of marriage and the disintegration of the family. Often the poor were even forbidden to marry, when it was feared that their children would fall on public relief, and when this actually happened, the children were taken away from them and farmed out to the parish to work. It is estimated that one third or more of the population of rural Europe remained single; in the towns the rates were even higher, especially among women; in Germany, 40 per cent were either 'spinsters' or widows.[31] Impoverished and disempowered as they might be, male waged workers could still benefit from their wives' labour and wages, or they could buy the services of prostitutes. Throughout this first phase of proletarianisation, it was the prostitute who often performed for male workers the function of a wife, cooking and washing for them in addition to serving them sexually. Moreover, the criminalisation of prostitution, which punished the woman but hardly touched her customers, strengthened men's power. Any man could now destroy a woman simply by declaring that she was a prostitute, or by publicising that she had given in to his sexual desires.

It is not surprising, then, in view of this devaluation of women's labour and social status that the insubordination of women and the methods by which they could be 'tamed' were among the main themes in the literature and social policy of the 'transition' to modernity.[32] Women could not have been totally devalued as workers and deprived of autonomy with respect to men without being subjected to an intense process of social degradation; and indeed, throughout the sixteenth and seventeenth centuries, women lost ground in every area of social life. A key area of change in this respect was the law, involving a steady erosion of women's rights.[33] One of the main rights that women lost was the right to conduct economic activities alone, as *femmes soles*. In France, they lost the right to make contracts or to represent themselves in court, being declared legal 'imbeciles'. In Italy, they began to appear less frequently in the courts to denounce abuses perpetrated against them. In Germany, when a middle-class woman became a widow, it became customary to appoint a tutor to manage her affairs. German women were also forbidden to live alone or with other women and, in the case of the poor, even with their own families, since it was expected that they would not be properly controlled. In sum, together with economic and social devaluation, women experienced a form of legal infantilisation.

The punishment of female insubordination to patriarchal authority was celebrated in countless misogynous plays and tracts. And in the Age of Reason, women accused of being scolds were muzzled like dogs and paraded in the streets, prostitutes were whipped, while capital punishment was established for women convicted of adultery.[34] It is no exaggeration to say that women were treated with the same hostility and sense of estrangement accorded 'Indian savages' after the Conquest of America. The cultural denigration, even demonisation of American indigenous people served to justify their enslavement and the plunder of their resources. The attack waged on women in Europe justified the appropriation of their labour by men and the criminalisation of their control over production. But none of the tactics deployed against European women and colonial subjects would have succeeded without a campaign of terror. In Europe this was the witch-hunt. The definition of women as demonic beings, and the atrocious and humiliating practices to which so many were subjected left indelible marks in the collective female psyche. From every viewpoint – socially, economically, culturally, politically – the witch-hunt was a turning point in the history of European women, a rehearsal of the historic defeat that Frederick Engels alludes to in *The Origin of the Family, Private Property, and the State* as cause of the downfall of the matriarchal world.[35] For the witch-hunt destroyed a whole world of female practices, collective relations, and systems of knowledge that had been the foundation of women's power in pre-capitalist Europe and the condition of their resistance in the struggle against feudalism. Out of this defeat, a new model of femininity emerged. By the end of the seventeenth century, after women had been subjected to more than two centuries of state terrorism, a new model emerged: the ideal-typical woman became the wife – passive, obedient, thrifty, of few words, always busy at work, and chaste.

Sex, race, and class in the colonies

While the response to the population crisis in Europe was the subjugation of women to enforced reproduction, in America, where colonisation had destroyed 95 per cent of the aboriginal population, the response was the slave trade, which delivered to the European ruling class an immense quantity of labour-power. As early as the sixteenth century, approximately 1 million African slaves and indigenous workers were producing surplus-value for Spain in colonial America. This rate of exploitation was far higher than that of workers in Europe, and contributed considerably to sectors of the European economy that were developing in a capitalist direction. By 1600, Brazil alone exported twice the value in sugar of all the wool that England exported in the same year.[36] Gold imported from Brazil re-activated commerce and industry in Europe too.[37] More than 17,000 tons were imported by 1640, giving the capitalist class an exceptional advantage in access to workers, commodities, and land.[38] But the true wealth was the labour accumulated through the slave trade – a mode of production that could not be imposed in Europe. It is now established that the plantation system fuelled the Industrial Revolution, and as Eric Williams has noted, hardly a brick in Liverpool and Bristol was not cemented with African blood.[39] In fact, capitalism may not even have taken off without Europe's 'annexation of America' and the blood and sweat that for two centuries flowed to Europe from the plantations. Slavery has been essential to the development of capitalism; and systematically, whenever this economic system has been threatened by a major crisis, the capitalist class has launched a process of 'primitive accumulation' – a large-scale drive to new colonisation and enslavement, just like the one we witness at present.[40]

In addition to this, the plantation system set in place a model of labour management, export-oriented production, economic integration and international division of labour, that have become paradigmatic for capitalist class relations. With its immense concentration of workers and a captive labour force uprooted from its homeland, the plantation prefigured not only the factory, but also the use of immigration and globalisation to cut the cost of labour. In particular, the plantation was a key step in the formation of an international division of labour that (through the production of 'consumer goods') integrated the work of the slaves into the reproduction of the European workforce, while keeping enslaved and waged workers geographically and socially divided. The colonial production of sugar, tea, tobacco, rum, and cotton – the most important commodities, together with bread, in the production of labour-power in Europe – did not take off on a large scale until after the 1650s. This was after slavery had been institutionalised and wages in Europe had begun to rise modestly.[41] There were two mechanisms involved in restructuring the reproduction of labour-power internationally. On one side, a global assembly line was created that cut the cost of the commodities necessary to produce labour-power in Europe. This linked enslaved and waged workers in ways that anticipated how 'advanced' countries use Asians, Africans, and Latin Americans to provide 'cheap consumer' goods – cheapened by death squads and military violence. On the other side, the metropolitan wage became the vehicle by which goods produced by enslaved workers went to the market, and by which the value of the products of enslaved-labour was realised.

What travelled then, with the goods 'exported' from the plantations, was not only the blood of the slaves but the seeds of a new science of exploitation, and a new division of the working class by which waged-work, rather than providing an alternative to slavery, was made to depend on it for its very existence. This functioned in parallel to the way in which female unpaid labour served to expand the unpaid part of the waged working day. So closely integrated were the lives of enslaved labourers in America and waged labourers in Europe, that in the Caribbean islands, where slaves were given plots of land or 'provision grounds' to cultivate for their own use, how much land was allotted and how much time was allowed to cultivate it, varied in proportion to the price of sugar on the world-market plausibly determined by the dynamics of workers' wages and workers' struggle over reproduction.[42] It would be a mistake, however, to conclude that slave labour created a community of interest between European workers and metropolitan capitalists – cemented by their common desire for cheap imported goods. Like the Conquest, the slave trade was an epochal misfortune for European workers, impacting on their wages and legal status – it is no coincidence that only with the end of slavery did wages in Europe increase and workers gain the right to organise. It is also important to remember that it was the anti-feudal struggle that had instigated the lesser nobility and merchants to seek colonial expansion, and that the slave traders, like the earlier conquistadors, came from the ranks of those most hated by the European working class.

That racism like sexism had to be legislated and enforced is demonstrated from the history of the American colonies. Until the mid-seventeenth century, when slavery was institutionalised, the status of African slaves in the New World was not significantly different from that of European indentured servants, with whom they worked side by side and often joined in their revolts. Low-class English women 'transported' from Britain as convicts or indentured servants were also a significant part of the labour gangs on the sugar estates. 'Considered unfit for marriage to propertied white males, and disqualified for domestic service' because of their insolence and riotous disposition, 'landless white women were dismissed to manual labour in plantations, public construction works, and the urban service sector. In these worlds they socialized intimately with the slave community, and with enslaved black men.'[43] They established households and had children with them. They also cooperated as well as competed with female slaves in the marketing of produce or stolen goods. Only with the institutionalisation of slavery, motivated by the fear of alliances between black and white servants, were racial boundaries drawn. Regardless of their social origins, some white women were upgraded, married into the colonial power structure, and even became owners of slaves themselves, usually employed for domestic work.[44]

A sexual division of labour also, was instituted among the colonised and slaved populations. Thus, in Mexico and Peru, the response to demographic decline was to recommend that female domestic labour in the home be incentivised. Spanish authorities, stripped indigenous women of their autonomy, and gave their male kin more power over them. Under the new laws, married women became men's property, and were forced (against the traditional custom) to follow their husbands to their homes. A *compadrazgo* system was also created further limiting their rights, placing the authority over children in male hands. In addition, to ensure that indigenous women reproduced the workers recruited to do *mita* work in the mines, the Spanish authorities legislated that no one could separate husband from wife. So women were forced to follow their husbands even to areas known to be death camps, due to the pollution created by mining.[45]

In the American plantations, until the abolition of the slave trade, as both Barbara Bush and Marietta Morrissey show, women and men were each subject to the same degree of exploitation; the planters found it more profitable to work and 'consume' slaves to death than to encourage their reproduction. Thus, neither the sexual division of labour, nor sexual hierarchies were as pronounced as in Europe. African men had no say concerning the destiny of their female companions and kin; and women were expected to work in the fields like men, especially when sugar and tobacco were in high demand. Ironically then, it would seem that in slavery women 'achieved' a rough equality with the men of their class.[46] But women were given less to eat, and unlike men, were vulnerable to their masters' sexual assaults. In addition to the physical agony of labour and punishment, women had to bear sexual humiliation and the damage done to the foetuses they carried. When the slave trade was abolished in 1807, the Caribbean and American planters adopted a 'slave breeding' policy. On Barbados, plantation owners had attempted to control the reproductive patterns of female slaves since the seventeenth century, depending on how much field labour was needed. But only when the supply of African slaves diminished did the regulation of women's sexual relations and reproductive patterns become more systematic and intense.[47]

Yet women's refusals of victimisation both reshaped the sexual division of labour and had a decisive impact on the culture of the white population, especially through their activities as healers, seers, experts in magical practices, and their 'domination' of the kitchens, and bedrooms, of their masters.[48] Not surprisingly, they were seen as the heart of the slave community. Visitors were impressed by their singing, their head-kerchiefs and dresses, and their extravagant manner of speaking, which is now understood as a means of satirising their masters. African and Creole women influenced the customs of poor female whites, whom a contemporary portrayed as behaving like Africans, walking with their children strapped on their hips, while balancing trays with goods on their heads.[49] But their main achievement was the development of a politics of self-reliance, grounded in survival strategies and female networks. These practices and the values attached to them, which Rosalyn Terborg Penn has identified as the essential tenets of contemporary African feminism, redefined the African community of the *diaspora*.[50] They created not only the foundations for a new female African identity, but also the foundations for a society committed against the capitalist attempt to impose scarcity and dependence as structural conditions of life. This political vision is alive today, and enjoined by women across the globe calling for reappropriation in women's hands of the means of subsistence, starting from land, the production of food, and the inter-generational transmission of knowledge and cooperation.

Notes

1. David Stannard, *American Holocaust: Columbus and the Conquest of the New World*, Oxford University Press, 1992.
2. Henry Kamen, *The Iron Century: Social Change in Europe 1550–1660*, New York: Praeger, 1972, pp. 32–3.
3. David Hackett Fischer, *The Great Wave: Price Revolutions and the Rhythm of History*, Oxford University Press, 1996, p. 91.
4. Michel Foucault, *History of Sexuality*, Vol. I, New York: Random House, 1978. 'Bio-power' describes the reach of states over individual bodies.
5. Bruce Curtis, 'Foucault on Governmentality and Population: The Impossible Discovery', *Canadian Journal of Sociology*, 2002, Vol. 27, No. 4, 505–33. 'Populousness' was an organic concept, used by mercantilists to talk about the part of the social body that creates wealth, that is, labourers; 'population' is an atomistic notion.
6. See Michel Foucault, *Madness and Civilization: A History of Insanity in the Age of Reason*, New York: Random House, 1973, pp. 38–64.

7. Giovanni Botero, *Delle Cause Della Grandeza Delle Citta*, Rome, 1588.

8. Margaret King, *Women of the Renaissance*, University of Chicago Press, 1991, p. 115.

9. Eli Heckscher, *Mercantilism*, Vol. I and II, London: Allen and Unwin, 1965, p. 158.

10. King, *Women of the Renaissance*, p. 10. On the new legislation against infanticide see John Riddle, *Eve's Herbs: A History of Contraception and Abortion in the West*, Cambridge University Press, 1997, pp. 163–6; Merry Wiesner, *Working Women in Renaissance Germany*, New Brunswick: Rutgers University Press, 1993, pp. 52–3.

11. King, *Women of the Renaissance*, pp. 51–2.

12. Wiesner, *Working Women in Renaissance Germany*, pp. 51–2. The same observation is made in Steven Ozment, *When Father Ruled Family Life in Reformation Europe*, Cambridge, MA: Harvard University Press, 1983, p. 43.

13. Ozment, *When Father Ruled Family Life in Reformation Europe*, pp. 42–4.

14. Ulinka Rublack, 'Pregnancy, Childbirth, and the Female Body in Early Modern Germany', *Past and Present*, 1996, No. 150, 84–110.

15. Karl Marx, *Grundrisse 1857–58*, London: Penguin, 1973, p. 100.

16. Karl Marx, *Capital*, Vols I and III, Chicago: Kerr, 1909, pp. 689ff.

17. Emily Martin, *The Woman in the Body: A Cultural Analysis of Reproduction*, Boston: Beacon, 1987, pp. 19–21.

18. Wiesner, *Working Women in Renaissance Germany*, pp. 83ff.

19. Ibid., pp. 84–5.

20. Emanuel Le Roy Ladurie, *Peasants of Languedoc*, Paris: Gallimard, 1974, pp. 112–13.

21. Marilo Vigil, *La Vida de La Mujeres en Los Siglos XVI y XVII*, Madrid: Siglo Veinttiuno de Espana Editores, 1986, pp. 114–15.

22. Nickie Roberts, *Whores in History: Prostitution in Western Society*, New York: Harper Collins, 1992, pp. 115–16.

23. King, *Women of the Renaissance*, p. 78; Wiesner, *Working Women in Renaissance Germany*, pp. 194–209.

24. See David Herlihy, *Women, Family and Society in Medieval Europe: Historical Essays*, Providence, RI: Berghahn Books, 1995, for a catalogue of women's expulsion from the crafts; also Wiesner, *Working Women in Renaissance Germany*, pp. 174–85.

25. Sigrid Brauner, *Fearless Wives and Frightened Shrews: The Construction of the Witch in Early Modern Germany*, Amherst: University of Massachusetts Press, 1995, pp. 96–7.

26. Martha Howell, *Women, Production and Patriarchy in Late Medieval Cities*, University of Chicago Press, 1986, pp. 182–3.

27. Carole Pateman, *The Sexual Contract*, Stanford University Press, 1988, argues that the 'social contract' theory of Hobbes and Locke rested on a more fundamental 'sexual contract', recognising men's right to appropriate women's bodies and labour. See also Zilla Eisenstein, *The Radical Future of Liberal Feminism*, New York: Longman, 1981; Margaret Sommerville, *Sex and Subjection: Attitudes to Women in Early Modern Society*, London: Arnold, 1995.

28. Ruth Mazo Karras, 'The Regulation of Brothels in Later Medieval Europe', *Signs: Journal of Women, Culture and Society*, 1989, Vol. 14, No. 2, 399–433: Karras notes that '"common woman" meant a woman available to all men; unlike "common man" which denoted someone of humble origins and could be used in either a derogatory or a laudatory sense' (p. 138).

29. Gordon Schochet, *Patriarchalism in Political Thought*, New York: Basic Books, 1975.

30. Brauner, *Fearless Wives and Frightened Shrews*, p. 96.

31. Ozment, *When Father Ruled Family Life in Reformation Europe*, pp. 41–2.

32. David Underdown, *Revel, Riot and Rebellion: Popular Politics in Culture and England 1603–1660*, Oxford: Clarendon, 1985, pp. 116–36.

33. According to Wiesner, *Working Women in Renaissance Germany*, p. 33: 'The spread of Roman law had a largely negative effect on women's civil legal status in the early modern period'.

34. Underdown, *Revel, Riot and Rebellion*, pp. 117ff.

35. Frederick Engels, *The Origin of the Family, Private Property, and the State*, New York: International Publishers, 1942.

36. James Blaut, *1492: The Debate on Colonialism, Eurocentrism and History*, Trenton, NJ: Africa World Press, 1992, pp. 42–6.

37. Jean De Vries, *The Economy of Europe in an Age of Crisis 1660–1750*, Cambridge University Press, 1976, p. 20.

38. Blaut, *1492*, pp. 38–40.

39. Eric Williams, *Capitalism and Slavery*, New York: Capricorn, 1944, pp. 61–3.

40. Kevin Bales, *Disposable People: New Slavery in the Global Economy*, Berkeley: University of California Press, 1999.

41. Nick Rowling, *Commodities: How the World was Taken to Market*, London: Free Association Books, 1987, pp. 51, 76, 85.

42. Marietta Morrissey, *Slave Women in the New World: Gender Stratification in the Caribbean*, Lawrence: University Press of Kansas, 1989, pp. 51–9.

43. Hilary Beckles, 'Sex and Gender in the Historiography of Caribbean Slavery' in Verene Shepherd et al. (eds), *Engendering History: Caribbean Women in Historical Perspective*, New York: St Martins, 1995.

44. Ibid., p. 74.

45. David Cook Noble, *Demograpic Collapse in Indian Peru*, Cambridge University Press, 1981, pp. 205–6.

46. Janey Momsen (ed.), *Women and Change in the Caribbean: A Pan-Carribean Perspective*, London: James Currey, 1993; Barbara Bush, *Slave Women in Caribbean Society 1650–1838*, Bloomington: Indiana University Press; Morrissey, *Slave Women in the New World*, pp. 42–4.

47. Beckles, 'Sex and Gender in the Historiography of Caribbean Slavery', p. 92.

48. Bush, *Slave Women in Caribbean Society 1650–1838*.

49. Beckles, 'Sex and Gender in the Historiography of Caribbean Slavery', p. 81.

50. Rosalyn Terborg Penn, 'Through an African Feminist Theoretical Lens: Viewing Caribbean Women's History Cross-culturally' in Verene Shepherd et al. (eds), *Engendering History: Caribbean Women in Historical Perspective*, New York: St Martins, 1995.

3

WHO IS THE 'HE' OF HE WHO DECIDES IN ECONOMIC DISCOURSE?

Ewa Charkiewicz

Before her untimely death, Teresa Brennan wrote a book on economic globalisation as war on human beings and nature – *Globalization and Its Terrors*.[1] The backbone of her analysis was the concept of energetics, in which she revised Marx's labour theory of value. As she argued, adding value to money requires the input of living nature (human and non-human) into products and services. As 'raw materials', nature and human labour are sources of energy and sources of surplus value. Both labour and nature give more than they cost. Capital does not pay the costs of reproduction of people, but transfers these costs to households (to the care economy, as some feminists would say). Nor does capital pay for the reproduction of nature (under substitution law), unless forced to do so.

> The real costs of nature are always deferred ... Speed of acquisition and spatial expansion increase pressures on living nature ... In the event that natural processes of reproduction cannot be speeded up, the cost of natural reproduction has to be reduced to make up for the drag on exchange-value.[2]

Hence, not surprisingly, income disparities increase, and new societal groups emerge, the hyper-rich and human-waste, disposed of to the 'death zones' as Achille Mbembe would say, or 'zones of social abandonment' according to João Biehl.[3] Life is consumed and killed in the accumulation of capital. In addition to dislocation from livelihoods and exploitation of human bodies to exhaustion,

Brennan wrote that 'new forms of immiseration relate to making a body ill with the constant bombardment of toxins'.[4] Her revision of the labour theory of value was first published in the ISEE journal, *Ecological Economics* in 1997.

Although it is very tempting to give more time to detailed exposition and further reworking of her analyses, in this chapter I would like to fit it into a portable ecofeminist interpretive machine that helps to make sense of how economic processes of production, and consumption, and each and all of us, are entangled with death and war. Relations between nature, labour, and capital, are but one of many domains in the social organisation of human existence through which violence, including its extreme form – the power to kill – is maintained and reproduced. By Michel Foucault's analysis, the economic is inseparable from the personal, the social, or political. Foucault was a French political philosopher, who focused on the mutually constitutive relations of truth, power, and knowledge. The question for Foucault, was not what is the truth, but how truth games (and rules for the production of truth) are connected with power relations, how the truth effects of knowledge coalesce with relations of power, and how they congeal over time to produce real and material effects. For Foucault power is always relational and anonymous, 'it is the name that one attributes to a complex strategical situation in a particular society'.[5] Deployed through a network-like organisation, power circulates through bodies, things and discourses that 'come into contention and struggle'. Its main vehicle of distribution is discourse. A discourse for Foucault is a set of statements about an issue that governs its object in the context of conditions, which 'enable, constrain, and define what passes for truth at a particular historical period'.

Economics as a seriality of truth games

In this sense, economics as a discourse that governs economic life is a seriality of 'truth games' (theories, arguments, calculation that make an object visible and shape it) that undergo transformations, and govern subjects, households, a market or national economy –

and which structure and entice the adjustment of bodies and social forms of organisation with economic rationalities. This never happens in a linear, teleological manner – 'discursive elements … can come to play in different strategies'.[6] The truth effects of discourse are always contingent and bound to an inter-discursive field, in which colliding, colluding, or annulling discourses compete with contingent outcomes.

To discern regularities in the complex field of relations between power and truth, Foucault deployed original strategies and conceptual devices to analyse power (like sovereignty – the right of death and power over life; pastoral power; biopolitics or the regulation and administration of life). His main analytical strategy was to study power from its effects, where it installs itself, in its most capillary applications, like the body or subjectivity. Applying this advice to the study of economic globalisation one could start for instance with a computer or a cut flower to see – beginning at this capillary application – how relations between people, things, forms of representation and capital flows in global toy or flower production and consumption networks are (re)organised.

Now, what has Foucault to do with Brennan and her re-working of Marx's labour theory of value – which Marx in turn, had re-worked from Ricardo, who took clues for his work from patristic teaching and economic theology? In Foucault's understanding power relations are interdependent with economic relations and relations of meaning (sign systems). But they have to be studied separately and in addition to other systems of relations. Brennan talks of energy, which flows through living (human and non-human) nature and is appropriated by capital. As producers and consumers, human subjects are involved in and sustain these flows. Foucault talks of the productivity of a network-like organised power, which is co-extensive with the 'social body', and gives it shape. In fact, power produces; it produces reality; it produces forms of knowledge, domains of objects, and rituals of truth; it produces discourses, and engages subjects in their own subordination. Foucault's analyses of discursively and historically organised relations between power and truth provide a far more complex picture of modern society than Marxism. To have a more complete picture of the mutual adjustment in the accumulation of people and the accumulation of capital, the second part of this equation, that is, mechanisms of the accumulation of capital have to be taken into account as well. In this sense, Brennan and Foucault provide complementary frameworks or strategies to 'walk around' the subject of this chapter, to view it from multiple sites, to bring in the analysis of economic relations as well as the analysis of discursive power of economic discourse.

To investigate the persistence of violence in how human societies are governed and govern themselves, I would like to revisit the analyses of relations between sovereignty and life developed by Foucault and philosophers, such as Giorgio Agamben and Achille Mbembe, who followed in his footsteps.[7] The point I want to argue is that sovereignty, defined by Foucault as a form of power endowed with the right and capacities to kill does not only operate through the state and law, it operates through the market, in particular, through capital's propensity to reproduce. My argument therefore, differs from Hardt and Negri, who associate sovereignty with capital, but trace the transmission of sovereignty from the nation state to the global empire.[8]

Economic discourse is one of several conduits accounting for the persistence of sovereignty. Historically, this discourse was devoted to the development of knowledge, rules, and techniques for management of the familial household and estate (*oikos* in Greek, *familia* in Latin), and subsequently, for management of a firm or national and global economy. Economic discourse has strong theological underpinnings.[9] From a feminist-Foucauldian perspective, sovereignty is co-extensive with patriarchy. At one extreme, the meeting point for patriarchy and sovereignty is theological – via legitimisation of the transfer of political power and laws from God, be it Allah, Jahweh, or the God of the New Testament.[10] At the other extreme, there are colluding applications of sovereignty and patriarchy in the management of political and economic life, or in the regulation and control of 'living nature'. This is where Brennan's concept of energetics derived from Marx, a Foucauldian analytics of power, and feminist critiques of patriarchy and economic discourse meet, to explain the integration of death in systems of production and consumption, and how life has to be killed or maintained in what Agamben calls the zone of indistinction between living and dying.[11] This is the easiest available course by which financial capital can expand, and by which patriarchal controls over women and wealth can be maintained.

How to train a wife and manage an estate

One of the opening statements in the history of economic discourse is Xenophon's tract the *Oeconomicus* (*The Economist*), written around 400 BC. It involves a dialogue between Socrates and Critobulus on profitable estate management where the former claims:

> We agreed that economy was the proper title of a branch of knowledge, and this branch of knowledge appeared to be that whereby men are enabled to enhance the value of their houses or estates; and by this word 'house or estate' we understood the whole of a man's possessions ... all that a man knows how to use and turn to good account.[12]

In Xenophon's account wealth comes from interaction with the economy of nature. 'She is the sweet mistress who, with smile of welcome and outstretched hand, greets the approach of her devoted one, seeming to say, Take from me all thy heart's desire ...'[13] The gift is designated for the 'devoted' manager. Transforming nature into wealth requires the knowledge of nature, skills in tilling the land, and knowledge and skills in the management of labour. The two meet in what is then called 'the art of husbandry'. It is the economist or manager as 'the husbander' who creates nature's utility.

The figure has its double, that of the skilful military leader, who arranges the right movement and distribution of bodies, and trains his troops for effective defence or attack:

> ... there is yet another lesson to be learnt in the public school of husbandry – the lesson of mutual assistance. 'Shoulder to shoulder' must we march to meet the invader; 'shoulder to shoulder' stand to compass the tillage of the

soil. Therefore it is that the husbandman, who means to win in his avocation, must see that he creates enthusiasm in his workpeople and a spirit of ready obedience; which is just what a general attacking an enemy will scheme to bring about, when he deals out gifts to the brave and castigation to those who are disorderly ...[14]

Xenophon goes on to say that Nature is not ploughed for personal economic gain alone: 'Earth, too, adds stimulus in war-time to earth's tillers; she pricks them on to aid the country under arms' ...[15]

The dialogue between Socrates and Critobulus includes 'a case study' of the management of *oikos* by Ischomachus. For Socrates, Ischomachus is a role model for 'the good and beautiful man'. What makes Ischomachus interesting to discuss is his 'innovative' project of training his wife to manage the household, and his wealth. As we find out from the dialogue, his ability to train the wife, and his wealth are related. Marriage is an economic-reproductive union:

... my wife, would seem to have exercised much care and judgment in compacting that twin system which goes by the name of male and female, so as to secure the greatest possible advantage to the pair ... underlying principle of the bond is first and foremost to perpetuate through procreation the races of living creatures; and next, as the outcome of this bond, for human beings at any rate, a provision is made by which they may have sons and daughters to support them in old age.[16]

Ischomachus marries his 15 year old wife by arrangement with her parents, saying that 'as regards control of appetite and self-indulgence, she had received the soundest education, and that I take to be the most important matter in the bringing-up of man or woman'.[17] While her mother had educated her about food, knitting and trained her in obedience, Ischomachus has to train the wife in new skills. In order to be 'capable of attending carefully to her appointed duties', she has to be empowered to perform her tasks with enthusiasm, dedication, and diligence. For that, Ischomachus solicits the support of gods, by taking her to pray together for her enlightenment. At the same time, he invokes gods and nature as the justification for the sexual division of skills, capabilities, and labour. Gods and nature make man strong, that is why he works outdoors, while a woman is weak, fragile and has to be protected, hence she stays at home. To generate her commitment, Ischomachus portrays her to herself as a queen bee who presides in the hive, and never leaves it. The house is common property. If the wife contributes to enhance its value, that will be to her benefit as well. 'We need not stop to calculate in figures which of us contributed most, but rather let us lay to heart this fact that whichever of us proves the better partner, he or she at once contributes what is most worth having.'[18]

In addition to 'empowerment' of the wife so that she performs her duties out of her own volition, the second component of training is the instruction on the right spatial and functional disposition of things and people (slaves). For this purpose, Ischomachus takes his wife on a tour through the house, which is divided into private quarters (the bedroom), and work and entertainment quarters. While the mistress and master enjoy a common bedroom, the slaves' sleeping quarters are segregated on the basis of sex, so that proper order is maintained and no children will be borne without prior decision of the master. In the working space of the house, each tool, each produce has its own allocated space. Tools are associated with the workers who use them, who in turn are assigned responsibility for their proper maintenance. The wife is expected to oversee that each person, and each thing is in its right place.

The 'wife' here, is constructed in dialogue as a thinking subject who is not dealt with by crude force but persuaded as to what is good for her, to make her strive to adjust. She is also a reproductive resource so that children can provide security in old age. And at the same time, she is part of 'a man's possessions … all that a man knows how to use and turn to good account'.[19] What we see here is an extremely durable, at least 2,500 years old paradigm for integrating women into the economy in a manner by which women are included as providers of labour, skills, and reproductive capacities. Yet through discursive power, women are excluded from outdoor wealth generating activities, from overall supervision of wealth production, and from design and decisions on 'the art of household management'. The wife of Ischomachus is portrayed as a diligent implementer of her husband's instructions. Her input to management and the multiplication of familial wealth, and therefore entitlements to wealth, are less than those of her husband (her wedded sovereign). The ultimate 'he, who decides', the Knower, the Owner in his own right, the Manager (not the co-owner of common property), is Ischomachus.

Sovereignty and patriarchy as *dispositif*

The discursive construction of women, created by 'gods and nature' as 'weak' and mentally less capable than men, provides justification for this arrangement as 'natural'. Meanwhile, the sovereign power articulated in laws on marriage, inheritance, and transfer of property supports patriarchal domestic arrangements.[20] It is the manager dedicated to enhancement of wealth, the citizen dedicated to his 'beautiful life', the soldier that meets in Ischomachus – the emblematic figure of an enlightened patriarchal sovereign. The powers at work are at the same time individualising according to categories of gender and class – while simultaneously operating through anonymous and interlocked networks of rule that produce the right disposition of people and things. The 'right disposition of things' allows sovereign and patriarchal right and duty to be enacted, enhancing wealth. Sexual and economic relations among people, and 'the right disposition of things' in the domain of the household and the estate have had matrices of reinforcement in the form of law. The study of Greek and ancient law points to the fact that the law-maker was concerned with regulating sexual and economic interactions, as well as interactions with nature. Sovereignty was established on and through the regulation of 'living nature'.

From the standpoint of the anonymous wife of Ischomachus, patriarchy is not only about the control of sexuality, or about the sexual division of labour alone. What further generates and sustains patriarchy is the establishment of discursive and material limits to the contribution of women to wealth, with a resulting delegitimisation from their entitlements to wealth. Patriarchy is not only prohibitive; it is also productive. It is a Foucauldian *dispositif* of power that produces relations and spatial arrangements between people, discourses, and things in such a manner as to assign sovereignty of men over women in the control of wealth and bodies, including controls over feminine sexuality. From this perspective, patriarchy is not just a rule of the father, it is a complex strategic and evolving system of relations through which male privilege and the subordination of women is produced. Foucault refers to the *dispositif* as a heterogeneous ensemble of material and discursive elements, which consists of 'discourses, institutions, architectural forms, regulatory decisions, laws, administrative measures, scientific statements, philosophical, and moral propositions'.[21] A *dispositif* is not only a heterogeneous collection of the above elements but also a system of relationships with an identifiable project. In this case, the project involves the reproduction of wealth and of patriarchal privilege. A *dispositif* has strategic (while not always predictable) effects. The *dispositif* can be likened to a landscape through which a body moves taking clues on how to proceed. Women and men are 'inside' the *dispositif*, hence what is at stake here is not only the validity of a woman centred approach in research, but gender relations as constitutive relations of power, and patriarchy as a complex system of power installing itself in bodies and at all sites of human existence. It is aligned with, rooted in, or superimposed by other forms of power, in particular via its archaic relation to sovereignty.

Within this understanding of patriarchy, women are not just victims or passive objects of domination, they are thinking, active subjects, who are exposed to and live within a patriarchal world, but have a degree of freedom to manoeuvre and react, to conform and to resist what in standard accounts is called patriarchal domination. Patriarchy was not abandoned with the advent of political rights and social contract. As Carole Pateman argues, patriarchy modernised itself, in new fraternal contracts among liberal and socialist brothers who liberated themselves from the dominion of the father but abandoned women to the household. Civil freedom coexists with patriarchal right over women.[22]

Moreover, as the politico-theoretical project of Hardt and Negri reveals, brothers endlessly engage in liberating themselves from reincarnated patriarchal empires. Taking a clue from Pateman's analysis and combining it with a Foucauldian analytic of power, I propose to demonstrate how patriarchy and sovereignty are alloyed with each other in the management of life.

In mainstream political discourse sovereignty takes definition from the Treaty of Westphalia 1648, which gave the sovereign state rights over its territory and populations. Nature has always been included in the sovereign juridical order. The social contract and liberal theory and eighteenth century juridical innovations such as the Declaration of Human Rights conceive of an autonomous sovereign individual who transfers his sovereignty to the body politic. Throughout Europe, the subject of political and economic discourse is the sovereign rational economic man, whose pursuit of self-interest generates global welfare. The two definitions of sovereignty are contradictory, however. On the one hand, the term implies control by the state, on the other, it implies freedom of the individual. As Isabella Bakker has proposed, patriarchal privilege for men is produced at both the macro level of the state and market, and the micro level of domestic activities.[23] Both sovereignty and patriarchy are attributed to God. Thus, whether legitimising the sovereign power of the modern nation state, making visible how it cleaves to capital or opposes it, the conceptualisation of sovereignty has been rooted in political theology.[24]

In the first volume of *History of Sexuality*, Part Five, entitled *The Right of Death and the Power of Life*, Foucault defines sovereignty as the ancient power of taking life or letting live.[25] Historically, Foucault derives sovereignty from *patria potestas*, a father's right to take the life of his children and of his slaves as codified in Roman law. The father, who gave life, could – under specified conditions – take it away. Foucault's understanding of sovereignty has to be extended to show how women were positioned in the Roman legal order. Corresponding to the patriarchal right to kill, Roman law inscribed *cura materna* – a woman's duty to care. Integrated with the juridical order, sovereignty, writes Foucault, evolved into 'the right of seizure, the right to seize things, time and bodies, and the privilege to seize hold of life in order to suppress it'.[26] In short: the discursive power of legal discourse, and its material effects, reproduced patriarchal privilege and maintained the subjugation of women.[27]

In the two lectures delivered at Stanford University in 1979, Foucault outlined a critique of modern political reason, in which he concentrated on another modality of power, co-acting with sovereignty – that is, pastoral power.[28] If the sovereign state was a centralised and centralising form of power, pastoral power, which Foucault described with the metaphor of shepherd and his flock, was individualising. This form of power provided a model of parochial organisation for the church and political institutions oriented to the care of the individual, including the welfare state. Without the flock, the shepherd cannot perform his role. The flock is his wealth. Hence reproduction of the flock is the shepherd's primary concern. The flock complies with the law, and follows the shepherd. In the Christian pastorate, the main practice is the segregation of good and bad, virtuous and sinful; mortification in this world, and government of individuals by self examination, obedience, and acquiescence to veridical and truthful – including subsequent transfer of acquiescence to the 'truthfulness' of scientific discourse. In the words of Maurizio Lazzarato: 'Government is a "human technology" that the modern State has inherited from the Christian pastoral technique ... liberalism has adapted it, changed it and enriched it from the government of souls to the government of men.'[29]

A national familial household

Albeit to a different degree, the sovereign power of the state was always engaged in the management of economic life. The oldest legal codes point out that the law-making sovereign – he, who decides – established himself by regulating interactions with nature and access to resources, sexuality (marriage), economic relations (property rights, damage claims). It was not by chance that in several European countries the name of the coin is a 'crown', and the representation on its face is that of a sovereign.

By the eighteenth and nineteenth centuries, processes that had been earlier set in motion, transformed the way people lived and viewed themselves and others, as well as societal institutions. One of these developments was the emergence of political economy; that is, the integration of the model of *oikonomia*, management of family, household, and estate, into the politics of the state. Populations and their economic activities were the source of wealth for the state, which had to be attended to and acted upon. Advances in science increased the productivity of agriculture and diminished the threat of death from hunger and disease. The modern discourses of man and society, including the economic discourse developed in a mutually constitutive relation with the state, governed population and political economy as a national familial household and estate.

To govern the economy, the administrative state required knowledge about wealth and about populations. In Foucault's account statistics, demographics, and economics evolved together with the modern state and market. In a mutually constitutive relation between knowledge of people and power over people, a new form of power over living human beings emerged that was geared to fostering life, enhancing its capacities, controlling and administering life. At one register bio-power centred on disciplining the individual body as the machine 'to integrate it in the system of efficient and economic controls'.[30] Disciplines developed in the monasteries were deployed in schools, barracks and factories. In another register, regulatory controls and the calculated management of life centred on the body of the species – the social body of the population. This new form of power, Foucault writes, was

> ... an indispensable element in the development of capitalism ... The adjustment of the accumulation of men to that of capital, the joining of the growth of human groups to the expansion of productive forces and the differential allocation of profits, were made possible in part by biopower in its many forms and modes of application.[31]

Although in Foucault's work there is hardly any attention to gender differences, a reading of *Omnes et Singulatim* together with feminist political theorists like Pateman, indicates that inherent in pastoral power (in particular, although not only through its control of sexuality and reproduction), is the reproduction of patriarchal advantage. Scientific discourse offers a secular form of guidance; patriarchal epistemologies preserve a male standpoint; women's economic activity is excluded from economic discourse or they are included in an asymmetrical way.[32] Each modality of power, sovereignty and pastoral power from which modern government adopted its techniques of administration of life, worked to kill or make live and exact a tribute from life, 'incite, reinforce, control, monitor, optimize, and organize forces under it'.[33] The 'forces under it', I would like to add, are the energies of 'living nature'.

Within political structures, institutions oriented to the care of individuals coexisted with the old sovereign right to dispose of the life of subjects and with new destructive mechanisms. In 'the games between life and death', Foucault proposes to analyse this modern predicament.[34] The state was at the same time 'the manager of life', and waged wars, massacres and wholesale slaughters in the name of the survival of populations, race, and life necessity. 'Since the population is nothing more than what the state cares of for its own sake, of course, the state is entitled to slaughter it, if necessary. So the reverse of biopolitics is thanatopolitics' – the politics of death.[35]

In time, the biopolitics of population or bio-economics – governmental action on political economy and population – evolved into a complex art of government that entailed the right disposition of the relationships between populations and environment, things and men to the effect of their adjustment with market and state. On the one hand, liberal political theory introduced equality of rights among (male) political subjects of the state. On the other hand, it brought forward as its subject *homo oeconomicus* – rational economic man, an entrepreneur, who competes with others over scarce resources to maximise profits. Women, as Pateman writes, were abandoned in the household. Investigating liberalism, not as an economic or political theory but as an art of government with its specific *savoir* and techniques, shows that liberalism cut off the king's head (albeit incompletely) and enthroned the market.[36] For as Lazzarato argues, in the liberal art of government the market was 'the test and means of intelligibility ... the truth and the measure of society'.[37] The egalitarian logic of rights is superimposed by the non-egalitarian logic of the market. The German *ordo-liberalen*, who were early twentieth century proponents of an economic order that makes the social support the market, and the Chicago School economists, who introduced the market as a regulatory ideal for all domains of human activity, each provided rationalities, *savoir* and techniques to transform the state and the social into the market.

Sovereign capital and social abandonment

The sovereign state has marketised itself, and with the sword of law, by fiscal and financial disciplines, and new finance centred management systems, it leads individuals and the public sector to marketise themselves. Each and every one has to function as a firm. Citizens are repositioned into entries into state budget, from the point of view of expenditures or revenue. The neoliberal politics and sovereignty of capital is established not only from above, that is, by monetary and fiscal disciplines, but also from below, by the implementation of regulatory systems that centralise all activities from the point of view of economic efficiency, and to ensure acceleration in the movement of financial capital. For instance, an analysis of UK governmental economic programmes, the reorganisation of firms and individual subjects in the 1960s–70s, suggests that

> ... the language of productivity of capital, and technique of DCF analysis [discounted cash flow analysis] as the way of translating this into individual investment decisions, would enable a fundamental transformation in the nature and quality of investment decisions ... a calculative norm would serve as a regulatory mechanism.[38]

According to Foucault, 'the market' is now positioned as 'permanent economic tribunal'. Competition and inequality as the measure of strategies and governmental interventions in the domain of political economy, introduced since the eighteenth century, have now been installed as a totalising and centralising global art of government. Hybridisations take place as well. For instance, the emerging Catholic neoliberalism rewrites the history of patristic teaching and Catholic social thought by framing 'the free market' as the state of nature.[39]

Neoliberal re-regulation exposed 'living nature' to global capital expansion. Consequently, the global population is divided into market citizens and human waste.[40] Reading the relationship between life, economy and politics with Foucault and with Brennan, it becomes clear that the market game, which is about competition, pursuit of self-interest, maximisation of utility, brings the model of war into the intersubjective, social, political, and environmental domains of governmental practice and social interactions. Hence, 'in the closed world' the advanced liberal art of government is war by other means. The market is about generation of wealth, (differential) maintenance of life, and the good life (for some), but this is inseparable from the death which comes with accelerated consumption of living nature and entails the disposal of human and non human waste. Thus 'the market mechanism', as defined in economic discourse, is the manager of life and the handler of death. By now the institutions oriented to care for individuals have been marketised. The new military market state engages in thanato-economics, wages war not only on distant others, but also, as Foucault and Brennan point out, war against their own populations.

For Foucault power operates through the triangle of sovereignty, discipline, government – the latter being a government of souls and the right disposition of things. Since the eighteenth century, direct engagement of the state in the administration of life is tantamount to state engagement in government of the political economy. Biopolitics is bio-economics. As human subjects and populations enhance the wealth and power of a nation state, the bioeconomic state cares for populations due to their utility. However, by the late twentieth century, the utility of human subjects as workers or soldiers has substantially declined. With advances in genomics and nanotechnology, and with the decoupling of profits from material production and services, the differential recategorisation of human subjects, increases. Thus, women as well as men are seen either as useful, fit, and virtuous market citizens and super-child reproducers – or they may be seen as redundant human waste.

Agamben is problematising this turn by making visible the ways in which death has become central to current political order. While Foucault focused on the emergence of biopolitics, that is, politics of the administration of life in the nineteenth century, Agamben points out that life (*zoe* – reproductive life) has always been regulated by political life (*bios*), such that the political is what gives life a form. In this sense, sovereignty has always been power over life. This was demonstrated in the sovereignty of Ischomachus as the citizen, the economic manager, the husbander and husband, articulated in his power to regulate and transform 'living nature' into wealth. Hence, Agamben's notion of the political expands into the juridico-economic sphere. Slaves or women, and 'nature' are included in the juridico-economic order – but at the same time, they do not have a voice, rights, entitlements, or possibilities to regenerate, and therefore, they exist in a state of suspension. Agamben calls this a zone of indistinction, existing between law and violence, between naked life and sovereign power to kill life.[41] The principle of *patria potestas* in Roman law not only codified the father's power to kill, but at the same time, it tied patriarchal law to the right to kill. The originary foundation of law is the inclusion of life by suspending itself as 'a state of exception'. In the zone of indistinction life can be killed with impunity.

From this perspective, not only economics, as Brennan would argue, but also politics, accounts for global civil war, or war on life. For Agamben the emblematic figure of modernity is *homo sacer*, the one who is banned from juridical protection, and can be killed with impunity. Not only resource wars in Africa, but neoliberal restructuring demonstrates how withdrawal of protection of life is central to the economic system. The abandonment of life is seen in resource wars and neoliberal restructuring – carried out as persuasive spectacles. It is seen in financial disciplines like structural adjustment and successor programmes: in the Netherlands as privatisation of public housing and health care, in the US as reduction of welfare benefits for single mothers. In Poland, it is seen in the cancellation of state guarantees for alimony funds. All such moves are tantamount to the legal abandonment of life. Life without political or economic value includes that of migrants or *sans papiers*, the elderly, the homeless, and the unemployed. Just as in an earlier plantation economy and in labour camps, this human waste is subject to sovereign policing, expulsions, or forced work for a remuneration that barely provides for biological reproduction. The shift in environmental policy from command and control measures or covenants, into 'market instruments', such as trading in pollution permits, is another legal abandonment of 'nature' under exploitation by capital. The new forms of immiseration that Brennan writes about, such as poisoning bodies with toxins, fall into the category of legal abandonment of life, too. Even the well off, momentarily secure, cannot escape the integration of their lives with the death of others. The global life-cycles of production, consumption, and disposal of computers, cars, cut flowers, clothes, toys, profits are dependent on death. Death became productive and is inextricably integrated in the juridico-economic realm. Life is available – on private subscription, but for how long?[42]

Patria potestas, cura materna

Given the pressures on living nature exerted by the speed of acquisition and spatial expansion of capital, it is not surprising that the propensity to take life – as it is embedded in economic discourse – creates 'death worlds' or 'zones of social abandonment'. Freely circulating through the planet, 'capital' – a metaphor for a certain way of managing life based on added value, a 'market mechanism' – is globalised as the universal regulatory ideal, creates *homo sacer* and *femina sacra*, killing him and her with impunity.

The economic war machine is supported juridically by a permanent state of exception.[43] The 'death worlds' are produced by the extraction of energy from living nature. What makes it possible is an economic system of production and consumption, and politico-economic discourses that arrange relationships between things, human subjects, and forms of truth. Capital endowed with sovereignty 'decides' who is disposable, and who can live. Even in this system, so saturated with and dependent on death, gender, race, and class, remain the key differential categories. Women are included in the economic and political, on condition that they fulfil caring duties. For the sovereign power was not only founded on *patria potestas*, a father's right to kill, but also on *cura materna* – the feminine duty to care. This duty takes form in women's prevailing responsibility for the care economy, absorbing social costs of the global war on living nature. Today the buffer function of the care economy is seriously overstretched.[44]

Agamben would solve the current predicament by severing the connection between violence and law. But does this mean the invention of a new law? He also recommends living a 'sufficient life, a life that has reached the perfection of its own power, and its own communicability – a life over which sovereignty and right no longer have hold'.[45] What is at stake is to undo the connection between violence and economic management. If a transformation and dethroning of the juridico-economic order is possible, then feminist and ecological economics need propositions for politico-juridical restructuring. Trans-disciplinary coalitions are essential to this task. But such propositions depend on a confidence that 'capital' can be politically reformed and subdued in order to meet the goals of social and ecological 'sustainability'. Given the speed of co-optation of ideas like 'sustainability' or 'gender equity', can such confidence be warranted? Does this mean, that nothing can be done? What kind of alternative economics would have something to say about livelihoods for people abandoned and expelled by the system?

Notes

1. Australian born scholar Teresa Brennan died in 2003. She was a transdisciplinary feminist academic who taught at CUNY, and at Florida Atlantic University, where she designed the first 'public intellectuals' PhD programme. Her books include *History After Lacan*, London: Routledge, 1993; *Exhausting Modernity: Ground*

for a New Economy, London: Routledge, 2000; *Globalization and its Terrors: Daily Life in the West*, London: Routledge, 2003.

2. Brennan, *Globalization and Its Terrors*, p. 128.
3. Achille Mbembe, 'Necropolitics', *Public Culture*, 2003, Vol. 15, No. 1, 11–40, p. 40; João Biehl, *Vita: Life in a Zone of Social Abandonment*, University of California Press, 2005, p. 35.
4. Brennan, *Globalization and Its Terrors*, p. 34.
5. Michel Foucault, *The History of Sexuality Vol. I*, London: Penguin Books, 1990, pp. 96ff.
6. Ibid., p. 100.
7. Francois Ewald et al. (eds), *Naissance de la Biopolitique: Cours au Collège de France (1978–1979) de Michel Foucault*, Paris: Gallimard, 2005; Giorgio Agamben, *Homo Sacer: Sovereign Power and Bare Life*, Stanford University Press, 1998; Giorgio Agamben, *Means Without Ends: Theory Out of Bounds*, University of Minnesota Press, 2000; Giorgio Agamben, *State of Exception*, University of Chicago Press, 2005.
8. Michael Hardt and Antonio Negri, *Empire*, Cambridge, MA: Harvard University Press, 2000.
9. On this point see: Agamben, *State of Exception*; Robert Nelson, *Economics as Religion: From Samuelson to Chicago and Beyond*, Pennsylvania State University Press, 2001; Wendy Brown, *Sovereignty and the Return of the Repressed*, Workshop in Law, Philosophy and Political Theory, School of Law, UCLA, 2006, Online Available HTTP: <www.law.berkeley.edu/centers/kadish/workshop_2006/brown.pdf> (accessed 11 October 2006).
10. Brown, *Sovereignty and the Return of the Repressed*; Carole Pateman, *The Sexual Contract*, Stanford University Press, 1988.
11. Agamben, *Means Without Ends*, p. 185.
12. Xenophon, *The Economist*, H. Dakyns (trans.), Project Gutenberg Association and Carnegie-Mellon University, 1998, p. 26, Online Available HTTP: <www.gutenberg.org/etext/1173> (accessed 31 May 2007).
13. Ibid., p. 23.
14. Ibid., p. 24.
15. Ibid., p. 23.
16. Ibid., p. 30.
17. Ibid., pp. 28–9.
18. Ibid., p. 30.
19. Ibid., p. 25.
20. Mary Lefkowitz and Maureen Fant, *Women's Life in Greece and Rome: A Sourcebook in Translation*, Johns Hopkins University Press, 1992; Mary Leftkowicz and Maureen Fant, *Women's Life in Greece and Rome*, Johns Hopkins University Press, 1997.

21. Hubert Dreyfus and Paul Rabinow, *Michel Foucault: Beyond Structuralism and Hermeneutics*, University of Chicago Press, 1982, p. 194.
22. Pateman, *The Sexual Contract*.
23. Isabella Bakker (ed.), *The Strategic Silence: Gender and Economic Policy*, London: Zed Books, 1994.
24. Brown, *Sovereignty and the Return of the Repressed*.
25. Foucault, *History of Sexuality Vol. I*, p. 136.
26. Ibid.
27. Carol Smart, *Feminism and the Power of Law*, London: Routledge, 1989.
28. Michel Foucault, *Omnes et Singulatim: Towards a Criticism of 'Political Reason'*, Tanner Lectures on Human Values, Stanford University, 1979, Online Available HTTP: <www.tannerlectures.utah.edu/lectures/foucault81.pdf> (accessed 21 May 2003).
29. Maurizio Lazzarato, *Biopolitics/bioeconomics: A Politics of Multiplicity*, undated, Online Available HTTP: <www.generation-online.org/p/fplazzarato2.htm> (accessed 22 April 2006).
30. Foucault, *History of Sexuality Vol. I*, p. 139.
31. Ibid., p. 141.
32. Gillian Hewitson, *A Survey of Feminist Economics*, La Trobe University, School of Business, Discussion Papers Series A, 01.01, 2001, Online Available HTTP: <www.latrobe.edu.au/business/assets/downloads/disc_papers/A01–01.pdf> (accessed 31 May 2007).
33. Foucault in Ewald et al., *Naissance de la Biopolitique*, p. 136.
34. Michel Foucault, 'Political Technologies of Individuals' in Luther Martin et al. (eds), *Technologies of the Self: Seminar with Michel Foucault*, Cambridge, MA: MIT Press, 1988, p. 148.
35. Ibid., p. 160.
36. Foucault in Ewald et al., *Naissance de la Biopolitique*.
37. Lazzarato, *Biopolitics/bioeconomics* (accessed 22 April 2006).
38. Peter Miller and Nikolas Rose, 'Governing Economic Life', *Economy & Society*, 1990, Vol. 19, No. 1, 1–29, p. 17.
39. See for instance, the essays by Robert de Sirico, Director of the Acton Institute for the Study of Religion and Liberty, Online Available HTTP: <www.acton.org/publicat/randl/author.php?pid=11>; and Michael Novak, Online Available HTTP: <www.michaelnovak.net/Module/Site/Biography.aspx> (both accessed 31 May 2007). This material inspired Polish debates in the Catholic weekly *Przegląd Tygodniowy Przewodnik Ucho Igielne*, about combining neoliberal free market ideology with a reinterpretation of Roman Catholic teaching on the virtue of multiplying and accumulating wealth.

40. Zygmunt Bauman, *Wasted Lives: Modernity and Its Outcasts*, Cambridge: Polity, 2004.
41. Agamben, *Homo Sacer* and *State of Exception*.
42. Jamie Skye Bianco, 'Zones of Morbidity and Necropolitics', *rhizomes*, 2004, Online Available HTTP: <www.rhizomes.net/issue8/bianco.htm> (accessed 31 May 2007).
43. William Scheuerman, *The Economic State of Emergency*, 2000, Online Available HTTP: <www.derechos.org/nizkor/excep/scheuerman.html> (accessed 31 May 2007).
44. Irene van Stavaren, 'Global Finance and Gender' in Jan Aart Scholte (ed.), *Civil Society and Global Finance*, London: Routledge, 2002.
45. Agamben, *Means Without Ends*, pp. 114–15.

4

THE DIVERSITY MATRIX: RELATIONSHIP AND COMPLEXITY

Susan Hawthorne

One of the key features of neoclassical economics is its simplicity. Economists set out to achieve 'objectivity, scientific rigour and universal applicability', but the level of abstraction used, conjures the illusion that economic activity takes place in a relationship vacuum and that the creation of value is solely determined by market mechanisms. Decontextualisation from the social and natural worlds is 'a given' in this reifying and reductive discipline. But the fact is that neoclassical economics is embedded in sex/gendered power structures and in colonial domination. As such, its practice has come to resemble politics more than it does science.[1]

Complexity economists, on the other hand, know that economic activity takes place across a number of different social worlds.[2] Furthermore, complexity economists recognise the interaction of social and natural worlds, even in highly urbanised contexts where the natural world can seem far away. Social and cultural diversity sit alongside biodiversity as important concerns. Complexity economists take account of concreteness and place, they consider the ways in which economics is embedded in time, in place, and influenced by the circumstances of peoples' lives. This quality of embeddedness takes account of the relationships between people, as well as the relationship people have with their environment, the land, the eco-social context. And finally, complexity economists take account of time, of the ways in which economic activity in one period has an effect on others in another period. These interacting relational systems mean that intergenerational sustainability of economic systems is also taken account of. Complexity economists 'connect' on many different levels and their concerns cross through the personal, the local, the biophysical, and the global. Theirs is a politicised economics in the sense in which feminists use the term, the personal is political. The economic is certainly political.

Living as part of the whole

Sabine O'Hara points to the importance of storytelling as a way in to understanding economics, and in this chapter I begin with a narrative that exemplifies O'Hara's statement that: 'In ecosystems, no part of the whole is unimportant. No member is, or can be excluded from participation in the interconnected whole.'[3] In 1984, I had the privilege to meet a number of indigenous women from Central Australia at the Fourth Women and Labour Conference in Brisbane. The manner of our meeting came about through a discussion over knowledge claims. I was presenting a paper which turned out to be controversial. The women from Central Australia, even though they were critical of the paper, nevertheless spent time discussing the issues with me and supporting me through a difficult conference. What this group of women showed me in the course of the weekend had to do with balancing the importance of the group, and supporting its weakest member. Their ability to acknowledge my context and theirs and thereby create a connection of understanding was extraordinary. I felt I had participated as a group member in a way that was beyond my experience.[4] Among this group of women there was both a sense of participation and interconnectedness that was new to me.

It is this just sense of connection and participation I have in mind as a way of approaching the methodology of economics. It means putting things on the table, not hiding externalities in low prices, and it means sharing knowledge, which can occur only in circumstances of trust and relationship. Any new economic system will have to increase the opportunities for participation

– from all parts of the diversity matrix – for without doing so we can expect to see more intense confrontations between those who are for and against globalisation.

The situation of indigenous women in Australia is at crisis level. This has been borne out by report after report on their circumstances. The level of violence experienced by Aboriginal women, their health outcomes, their lack of access to education structured within frameworks that match their cultural needs, their mortality rates, and lack of access to sustaining work all point to severe economic deprivation in the midst of a country known for its prosperity. Mary Mellor notes that when externalities are not costed in, someone pays the price – 'they will die before their time, sleep on the street, be nursed by a relative, go without shoes, walk miles to the well'.[5] This is the case with indigenous women in Australia. They die 'before their time' because of the compounding effects of poor health care and nutrition throughout their lives, the cumulative effects of violence, and lack of medical care during times of health crisis. The women I met in 1984 belonged to communities that suffered and continue to suffer the afflictions of colonisation, dispossession, missionisation, commodification of their religious and artistic culture, and the privatisation of intellectual property rights by transnational corporations.[6] These concrete realities indicate some of the ways in which a wild economics might develop if it is to take serious account of these women's lives and of the lives of women in other places and times whose needs are not even at the horizon of those working within the neoclassical economic tradition.

Again, at the World Social Forum in Mumbai, January 2004, political activism was being pursued by a number of groups whose lives fall well beyond the horizons of most economists, even beyond the experience of many anti-globalisation activists. Two among them touched a chord in me: a group of young Dalit artists in their twenties from Safai Karamchari-Arunthathiyar Community in Madurai, Tamil Nadu, who come from families where a child can barely dream of more than a life as a sweeper, a coolie, or as a scavenger. But this group is struggling for the possibility of being artists. They are graffiti artists, cut-out artists and poster artists, creating political and outsider art. The second was a group of children aged between about eight and 13 who belonged to the children's rag-pickers union, Bhima Sangha. The vice-president, was a 13-year-old girl standing up to present their demands. Complexity economists will advance the principle of difference as they build inclusivity.

Indigenous, feminist, and ecological economics

I want to highlight just a few examples of complexity economics as expressed by three challenges to neoclassical economics – indigenous, feminist, and ecological. In many instances this theoretical work overlaps, so I am suggesting that these lenses offer interweaving aspects of complexity economics.[7] The insights from all three are important to the development of a decolonised wild economics. In order to systematically decolonise economics, it is critical to begin with who it is that is involved in economic activity. While 'economic man' may still exist in a few rarified quarters, at the centre of wild economics is the group I name the diversity matrix:[8] women, indigenous people, the poor, and the socially marginalised (ethnically and religiously marginalised people, the disabled, lesbians, and refugees are just some of the possible groupings).[9] The diversity matrix represents the enmeshing of different kinds of oppressions recognising that individuals may inhabit several different worlds simultaneously or serially. It also implies that some locations are suited to the making of alliances across boundaries without falling into the postmodern fantasy of a borderless world filled with transgressed boundaries (mad cow disease, GM foods, and globalisation, are all examples of transgressed boundaries with negative impacts on ordinary people). It is no accident that in an era of global market liberalism, the number of refugees in the world has increased. They are an increasingly significant grouping in the global economy; one that unlike indigenous peoples, loses all sense of ecological grounding. Moreover, the abstract, globalised world, ushers in an era in which the connection to place is considered passé, although in reality it is irrelevant only for those who have mobility, frequent flyer points, and access to a range of infotech resources.[10]

A sense of 'locatedness' is critical from the perspective of social justice and ecological sustainability. As Linda Tuhiwai Smith points out in her book *Decolonising Methodologies* (1999): who we are and where we are located largely determines what questions are asked and what outcomes are accepted.[11] Tuhiwai Smith's concern to decolonise research methodology is echoed by those involved in protecting the intellectual property rights (IPRs) of indigenous peoples. IPRs are presented as the *sine qua non* of indigenous people, as the way to prosperity. But IPRs as they are currently structured in the setting of the World Trade Organisation (WTO) take no account of the issues raised by Tuhiwai Smith. The WTO model of IPRs does not take account of the fact that in indigenous communities knowledge systems are nuanced in complex ways and therefore a universalised system of IPRs does not take account of the local system, nor does it recognise 'undocumented traditional knowledge'.[12] Documentation involves having the knowledge validated by scientists and written up in academic journals or other public forums. When access to knowledge is earned, as it is in many indigenous communities, these communities are faced with a Catch-22 when dealing with IPRs. If they maintain the system of earned knowledge then it cannot be written up in scientific publications, and therefore it cannot be formally protected by the current global system of IPRs. If they agree to have the knowledge made public, then the community betrays an important element of their own system of protecting intellectual property: a system based not on money but on responsibility. Here one can see the tension between universality and a concern for the specific needs of a particular community, the eco-social system.[13] These are concrete needs tied to a particular place and a particular culture.[14]

In a series of articles on ecological economics, Sabine O'Hara suggests that the attempt to 'analyse bio-diversity or socio-diversity from [a] market-centered perspective would be a contradiction in terms'.[15] Within O'Hara's framework the WTO IPR rules simply do not meet the criteria necessary for ecological coherence. Indigenous communities confronted with scientists looking for 'new' medicinal plants from which to create novel life forms in laboratories, followed by patenting and commercialisation through the pharmaceutical industry, are participating in O'Hara's 'contradiction in terms'. O'Hara looks instead to what might be the essential features of an economics in which bio- and socio-diversity are placed at the centre. She comes up with a number of features which all tend in the direction of specificity: concreteness is more important than abstraction, location more important than generalisation, relationship more important than distribution, specificities of conditions, time and attention to the limits of mortality and growth.[16] In proposing a methodology suited to indigenous needs, Tuhiwai Smith calls for 'a "local" theoretical positioning', which enables the researcher to draw on her own very 'specific historical, political and social context' to develop an embedded critical theory. It is in this way, she argues, that 'oppressed, marginalised and silenced groups' will gain something from research and from the knowledge created by these means.[17]

Such local positioning can be found in feminist scholarship on indigenous women in Australia. For instance, Diane Bell connects the ritual maintenance of land with its economic importance. The economic relations arise from a deep and embodied knowledge of the land, and reciprocal behaviours of obligation and responsibility for the wellbeing of the land, and by extension, of the people who inhabit the land.

> Ancestral activity in country provides a metaphor for relations between the living: the comings and goings of the dreaming animate the landscape, infuse it with significance, and provide paths along which links between living people may be traced. Each individual has a unique complex of relations to land, its sites and dreamings, but it is the corporate nature of interests in land which is emphasized.[18]

Bell uses the concept of *jukurrpa*, usually translated as 'dreaming' and widely used by central Australian desert peoples like the Aranda and Walpiri.[19] The *jukurrpa* is not only time past, but also the present, and the framework of knowledge provided by the ancestral beings that determines relationships and responsibilities to land, nature, culture, and spiritual life. The *jukurrpa* is not a fixed law/lore, but rather a fulcrum from which change within the culture can occur. It provides 'the structural potential for change' within a particular framework of social and cultural forms. In the *jukurrpa* was established an all-encompassing Law which binds people, flora, fauna, and natural phenomena into one enormous interfunctioning world.[20] The way in which the Law works is to allow classification within this system of things and concepts not previously encountered – a crowbar can be classified as a digging stick; money can take on ritual significance; and the *jukurrpa* can be renewed through new acts of dreaming, song and ritual.

Particularity, concreteness, and place

The 'interfunctioning' quality of central Australian epistemology means that there is a direct engagement and relationship between the people of a community and their environment. This is reflected in the land tenure systems of both the Aranda and Walpiri peoples, each of which is adapted to the nature of the 'country' which a particular person or group is responsible for. The relationship with the land is one of responsibility, which is characterised by ritual maintenance, knowledge of resources and areas where food may or may not be harvested. Intimate and detailed knowledge is integral to the sustenance of the land, and in turn, to the culture. Plants, animals, rocks, the nature of the landscape and soil, its watercourses, and the people all play a part in the interfunctioning system of the *jukurrpa*. In developing a theory of wild economics, considerations must be made about relationship to land – and this embodied relation is implied in the indigenous word 'country'. In the dominant global capitalist system, land is more and more disconnected from people. Through investment, through superannuation schemes, through internet auctions, it is possible for more and more people to 'own' land and never to have seen that land, or sometimes not even know about it. The distinction is between Western property ownership rules – disconnected, purchased with money, located anywhere – and indigenous perspectives on property, where an intimate relationship between land and people is maintained by personal presence, ritual maintenance, and responsibility.[21]

By indigenous reasoning, land cannot be purchased and it has a pre-determined location. Water cannot be purchased either. Near the mouth of the Murray River, which drains the Murray–Darling Basin – the most important river system in southeast Australia, a battle is underway between those who call for 'economic benefit' and those who call for 'ecological and economic sustainability'. The former group includes government, developers, and overseas based water corporations – which incidentally, now control the scarce drinking water supply of the city of Adelaide. Against these corporate and official interests stands an alliance of indigenous peoples, feminists, local food producers, fishers, land owners, wine makers, and environmentalists. Many of these voices 'for life' are documented in *Listen to Ngarrindjeri Women Speaking: Kungun Ngarrindjeri Miminar Yunnan*.[22] In conventional terms, the battle is between economic gain versus ecological, cultural, and justice issues. The proposed construction of an expensive weir will have profound effects on the ecosystem, and on places of importance to indigenous peoples. Moreover, in the longer term, this weir will also affect the viability of fishers, farmers, and other business producers. Ellen Trevorrow, a Ngarrindjeri elder and a weaver speaks of her relationship with the Murray River:

> The River is in a bad way. Now there's talk about a weir down the end, there past Wellington at Pomanda Island. What's our direction? It's very important for us to look after what we've got because we're leaving something behind.[23]

All of this political talk is going on in an environment in which land and water have been separated through a history of water trading, one on the Murray River that has been in place since 1983.[24] The abstract and artificial separation of water from land, the commodification and pricing of water, results in it being treated in a way that is comparable to intellectual property. Water ceases to be a physical entity and instead is turned into a licence or a right to trade an allocation.[25] In the words of activist Mike Smith: 'We're trading a right. We're not trading volumes of water up and down the River. We are trading a right.'[26] For indigenous people, land and intellectual property are inseparable. For land is knowledge, and knowledge is located in land. In South Australia, the Ngarrindjeri have been well schooled in battles with developers over women's sacred sites. To quote Ngarrindjeri woman, Eileen McHughes:

> There are special places where we can show our kids Ngarrindjeri *ruwi* and keep our culture alive, teach them about bush tucker and bush medicine. There are places with long uninterrupted histories of Ngarrindjeri care ...[27]

The principles underlying this discussion can be applied, not just to indigenous cultures, but also to the global economy. Feminist economists and ecological economists are engaging in similarly transformative discourses about the changes that could take place if the world were organised around the principle of multiversity rather than homogeneity and profit.[28] But at the same time, it has to be acknowledged that feminist economists range from liberals who argue that women should become more and more active in the market economy to those who argue that women are already, to some extent, practising an alternative economic system. Liberal feminists myopically see what they call 'gender equity' in the global market as an advance; so too, some short sighted indigenous people support IPRs on traditional knowledge, failing to see the losses this entails for the communities affected.[29]

Eco-social systems and 'life'

Maria Mies is a proponent of the 'alternative economy' thesis. She believes that the most important feminist political principle is 'Autonomy over our bodies and lives'.[30] Moving from the personal and the local, to the broad global view, Mies connects the violence of men with the violence of capitalist patriarchy, and maintains that abandoning this violence is the first step in abandoning exploitation. Like Susanne Kappeler, Mies stands firmly for men taking up a sense of responsibility, and further, that men begin to participate in the informal economy, the unpaid and unnamed domestic economy.[31] Mies makes a plea for what she calls global economic autarky based on local self-sufficiency and only trading where something important cannot be produced regionally. She recognises that such a shift would result in 'a contraction of world trade and of export-oriented production' but that it would also reduce exploitation and non-reciprocal relations between nations.[32] It might also result in the reduction of the unnecessary spread of diseases directly caused by large scale transport of livestock – BSE and foot-and-mouth disease are examples. Globalised free trade and customs relaxation is also a potential purveyor of the genetic contamination of wild types through the import of GM crop seed manufactured by transnational companies.[33]

Mies looks for a reduction in the 'gap between production and consumption' through the development of closer relations between producers and consumers, and a sense of responsibility for waste.[34] With co-author Veronika Bennholdt-Thomsen, she extends this analysis in *The Subsistence Perspective*. Mies has always been interested in the parallels between the sexual division of labour and the international division of labour, arguing that in order for one to change, the other must also. Globalisation pulls women into international trade, into the market economy, into the privatised and commodified world of capital, and in the process women's labour is appropriated not in ways that benefit them, but in ways that benefit markets.[35] The market economy is primarily Western and modern in its orientation. This means that anyone, anywhere, can participate in it, so making it context insensitive. In addition, because of the ways in which power is dispersed from the Western economies to former colonies it tends to draw men into the cash/market economy more quickly than it does with women.[36] Other marginalised peoples such as refugees and indigenous peoples are also less likely to be entirely dependent on the market economy for their sustenance. Even women from within the Western and modern societies lag behind men in their participation, being more likely to engage in part-time or unpaid labour.

In 1988, Marilyn Waring argued that women were structurally disappeared from economic figures because of the way in which the United Nations System of National Accounts (UNSNA) figures are collected. The disappearing work includes all subsistence work, giving birth, home caring, gardening or other domestic work such as educating children, keeping to a family budget, voluntary work or work done because of friendship or reciprocal or community responsibilities, all work done within the domestic premises without payment. But without this work, the world would come to a standstill. This is work whose aim is 'life', rather than the production of capital.[37] The convergence of the economic invisibility of women's work and its clear importance to the daily functioning of economies is a major disconnect for neoclassical economics. It suggests the need for a total rethink of how economic activity is rated. If we were to take work whose aim is life, rather than the production of capital, if we were to consider work whose outcome was the maintenance of biodiversity and cultural diversity (multiversity) rather than the production of capital, then the world's women would be seen for their massive productivity. No longer would prostitution raise the GNP.[38] No longer would populations of women domestic workers be obliged to move from the Philippines to Japan and Saudi Arabia in order to send home a foreign exchange contribution of US$3 billion annually.[39] No longer would investment in reproductive technologies contribute to the economy but have negative bodily and social effects on women in both rich and poor worlds.[40] No longer would the development of resorts and eco-tourism threaten the livelihood of indigenous communities.[41] No longer would the speed of production and distribution outpace the ability of humans and the environment to regenerate.[42]

It is true that many men in non-Western cultures are induced to participate in and assimilate masculine Western culture frequently at the expense of the women in their own culture. The inducements begin as men become producers of cash crops, goods for export and they move on to becoming consumers of luxury goods such as tobacco, alcohol, motorised vehicles, and women.[43] To the extent that women belong to dominant white, European-derived, heterosexual, wealthy and mobile groupings, they too are drawn into modes of production, consumption, and theorisation that reflect the model of economic man – discrete, non-relational, individualistic, and universalised. But if some aspects of feminist economics reflect liberal ideology, there are similar tendencies in the fuzzy area that exists between environmental and ecological economics. The work on natural capitalism, for example, can be seen as a parallel absorption of critical objectives to that of 'gender equity' advocates within feminist economics.[44] Even the term 'natural capital' has problems, as it turns a complex, situated and contextualised system (natural) into a homogenised unit of measurement (capital). The politically conservative character of some ecological economics is clear from its unquestioning application of neoclassical principles and assumptions to 'single issues' such as climate control, conservation, and pollution. Or again, in its focus on 'sensible allocation of resources' through carbon taxes, and the use of property based instruments (IPRs) to regulate biodiversity.[45] This kind of environmental economics contains no challenge to the neoliberal economic paradigm.

Towards a wild economics

On the other hand, for many ecological economists 'development' has become an uncomfortable word, and 'sustainable development' is acknowledged as part of the neoclassical armoury.[46] Joan Martinez-Alier is one who suggests that the question of whether economic growth improves or harms the environment is a central one.[47] Herman Daly points out that 'sustainable growth' is an 'economic oxymoron', while Robert Goodland argues that growth has already reached its limits.[48] These are continuations of the critiques first put forward by Donella Meadows et al. (1972) in the highly influential report *Limits to Growth*.[49] Goodland and Daly also note the shortcomings of GNP as a measure of human wellbeing and of the connections between consumerism in the North and poverty in the South. Ecofeminist Vandana

Shiva talks about development as a 'continuation of the process of colonisation', and she goes on to talk about Western-style development as a form of 'maldevelopment', wherein 'nature and women are reduced to being resources'.[50] Once again the same concerns are raised by indigenous, feminist, and ecological economists. The 'free' resources of nature, of indigenous peoples, of women – any element of the diversity matrix not yet colonised – are hunted down by the free traders for commercial gain by transnational corporations. And, Tuhiwai Smith tells how 'the other' has become a tradeable commodity and a profitable one. Likewise, the 'interesting little backwaters, untapped potentials' are themselves markets for other global products.[51]

Feminists have insisted on the connection between the personal and the political. In a similar way, ecology cannot extricate itself from ecosystems and context, and indigenous systems of knowledge rely heavily on the specificities of location and cultural tradition. This integral connectedness is what feminists, indigenous peoples, and ecologists are bringing to economics. And it comes with a number of other important elements that O'Hara lists as 'reciprocity, mutual support, respect and awareness of the context of human sociality within the larger ecosystem ...'[52] The challenge to neoclassical economics is coming from those whom I call complexity economists – indigenous, feminist, and ecological thinkers. In an attempt to draw together their perspectives, I suggest using the term wild economics. The wild includes complexity at its core, but it is also more than this. The wild is a life-based concept. It is not containable and it is uncontrollable. One cannot predict the wild, and in this sense it has an unfettered freedom. A freedom based on imperfect knowledge. It is imperfect knowledge that allows us to be inventive, to move along paths not previously taken, to adapt to new and changing circumstances. The wild is also multiple and can only be understood in relation to the things and processes around it. So context and relationship are critical to understanding the wild. The wild is multiple in the sense that biodiversity is multiple. It is multiversal, with no single centre. Life, including economic life, can erupt where conditions are best suited to it, and as O'Hara points out eco-social systems 'vary with location, biophysical, climatic, social and cultural contexts'.[53]

In a wild economics, people of all kinds come to question the view of 'economic man' as singular, universal, and thoroughly in control of 'his life'. A wild economics moves towards 'an open discursive ecosystem', a system that allows for a multiplicity of perspectives, including dissent. As Ariel Salleh notes: 'We do not challenge the monoculture of corporate savages by denying "difference" and the "wild".'[54] And O'Hara adds, although we may not all be able 'to cope with the messiness of an open discursive ecosystems valuation process, this messiness is where the power lies'.[55] Indeed, we need to relish the complexity of such terms and use them as concepts on which to build theory. An economics based on the wild has many centres and models of humanity. One of these models is female and poor. She is coming into being carrying the baggage of her body – whether lesbian or heterosexual, mobile or disabled. She also carries the baggage of her particular culture, a culture of class, religion, ethnicity, a culture that is ecologically embedded in time and place – just as the men who theorise economics are culturally embedded ... somewhere.[56]

Economists who acknowledge such embeddedness will have very different assumptions from the universalised neoliberal economics currently invading every corner of the world. In proposing a different approach to economics, the emphasis has to shift from the simplified decontextualised world of perfect information. Instead, as Bell, Tuhiwai Smith and O'Hara maintain, relationship is central, as is a sense of connectedness that takes account of real needs, rather than marketing generated consumer needs. Today, an international cadre of women scholars like India's Vandana Shiva and Africa's Marimba Ani challenges the false universalism of eurocentric assumptions behind global systems of power and knowledge.[57] The time sensitive, intergenerational quality of wild economics is perhaps best exemplified by the words of Lilla Watson. In a 1984 talk on 'Aboriginal Feminism', Watson pointed out that for Aboriginal people the future extends as far forward as the past.[58] This, she said, means a 40,000-year plan.

By envisioning a future of this length, it becomes essential to consider how resources can be maintained, as if permanently. So too the Ngarrindjeri women of South Australia, are clear about what they want for the future. As Rita Lindsay, Ellen Trevorrow, Alice Abdulla, and Margaret Dodd emphasise:

> We want our young people to be educated so they can be part of managing our lands and waters, so they will have employment, so land and waters will be cared for according to Ngarrindjeri laws, for future generations.[59]

This community is looking for economic independence and that depends on retaining their intellectual property and their land. The interfunctionality of a healthy environment and economic sustainability is quite evident when looking at indigenous social forms. Indeed, Ngarrindjeri women say that the desecration of land registers on their bodies – 'just like we'd been stabbed in the heart'.[60]

Notes

1. Marimba Ani, *Yurugu: An African-Centered Critique of European Cultural Thought and Behavior*, Trenton, NJ: Africa World Press, 2000.

2. I use 'worlds' in the sense of Maria Lugones, *Pilgrimages/ Peregrinajes: Theorizing Coalition Against Multiple Oppressions*, Lanham: Rowman and Littlefield, 2003, pp. 77ff.

3. Sabine O'Hara, 'Valuing Socio-diversity', *International Journal of Social Economics*, 1995, Vol. 22, No. 5, 31–49, p. 37 and Sabine O'Hara, 'Sustainability: Social and Ecological Dimensions', *Review of Social Economy*, 1995, Vol. LIII, No. 4, 529–51; also Sabine O'Hara, 'Discursive Ethics in Ecosystems Valuation and Environmental Policy', *Ecological Economics*, 1996, Vol. 16, No. 2, 95–107; Sabine O'Hara, 'Toward a Sustaining Production Theory', *Ecological Economics*, 1997, Vol. 20, No. 2, 141–54.

4. I tell this story because real-life narratives can sensitise economists to the complexity of local conditions: see also O'Hara, 'Toward a Sustaining Production Theory', p. 151 and O'Hara, 'Sustainability: Social and Ecological Dimensions', pp. 540–6.

5. Mary Mellor, *Breaking the Boundaries*, London: Virago, 1992, p. 3.

6. On Australian indigenous peoples: Diane Bell, *Daughters of the Dreaming*, Melbourne: Spinifex Press, 1983; Deborah Bird Rose, *Dingo Makes Us Human*, Cambridge University Press, 1992; Diane Bell, *Ngarrindjeri Wurruwarrin: The World That Is, Was, and Will Be*, Melbourne: Spinifex Press, 1998; Jean Christie, 'Enclosing the Biodiversity Commons: Bioprospecting or Biopiracy?' in Richard Hindmarsh and Geoffrey Lawrence (eds), *Altered Genes II: The Future*, Melbourne: Scribe, 2001; Judy Atkinson, *Trauma Trails, Recreating Song Lines: The Transgenerational Effects of Trauma in Indigenous Australia*, Melbourne: Spinifex Press, 2002; Zohl dé Ishtar, *Holding Yawulyu: White Culture and Black Women's Law*, Melbourne: Spinifex Press, 2002; Marcia Langton, 'The "Wild", the Market and the Native: Indigenous People Face New Forms of Global Colonization' in William Adams and Martin Mulligan (eds), *Decolonizing Nature: Strategies for Conservation in a Post-colonial Era*, London: Earthscan, 2003.

7. Ariel Salleh, *Ecofeminism as Politics: Nature, Marx, and the Postmodern*, London: Zed Books, 1997, has a thoroughgoing analysis of the complex interaction between feminist, indigenous, socialist, and ecological, attitudes to land, ecology, human relations, and responsibility.

8. I first used this term in Susan Hawthorne, *Wild Politics: Feminism, Globalisation and Bio/diversity*, Melbourne: Spinifex Press, 2002. A matrix also has generative and creative aspects that I see as central to the survival of those caught up in a matrix of oppressions.

9. The literature on economic marginalisation is extensive. Prue Hyman, 'Lesbians and Economic/Social Change: Impacts of Globalisation on Our Community(ies) and Politics', *Journal of Lesbian Studies*, 2001, Vol. 5, No. 1/2, 115–32; Gregor Wolbring, 'Disability Rights Approach Towards Bioethics', *The Journal of Disability Policy Studies*, 2003, Vol. 14, No. 3, 154–80.

10. On refugees: Saskia Sassen, *Globalization and Its Discontents: Essays on the New Mobility of People and Money*, New York: The New Press, 1998; on place see O'Hara, 'Valuing Socio-diversity', pp. 38–40.

11. Linda Tuhiwai Smith, *Decolonising Methodologies: Research and Indigenous Peoples*, London: Zed Books, 1999.

12. Graham Dutfield, *Intellectual Property Rights, Trade and Biodiversity*, London: Earthscan Publications, 2000, p. 64; Bell, *Ngarrindjeri Wurruwarrin*.

13. For an example of the misuse of universalised patent laws to the detriment of people in Africa: Beth Burrows, 'Biodiversity Mystery

Theatre #4: The Case of the Pentagon's Big African Knowledge Grab', Diverse Women for Diversity Listserve, 29 July 2003.

14. There are numerous discussions in the literature about how IPRs should be protected in indigenous and other communities. Vandana Shiva, 'Golden Rice and Neem: Biopatents and the Appropriation of Women's Environmental Knowledge', *Women's Studies Quarterly*, 2003, Vol. 29, No. 1.2, 12–23; Dutfield, *Intellectual Property Rights, Trade and Biodiversity*; Langton, 'The "Wild", the Market and the Native'; Hawthorne, *Wild Politics*.

15. O'Hara, 'Valuing Socio-diversity', p. 33.

16. Ibid., 'Sustainability: Social and Ecological Dimensions', 'Discursive Ethics in Ecosystems Valuation and Environmental Policy', 'Toward a Sustaining Production Theory'.

17. Tuhiwai Smith, *Decolonising Methodologies*, p. 186.

18. Bell, *Daughters of the Dreaming*, p. 137.

19. Ibid., pp. 90–4.

20. Ibid., p. 91.

21. For an extended discussion of land, see Hawthorne, *Wild Politics*, pp. 162–205.

22. Ngarrindjeri concepts of cultural property are described in Diane Bell (ed.), for the Ngarrindjeri Nation, *Listen to Ngarrindjeri Women Speaking: Kungun Ngarrindjeri Miminar Yunnan*, Melbourne: Spinifex Press, 2008.

23. Trevorrow in ibid., p. 10.

24. Smith in Diane Bell and Gloria Jones (eds), *All about Water: All about the River*. A symposium held at Strathalbyn Town Hall, South Australia, 13 April 2007, p. 17.

25. The resemblance to trade in copyrights or patents is close. In the case of a copyright, it is not the book or CD that is being traded, but the right to trade in that licence.

26. Smith in Bell and Jones, *All about Water*, p. 18.

27. McHughes in Bell, *Listen to Ngarrindjeri Women Speaking*, pp. 12–13.

28. Multiversity is an epistemological approach that takes account of the location and context of the knower. The term is also used in the resistance to modernisation and colonisation of knowledge, see: Paul Wangoola, '*Mpambo*, the African Multiversity: A Philosophy to Rekindle the African Spirit' in George Dei et al. (eds), *Indigenous Knowledges in Global Contexts: Multiple Readings of Our World*, Toronto: OISE/University of Toronto Press, 2000.

29. On the problem of liberal feminism and the institutionalisation of gender mainstreaming see: Salleh, *Ecofeminism as Politics*, pp. 103–17; Susan Hawthorne, 'The Political Uses of Obscurantism:

Gender Mainstreaming and Intersectionality', *Development Bulletin*, 2004, No. 89, 87–91, Online Available HTTP: <www.devnet.anu. edu.au/GenderPacific/pdfs/20_gen_mainstream_hawthorne.pdf> (accessed 4 March 2008).

30. Maria Mies, *Patriarchy and Accumulation on a World Scale: Women in the International Division of Labour*, London: Zed Books, 1986; Maria Mies, 'Women and the Security of the Commons', paper presented at the World Social Forum, Mumbai, January 2004.

31. Susanne Kappeler, *The Will to Violence: The Politics of Personal Behaviour*, New York: Teachers College Press, 1995.

32. Mies, *Patriarchy and Accumulation on a World Scale*, pp. 220–2. Compare the statements of Martinez-Alier, Daly, and Goodland, below.

33. Susan Hawthorne, 'Dependent on Monsanto for Our Food?', 2007, Online Available HTTP: <www.onlineopinion.com.au/view. asp?article=5955> (accessed 4 March 2008).

34. Mies, *Patriarchy and Accumulation on a World Scale*, p. 221. Veronika Bennholdt-Thomsen and Maria Mies, *The Subsistence Perspective: Beyond the Globalised Economy*, London: Zed Books, 1999.

35. For a discussion of globalised production: Hawthorne, *Wild Politics*, pp. 273–82. In her talk at the World Social Forum in Mumbai, 2004, Maria Mies pointed out that the word private, comes from the Latin root, *privare* – the verb that means to rob, to steal, to deprive.

36. Hawthorne, *Wild Politics*, pp. 232–3, 285–6.

37. Bennholdt-Thomsen and Mies, *The Subsistence Perspective*, p. 20.

38. Janice Raymond, *Legitimating Prostitution as Sex Work: UN Labor Organization (ILO) Calls for Recognition of the Sex Industry*, Amherst, MA: Coalition Against Trafficking in Women, 1998, p. 2. See also Marilyn Waring, *Counting for Nothing: What Men Value and What Women are Worth*, Sydney: Allen and Unwin, 1988, p. 124; Kevin Bales, *Disposable People: New Slavery in the Global Economy*, University of California Press, 2000, p. 57.

39. Yayori Matsui, *Women in the New Asia*, London: Zed Books, 1999, p. 47.

40. Farida Akhter, *Seeds of Movements: On Women's Issues in Bangladesh*, Dhaka: Narigrantha Prabartana, 2007; Renate Klein, 'Globalized Bodies in the 21st Century: The Final Patriarchal Takeover?' in Veronika Bennholdt-Thomsen et al. (eds), *There is an Alternative: Subsistence and Worldwide Resistance to Corporate Globalization*, London: Zed Books, 2001.

41. Ngahuia Te Awekotuku, *Mana Wahine Maori: Selected Writings on Maori Women's Art, Culture and Politics*, Auckland: New Women's Press, 1991; Konai Helu Thaman, 'Environment-friendly or the New Sell? One Woman's View of Ecotourism in Pacific Island Countries' in Atu Emberson-Bain (ed.), *Sustainable Development or Malignant Growth: Perspectives of Pacific Island Women*, Suva, Fiji: Marama, 1994; Deborah McLaren, *Rethinking Tourism and Ecotravel: The Paving of Paradise and What You Can Do to Stop It*, West Hartford, CT: Kumarian Press, 1994.

42. Teresa Brennan, *Globalization and Its Terrors: Daily Life in the West*, London: Routledge, 2003.

43. Patricia Hynes, 'Consumption: North American Perspectives' in Jael Silliman and Ynestra King (eds), *Dangerous Intersections: Feminist Perspectives on Population, Environment, and Development*, Cambridge, MA: South End Press, 1999; Hawthorne, *Wild Politics*.

44. Hawthorne, 'The Political Uses of Obscurantism'.

45. See Alan Gilpin, *Environmental Economics: A Critical Overview*, Chichester: Wiley, 2000.

46. Helena Norberg-Hodge, 'The Pressure to Modernize and Globalize' in Jerry Mander and Edward Goldsmith (eds), *The Case Against the Global Economy and For a Turn Toward the Local*, San Francisco: Sierra Club Books, 1996, p. 40.

47. Joan Martinez-Alier, 'Environmental Justice as a Force for Sustainability' in Jan Nederveen Pieterse (ed.), *Global Futures: Shaping Globalization*, London: Zed Books, 2000, p. 148.

48. Herman Daly, 'Sustainable Growth: An Impossibility Theorem' in John Dryzek and David Schlosberg (eds), *Debating the Earth: The Environmental Politics Reader*, Oxford University Press, 1999, pp. 285–6; Robert Goodland, 'Growth has Reached its Limit' in Mander and Goldsmith (eds), *The Case Against the Global Economy*, pp. 207–17.

49. Donella Meadows, Dennis Meadows, Jørgan Randers and William Behrens, *The Limits to Growth*, New York: Universe Books, 1972.

50. Vandana Shiva, *Staying Alive: Women, Ecology and Development*, London: Zed Books, 1989; Vandana Shiva, *Biopiracy: The Plunder of Nature and Knowledge*, Boston, MA: South End Press, 1997, pp. 2–6.

51. Tuhiwai Smith, *Decolonising Methodologies*, pp. 90–8.

52. O'Hara, 'Valuing Socio-diversity', p. 37.

53. O'Hara, 'Toward a Sustaining Production Theory', p. 151.

54. Salleh, *Ecofeminism as Politics*, p. 194.

55. O'Hara, 'Discursive Ethics in Ecosystems Valuation and Environmental Policy', p. 102.

56. Leila Ahmed, *Women and Gender in Islam: Predicament and Promise*, New York: Routledge, 1992; Hawthorne, *Wild Politics*; Hynes, 'Consumption: North American Perspectives'.

57. Shiva, *Staying Alive*; Ani, *Yurugu*.

58. Lilla Watson, 'Aboriginal Feminism', paper presented at the Fourth Women and Labour Conference, University of Queensland, July 1984.

59. Rita Lindsay, Ellen Trevorrow, Alice Abdulla, and Margaret Dodd, in Bell, *Listen to Ngarrindjeri Women Speaking*, p. 15.

60. Eileen McHughes in Bell, *Ngarrindjeri Wurruwarrin*, p. 266.

Part II

Matter

Francis Bacon (1561–1626), a celebrated 'father of modern science', transformed tendencies already extant in his own society into a total program advocating the control of nature ...

Much of the imagery Bacon used in delineating his new scientific objectives and methods derives from the courtroom, and, because it treats nature as a female to be tortured through mechanical inventions, strongly suggests the interrogations of the witch trials ...

Although a female's inquisitiveness may have caused man's fall from his God-given dominion, the relentless interrogation of another female, nature, could be used to regain it ...

Bacon frequently described matter in female imagery as a 'common harlot'. 'Matter is not devoid of an appetite and inclination to dissolve the world and fall back into the old Chaos' ...

Mechanics, which gave man power over nature, consisted in motion; that is, in 'the uniting or disuniting of natural bodies'. Most useful were the arts that altered the materials of things ...

Carolyn Merchant, *Earthcare*,
New York: Routledge, 1995, pp. 80–3.

5

DEVELOPMENT FOR SOME IS VIOLENCE FOR OTHERS
India's Fisherfolk

Nalini Nayak

In India, the evolution of global neoliberalism through colonisation and 'modernisation', has taken a toll on the environment, on the poor in general, and on women in particular. Marketised development leads to people losing their livelihood as traditional occupations get eroded and as their common lands get privatised. The resulting exodus from rural to urban areas provides a convenient supply of cheap labour for capital. At a deeper level, long established systems of gender relations, together with patriarchal religions, sanction if not sanctify, the exploitation of women's sexuality and labour. The reproduction of life is relegated to the private sphere and considered a woman's respon- sibility. The many kinds of labour that go into sustaining life are thus invisible and kept out of economic calculations like the GNP. So entrenched is the exclusion of women from what passes for economic production, that international development agencies increasingly ask governments to bring women 'into the mainstream', as if they otherwise had no economic role at all. The new wisdom is that women's labour should be marketed and marketable no matter what it consists in.

In this 'inclusionary' effort, there are major gains for the modern capitalist patriarchal system of production. For instance, employment of women brings down the general price of labour, since thanks to the sex/gender ideology that devalues women, their labour is cheaper than men's. Secondly, women's labour is less organised and less resistant to manipulation by management. The reason for this is that most women are already burdened with family maintenance roles, so that the struggle for workplace rights is abandoned. Thirdly, women's wage labour softens the global economic crisis, as women with access to cash can purchase their needs. Fourthly, with women expected to earn their own family support, this reduces pressure on the state to provide welfare. As ecofeminist Maria Mies puts it, class exploitation and sex/gender exploitation are interlinked:

> It is my thesis that capitalism cannot function without patriarchy, that the goal of this system, namely the never-ending process of capital accumulation, cannot be achieved unless patriarchal man-woman relations are maintained or newly created. We could, therefore, also speak of neo-patriarchy. Patriarchy thus constitutes the mostly invisible underground of the visible capitalist system.[1]

Mies goes on to explain that the strategy of dividing the economy into 'visible' and 'invisible' sectors has characterised the capitalist accumulation process right from its origins. The invisible parts were by definition excluded from the 'real' economy; but in fact, they constituted the very foundation of the visible economy. Just as sex/gender ideology serves an economic purpose, so the ideology of race inferiority projected on to subaltern peoples, has functioned to disguise the visibility of racialised labour exploitation in colonial contexts.

Fishing for export or livelihood?

Today, in the global South, access to the commons as a source of livelihood is diminishing and traditional occupations are displaced by imported economic models and technologies – the United Nations Millennium Development Goals are a case in point. Now it becomes imperative for women to enter the marketised economy to keep households going. The cash nexus is justified in the jargon of modernisation as – 'the empowerment of women' – 'gender mainstreaming' – 'sex as work' – 'banking on women' – 'women as most credit worthy' – 'micro-finance for a strapped economy'. With the regularisation of globalisation, the dominant mindset is 'There Is No Alternative'. In this context, a proliferation of women's groups, NGOs, and governments are taking 'gender' seriously. Yet ironically, this trend coincides with the changing form of the capitalist patriarchal state from a centralised power to a more fluid innocuous dummy power. The corporate driven neoliberal trend is decentralisation of power, more 'freedom of choice', and a rush to draw women into the labour market. Money is made available for groups to work on domestic violence issues and on measures to ensure the political and economic empowerment of women. While all this is necessary and commendable, it is disassociated from the exploitative structures of globalisation.

In fact, women are generously brought into political decision-making, just as the state is pulling out of welfare, privatising care services beyond the reach of the masses. Women are allowed into political decision-making at a time when the control of economic power moves from the state to multinational financial institutions like the World Bank and World Trade Organisation. In market driven India, scandals surrounding the building lobby in Kolkota are constantly in the press; and the public watches in outrage as the Supreme Court puts corporate interests before their rights. Favourable judgments have been handed down to Coca-Cola versus the Plachimada community, and to the Jambudwip shrimp industry, allowing its appropriation of West Bengal wetlands.[2] This tendency is reinforced by the Special Economic Zones Act passed in 2005, which creates foreign enclaves for industrial use, through privatisation of extensive tracts of land. People across India are protesting such developments, only to be met by state violence – as in West Bengal and Orissa, where people have been killed. In the name of economic growth, commercial developments have displaced thousands of people from their means of livelihood.

In the post independence era, the government of India chose 'modernisation' with the aim of increasing production, and in the case of fisheries, the availability of cheap protein food for the masses. The modernisation of fisheries took off in the late 1960s and by the mid 1970s fish production had grown phenomenally.

In traditional coastal communities, where fishing is a commercial activity in addition to subsistence, the sexual division of labour is clear cut. Men do the harvesting and women do the post harvest work. Both men and women are generally involved in the pre harvest activity of preparing the nets and tackle for work. Women also prepare the food for long fishing trips. This is achieved on top of all the services that village women render gratis to their husbands and family. With this division of labour, women have access to markets and are in control of cash, because it is they who convert the fish into money. This access to the economic world, also gives the women a wider perspective, as they relate not only to vendors in markets, but to many kinds of people through consumer interaction. Many coastal communities in Kerala are matrilineal, and matrilocal, and the women are also known to inherit the fishing gear in marriage.[3] This gives them a share of the catch, and where a woman may not go to market, her own access to fish, either for food or for resale at the seashore is assured, thereby giving her an income.

However, the active economic role that women have played in traditional communities does not necessarily give them an equal say in decision-making. The fishing villages have been patriarchal for several generations now and religious norms govern social life. The communities have active local governance systems but women do not feature on such committees. In Christian fishing communities, it is the church that controls social life and plays a unifying role. In Muslim communities, it is the *jamaat*, and in the Hindu communities, it is the caste *panchayat* or *samaj*, that regulates social life. All these bodies are profoundly patriarchal in philosophy. And while controlling gendered interactions in the community, these local institutions give little attention to women's practical and economic needs like toilets, fuel for cooking, water, or minimal health facilities. Nevertheless, one patriarchal practice that these coastal communities did not have was the marriage dowry system. Since a girl was not considered a burden on her family, this allowed women a certain self-respect. Moreover, it is clear that subsistence livelihood was not a problem. The traditional community met the needs of the poor, the old, and the destitute. Such people had access to fish when it was landed and they could take freely for their day's need. A tolerance of diversity and interdependency prevailed. This was so until the mid 1970s when states like Kerala and Tamil Nadu attained stable population growth rates – a progressive development indicator. Even so, large sections of the population still made their livelihood in traditional occupations, for modernisation had not taken over the countryside, and technological change in the fisheries was only found in the larger landing centres.

Things changed dramatically with modernisation. The traditional fishing community has been very open to technology transfer and creative innovation in their own way. Although, initially, new craft and gear were tried and tested and uptake was slow – the pace was such that it avoided destructive impacts on fish stocks or on the organisation of labour. But state subsidies stimulated adoption of new technologies and attracted non-fishers into the industry. The main features of this development have been that

- the boats got larger,
- they began to be propelled by engines dependent on oil,
- the gear got larger,
- it was more efficient, so fishers became less selective in what they caught,
- the landings got larger and more centralised, and
- the fishing operation became more capital intensive.

This state economic intervention met the needs of technology innovators and exporters in the global North and anticipated an expanded market demand for fish product. It was no longer a question of meeting the need for food in communities that depended on this resource.

Such changes took place in Kerala and Tamil Nadu in the mid 1970s; but the political pursuit of modernisation and growth has had disastrous sociological consequences. As fishing boats got larger they required better landing facilities. The fishers were now obliged to land their catch away from the village. This meant that women had to travel during the day in order to keep their traditional access to the catch. If the new landing site was too far away, women with children or the elderly, had to forfeit their access to the catch. Bigger boats and more efficient nets also meant larger catches. Sometimes these were so large that women were not equipped to handle them as they did before. The capitalist patriarchal state gave credit and technical support to the fishermen, but it rarely intervened to assist the fisherwomen in their work. Cold storage for caught fish, or credit to handle larger volumes of fish, might have been ways in which the state could reach out to women. But this gap has been taken up by merchants, who move into women's traditional economic activities and impinge on their livelihood rights. In Kanyakumari, hundreds of women were displaced from the work of net making between 1979 and 1980 when the state of Tamil Nadu introduced the net making machine. Nylon nets and the machine made net were a threat to the subsistence wages of women and to the otherwise destitute.[4] In all this, fishermen did not stand by their women in their economic struggle; rather, they identified with the power of the machine and the status it gave them.

Technologies of abandonment

The state subtly dispossesses women through its occasional interventions. For example, in the areas where the matrilineal system existed women inherited the fishing equipment. But with the development process, the state offered credit facilities only for men to buy new boats and nets. The banks through which credit was channelled, recognised men as the economic agent, and made loan advances in their names. With this system in place, the women lost ownership rights in the craft and their right to a share of the catch.[5] On the other hand, when a man desired to acquire a larger number of boats with state subsidies in Veraval, Gujarat, for example, he transferred the older boats into the name of his wife, although she in reality had no say over the management of the boat.

The mid 1980s was a time when the best varieties of fish like pomfret, seer fish, perch, shrimp, squid, were transported to urban markets and even distant countries to fetch top prices. This expansion of trade brought fishermen increased cash returns to invest in newer technologies – boats, nets, motors – and enabled them to meet higher fuel costs. But at the same time, it limited women's access to such fish for sale and for food. In exceptional cases where women, for instance, from Vishakapatinam, entered into larger trading arrangements, fish was despatched by train to Mumbai. A few women in Maharashtra and Mangalore did the same. But these were rare cases, and the quantity of fish handled was insignificant in comparison with the amount that merchant men dealt with. Some women have found a role as commission agents, supplying fish to bigger wholesalers. But again this is not a significant number. Nevertheless, as the International Collective in Support of Fishworkers (ICSF) reports: the fact that women do this is proof enough to show that they would have been able to remain in the market chain, had they been supported by the state. In the mid 1980s, women in south Indian states began to organise for state recognition of their rights to fish for marketing.[6]

Globalisation and the export trade has affected women in other ways as well. Formerly all fish that was landed in bulk and did not fetch a good price, was dried and salted. This fish was the lean season insurance for women. They could sell dried fish in bad times. In India, dried fish moved across the country creating a huge chain of economic dependants, both as agents of transfer and as retailers, the majority of the latter were women. Ribbon-fish from Gujarat provided livelihood to south Kerala vendors in the months of June, July and August, and cheap fish for consumers in lean months. In north and northeast India, landlocked areas, were served by similar chains. But the opening of the export market in the mid and late 1990s, saw this entire Indian food supply chain disrupted. During 1995–98, ribbon-fish was airlifted fresh to Hong Kong, so there was no fish for local drying, no fish for local women vendors in south and northeast India, and no cheap fish for poor local consumers.[7] As a 1995 Public Hearing organised by the National Fishworkers Forum revealed, women who lose access to fish at local landing places, are now forced to travel further for it. Many now fall into wage work, either cleaning shrimp for the processors or drying trash fish landed by the trawlers. However, once they have experienced the difference in earnings between self-employed fish vending versus exploited wage work, they will continue to fight all odds, putting even greater pressure on themselves, to remain in the fish trade.[8]

It is said that improved technology creates new work opportunities, but history has proven that this is not always true. With modernisation of the Indian fishing industry and the ousting of women from the post harvest disposal of fish, it was not local women who found work in the processing plants of Gujarat and Andhra.[9] As women were thrown out of work in Kerala and Kanyakumari, they became cheap migrant labour for fish-processing plants in Gujarat and other states of India. The entire industrialised fish-processing industry of Vishakapatinam, and later Maharashtra, and Gujarat, was established on the backs of these women. Only twenty years after its inception did the industry open up to local labour, although migrants still continue to arrive, even from as far away as northeast India. However, the 1995 Public Hearing into the conditions of migrant women workers, and several reports by women's organisations raised the alarm in State Assemblies drawing public attention to their dire state. Fish-processing plants were forced to review the employment situation. Coincidental with these local political moves, the global market imposed new sanitary standards on the export industry. Processors were required to improve standards inside the plants, and – in order to cut costs – they began employing locals, minimising migrant labour, and providing better working standards.

Ironically, after the concerted effort of government and research institutions to increase the fish catch and thereby earn foreign exchange, the catch began to decline. Across the globe, the ecological habitat and nursery grounds for fish have been ruined – directly by the introduction of industrial-scale fishing technologies, and indirectly through other development activities like pollution from land clearing, erosion, and run off. All this has made fishing uneconomic for small fishers, who have either been thrown into debt, or had to leave fishing altogether.

Patriarchal cultures old and new

If the 'development' and then decline of fisheries has had a devastating socio-economic impact on women, they have also been subjected to cultural changes working in favour of capitalist patriarchal economics. In the 1980s, the dowry system slowly crept into fishing communities. This was a period when coastal birth rates were falling in Kerala and Tamil Nadu. The conjunction of new fishing technologies, decreasing natality, and practice of the dowry system, was significant. If a girl was marrying a good fisher, then his demand was for money to buy better equipment. If a girl was marrying a man with little or no fishing skills or no equipment, the dowry was sought for a passage to employment in the Arabian Gulf states. Now at the start of the twenty-first century, the practice of dowry exchange has grown phenomenally. A study of the vibrant fishing village of Thoothur shows that the female sex ratio is way below the general rate of the Kanyakumari district as a whole. Dowries for a shark fisherman in Thoothur are anywhere between Rs.2–3 *lakhs*. When dowries are this high, girl children are discriminated against, and that can result in female foeticide. In general, women are forbidden to break out of the tightly bonded community or to enter marriage alliances on their own. Women, through the marriage cycle, are stabilisers not only of the caste system, but of the patriarchal family system as well. Dowry payments keep a fragile economy afloat.[10]

Following from the ecological decline of fish stocks, and social disorganisation of the 'developed' fishing industry, indebtedness and alcoholism now plague fishing communities. This results in violence against women. The highest rates of violence are reported from areas where the fishing is poor and there is a pressure to repay debts. When fishing no longer promises returns, the state looks to other ocean resources like oil, but also chemical resources, or it sees the coast as an earner of income through tourism.[11] In 2005, the Indian government enacted a law for Special Economic

Zones permitting the privatisation of large areas of coastal land for industrial development. Today, natural harbours and estuaries are being converted into commercial harbours for ocean trade. Fishing and coastal communities may be dislodged or their ocean commons polluted. At Adhani, a port in the Gulf of Cutch, displaced communities now exist as ready colonies of cheap labour for capital. Hundreds of women move into the liquor or sex trade as the only opening for the poor and uneducated. A few years ago, the author was told by women who come into Trivandrum city from a fishing village that they service men for as little as Rs.5 per person and need at least ten clients a night to buy food for the family next morning. Subsequently, rates for these services have increased but so has the number of AIDS cases in coastal towns.

The modernisation of fishing in India shows that development by means of market economics is neither just, nor sustainable. A technologised and globalising fishing industry has not benefited coastal people, nor has it taken care of the complex ocean ecosystem which is the key to life in these communities. In fisheries, the call of the hour is the co-management of coastal resources where those who depend on them for their livelihood will be their custodians. If tackled in good time, the ocean ecosystem will respond and at minimal cost. Meanwhile, the presence of women in co-management regimes will ensure their economic role; for 'Without Women in Fisheries, No Fish in the Sea'. At stake is a reconstitution of the idea of 'development' around a life-centred political economy, based on principles of participatory democracy. The statement of Asian fishworkers who met together recently at a Cambodian workshop, organised by the ICSF, entitled 'Asserting Rights, Defining Responsibilities' highlights this:

> ... believing that natural resources of bays, seas, rivers and inland water bodies are the common heritage of all and that they should not be privatised for the benefit of a few, and that these resources should be equitably and responsibly shared for sustaining life and livelihood and towards the greater benefit of all artisanal fishing communities ... [We]

> stress that just, participatory, self-reliant and sustainable development of
> coastal and inland fisheries is of vital importance to us.[12]

Several other communities that depend on local ecosystems for
their livelihood joined the fishworkers in this statement. These
communities have survived for the most part without the support
of the state. All that they demand is their customary right to
'the commons' and pledge their commitment to conserve them
for future generations. They thus throw down a challenge to
the logic of economic modernisation – a logic that is based on
the principle of greatest accumulation for the smallest number.
They cry halt to this process of mal-development as it impinges
on their material base of survival. These experts in subsistence
teach us how production systems that focus on life and its needs
can eventually contribute to the greater good. A number of micro
programmes functioning in India now bear witness to this.[13]

Notes

1. Maria Mies, *Patriarchy and Accumulation on a World Scale*,
   London: Zed Books, 1986, p. 38.
2. *Perumatty Grama Panchayat* vs *Hindustan Coca-Cola Beverages
   Ltd*, Kerala High Court Ruling, 1 June 2005; Report of the Central
   Empowerment Committee on Jambudwip, 20 December 2002;
   Interim Direction of the Supreme Court of India, IA No: 920, 25
   August 2003.
3. Nalini Nayak, *Continuity and Change in Artisanal Fishing
   Communities*, Trivandrum: Programme for Community Organisation
   and the South Indian Federation of Fishermen Societies, 1993.
4. As reported in Joseph Lukas, 'Fish Vendors Meet Their Own Credit
   Needs' in A. Vijayan and N. Nayak (eds), *Women First*, Chennai:
   ICSF, Samudra Dossier, Women in Fisheries Series, 1997, No. 2.
5. Nalini Nayak, 'Transition or Transformation: A Study of the
   Mobilisation, Organisation and Emergence of Consciousness
   among the Fishworkers of Kerala, India', Unpublished manuscript,
   Department of Social Analysis, Tamil Nadu Theological Seminary,
   Madurai, 2002, pp. 6–8.
6. Nalini Nayak, 'Women in Movements' in Vijayan and Nayak,
   Women First, pp. 97–9.
7. Sebastian Mathew, 'Gujarat Fisheries: Time to Move from
   Exploitation to Conservation and Management Regimes', paper

presented at the workshop Towards Sustainable Fisheries in Gujarat, Gujarat Institute of Development Research, Ahmedabad, 2002.

8. Aleyamma Vijayan, 'The Invisible Women in Fisheries, Kerala' in Vijayan and Nayak, *Women First*, p. 23.

9. Aleyamma Vijayan, 'Public Hearing on the Struggles of Women Workers in the Fish Processing Industry in India', Chennai: ICSF, Samudra Dossier, Women in Fisheries Series, 1995, No. 1.

10. Nalini Nayak, D. Nandakumar, and A. Vijayan, *Coastal Population Dynamics and Ecosystem Changes: How Markets, Technology and Institutions Affect this Process Along the West Coast of India*, Thiruvananthapuram: Protsahan, 2006, pp. 229–33. Literacy rates and birth rates can be a good indicator of women's oppression. In the coastal town of Veraval, Gujarat, despite a booming fishing industry in the 1990s, the 2001 Census revealed only 54 per cent literacy for women in the coastal wards, whereas it was 71 per cent in the town. The female sex ratio in the 0–6 age group is 925 to 1,000 males in coastal wards, despite the fact that under natural conditions, more girl babies than boys will survive birth.

11. Janpath and Partners, *Report of the Coastal Jathra of the Gujarat Coast*, Ahmenabad: Janpath, 2005.

12. Siem Riep Statement, 'Asserting Rights, Defining Responsibilities: Perspectives from Small-Scale Fishing Communities on Coastal and Fisheries Mangement in Asia', ICSF Workshop, Siem Riep, May 2007.

13. South Asian Network for Gender Training – SANGAT, *Feminist Activism in the 21st Century: Report of a South Asian Feminist Meet*, New Delhi: SANGAT, 2007, pp. 82–3.

6

NUCLEARISED BODIES AND MILITARISED SPACE

The US in the Marshall Islands

Zohl dé Ishtar

Women have experienced many reproductive cancers and abnormal births. They gave birth, not to children as we think of them, but to things we could only describe as 'octopuses', 'apples', 'turtles' and other things in our experience. We do not have Marshallese words for these kinds of babies. These babies are born with no bones in their bodies and with transparent skin. We can see their brains and their hearts beating. There are no legs, no arms, no head, nothing. Many women die from abnormal pregnancies and many of those who survive have given birth to what looked like strands of purple grapes.

Lijon Eknilang, Rongelap Atoll, 2005[1]

The small, sea-swept islands and coral bars of the Marshall Islands, scattered across the mid-Pacific just north of the equator, are unknown to most people, except those who call them 'home'. What better place to develop nuclear bombs as the world entered the Nuclear Age? A year after the US had dropped the atomic bombs which devastated Hiroshima and Nagasaki, they began developing the next generation of nuclear weaponry in the Marshalls. It is here that the Pentagon tested all of their missile delivery systems, and where they are now developing Ballistic Missile Defence systems and preparing for the militarisation of space.

The US security relationship with the Marshall Islands started in 1946 with 67 nuclear detonations occurring in the twelve years to 1958.[2] Prior to detonating the first nuclear bomb, the US removed the people of Bikini and Enewetak Atolls from their ancestral commons. In March 1946, residents of Bikini Atoll were relocated from their resource-rich atoll to the solitary and infertile sandbar island of Rongerik. By May, the residents of Enewetak, Rongelap and Wotho Atolls had also been temporarily relocated. Then, on 30 June 1946, the US detonated the first post-Second World War nuclear bomb on Bikini Atoll. Called 'Operation Crossroads' this initial testing programme consisted of two bombs, each equal in explosive force to the bomb dropped on Hiroshima. As if oblivious to these developments, barely a year later, on 18 July 1947, the United Nations agreed to commit the Marshallese along with other Micronesian nations (north of the equator) to the United States as the world's first 'Strategic Trust' – not a strategic advantage to the Marshallese, of course. The US aspiration to claim Micronesia following the battles of the Second World War had been expressed by Democrat Representative Edward Herbert in 1945, when he argued that: 'We have fought for them. We have got them. We should keep them. They are necessary for our safety.'[3] The US relationship to and involvement in Micronesia has been informed by that standpoint ever since.

The UN Trusteeship Agreement placed 'no limitation ... upon the utilization of all or any part of the area for United States security purposes' but obligated the US to:

> Promote the development of the inhabitants of the trust territory towards self-government or independence as may be appropriate ... and to this end shall ... promote the economic advancement of the inhabitants ... encourage the development of fisheries, agriculture and industries; protect the inhabitants against the loss of their lands and resources ... [and] protect the health of the inhabitants.[4]

The US government agreed to not subject the Trust Territory residents 'to perceptibly greater danger than, say, the people of the United States'.[5] The UN handed free rein to the US by placing the newly constituted 'Trust Territory of the Pacific Islands' under the Security Council where the US has veto power. This single act limited the UN's own role in Micronesia *and* superseded its own obligations to the Micronesians, handing these wholesale to US control. The US was granted the right to establish naval, military and air bases and to erect fortification in the Territory. This is exactly what the Japanese had done when they took most of Micronesia from the Germans at the start of the First World War. The Japanese had the islands mandated to them under the League of Nations in 1920 and subsequently on their withdrawal from the League in 1935, constructed an array of naval and air bases in preparation for the Second World War. But the US was different: it was a nuclear force, and the Marshallese were to experience the full brunt of US nuclear ambitions.

One bomb vapourised an entire island

The year had not come to a close before the US government removed the people of Enewetak from their home islands once again, relocating them to Ujelang Atoll. Meanwhile the Bikinians were still on Rongerik where they had been sent two years earlier. There was little food on Rongerik because the expected ship had not arrived with promised food aid and people were on the brink of starvation. There was global outrage as the world's media picked up the story, but this subsided when the Bikinians were moved to Kwajalein in March 1948, and from there sent on to Kili Island, a single island with no lagoon or harbour where they remain today. From 16 April to 16 May 1948, the US conducted three nuclear tests at Enewetak as part of the 'Operation Sandstone' series of tests. The next month, the US House of Representatives and Senate assured the people of the Trust Territory of 'justice, peace, and tranquillity, a voice in their civic affairs and government, and the development of their economies and the protection of their civil rights, all with due regard to the established customs of such peoples'.[6] Two months later, on 1 August 1948, US President Truman announced that Enewetak and Bikini would be the Proving Ground for their nuclear arsenal. A total of 47 nuclear bombs were subsequently detonated on Enewetak, and 20 on Bikini Atoll.

The Trust Territory was administered by the US Navy until 1951 when it transferred this authority to the US Department of the Interior, but the Marshallese did not become independent until

1986, although they did establish a legislature – the Nitijela – in 1950. In 1951 the US detonated another four tests on Enewetak in their efforts to develop a thermonuclear device. They also detonated the first of 928 tests in the deserts of Nevada. By November 1952, they had returned to Enewetak, under 'Operation Ivy', to detonate the world's first hydrogen bomb, named 'Mike', and the largest pure-fission bomb, named 'King'. These two bombs had a total force of 10.4 megatons: 750 times larger than the Hiroshima bomb. The 'Mike' detonation vapourised an entire island. In January 1953, the US Atomic Energy Commission (AEC) confirmed its intention to keep Bikini and Enewetak indefinitely as their 'Pacific Proving Ground', while simultaneously recognising that the former indigenous residents may have common land rights to the islands. Meanwhile the AEC set about preparing for the 'Castle' test series on Bikini Atoll. This time they decided against evacuating the people off Rongelap because of the unavailability of equipment for evacuations. Bikinians were already out of the way on Kili Island. The military argued that all indications suggested the impact of detonations would be minimal. This was to be a high altitude test and the US pinned safety precautions on the complicated nature of wind direction and speed at the time of the shot. If there was a need for an evacuation this could be achieved at the last moment.

Then, on 1 March 1954, the US detonated the 'Bravo' shot at Bikini. The explosion was far greater than what the US had predicted and prepared for: it was 15 megatons, that is, 1,000 times larger than the Hiroshima bomb. Fallout ash covered Rongelap and nearby Ailinginae Atolls and a 'mist' fallout enveloped Utirik and other islands.[7] US meteorologists stationed on Rongerik were also exposed to the fallout. The US described this unprecedented fallout as the result of an 'unexpected shift in wind conditions'.[8] However, it is believed by many servicemen that the military had intentionally ignored their own meteorologists' warning that the wind had shifted course and was blowing towards the inhabited islands, including the one where they were stationed. The fallout was so intense that the US directed the ships standing by for last minute evacuation of the Marshallese out of the fallout zone. It was 48 hours before the 86 Rongelap people were evacuated. Rongelap islander Lijon Eknilang, whose eighth birthday was the day of the Bravo shot, remembers:

> There was a huge, brilliant light that consumed the sky. We ... heard a big loud noise, just like a big thunder and the earth started to move – the ground started to sway and sink ... A little later in the morning we saw a big cloud moving to our islands. It covered the sky. Then it started to snow in Rongelap ... For many hours poison from the bomb kept falling on our islands. We kids played in the powder, having fun, but later everyone was sick ... The fallout was in the air that we breathed, in the fresh water that we drank, and in the food we ate during the days after Bravo.[9]

The 154 Utirik people were not removed from their island for a further 24 hours. By that time most islanders, including the Rongelapese, were suffering from radioactive-related illnesses: nausea, vomiting, and rashes.[10] The evacuees were taken to the US naval base at Kwajalein Atoll where a medical team studied their physical responses to the detonation. This was the first of many medical surveys which Marshallese would be subjected to over the next fifty years. Many of the evacuees developed sores, and experienced hair loss, stomach aches, and headaches. Children had absorbed high levels of radioactive iodine into their thyroid glands.[11] The Rongelap and Utirik people were understandably terrified. They had no way of knowing what was happening to them, and the US military was not pro-active in informing them: partly perhaps because it didn't really know itself. When the Marshallese asked to return home they were told that they could return in 'two or four weeks'. Meanwhile the military proceeded to detonate the remaining five 'Castle' detonations. On 27 April, five days after the US completed their series, the Rongelapese were evacuated to a tent camp on Ebeye Island, and later Ejit Island in Majuro. They were to stay there for three years. The Utirik people were returned home because the US scientists had found their island to be 'only slightly contaminated and considered safe for habitation'.[12]

Radioactive ecosystem: human guinea pigs

When in July 1957, the US encouraged the Rongelap people to return home despite lingering radiation, the Department of Energy's Brookhaven National Laboratory released an internal report explaining the logic behind its encouragement:

> Even though the radioactive contamination of Rongelap Island is considered perfectly safe for human habitation, the levels of activity are higher than those found in other inhabited locations in the world. *The habitation of these people on the island will afford most valuable ecological radiation data on human beings.*[13]

Unaware of US intentions, the Rongelap people remained on their island until 20 June 1985 when they made the decision to relocate themselves to the small coral island in Kwajalein Atoll. By this time most of the 327 Rongelapese were experiencing increasing health crises. They had requested repatriatriation in 1983 but had been ignored by the US government which insisted that Rongelap was safe. It was a brave act, said community activist Darlene Keju-Johnson, founder of the group Youth to Youth in Health:

> By doing this, the Rongelap people said that they don't want to be part of this whole nuclear craziness. And that their bottom line is: 'We care about our children's future'. Because they know that they are contaminated. They know that they'll be dying out soon. They are dying now – slowly.[14]

Although the US detonated their last bomb in the Marshalls on 18 August 1958, they have continued their military presence there to this day.

Kwajalein Atoll became 'the primary range for testing the accuracy of intercontinental ballistic missiles and developing anti-ballistic missile systems'. According to Giff Johnson, it has been so essential to US development of ballistic missile delivery systems, that it may have 'contributed more to the arms race than any other spot on the earth'.[15] On 23 March 1983, US President Reagan announced his Strategic Defense Initiative (SDI) or 'Star Wars' – a space based system designed as a total ballistic missile defence (BMD) to protect the US from missile attacks. US Army Kwajalein Atoll (USAKA) and Kwajalein Missile Range (KMR) became instrumental to US space warfare ambitions. On 1 October 1997, the Clinton administration restructured and revamped the programme as US Army Space and Missile Defense Command. On 1 May 2001, President George W. Bush committed the US to developing a 'layered' missile defence system that would extend Reagan's BMD system, and withdrew from the Anti-Ballistic Missile Treaty between the US and Soviet Union.

The US extension into space warfare technology is heavily dependent on maintaining its position at Kwajalein. As Assistant Secretary of State for East Asian and Pacific Affairs Stanley Roth told US Congress in October 1998:

> According to a Department of Defense assessment, the USAKA / KMR is a 'national asset' – currently the only facility in the world with an arena suitable for full scale testing of long-range missiles. The study also determined that Kwajalein is uniquely situated for intelligence gathering and provides important support for our space programs.[16]

In 1998, the head of the US Army's Space and Missile Defense Command, Lieutenant-General John Costello described Kwajalein as the 'gem in the crown'.[17] He said that: 'Kwajalein is the singular place where all the capabilities exist to gauge the success or failure of missile defence systems ... The only place in the world to do precision testing is Kwajalein.'

The current US lease on Kwajalein expires in 2016. But in 2003 the US and Republic of the Marshall Islands governments signed an agreement extending the lease for 50 years up to 2066, with a 20-year option.[18] This means that the Marshallese government has signed a lease granting the US control over Kwajalein Atoll until 2086. However, the Kwajalein landowners have consistently rejected the terms of the US agreement, and insisted that the Marshall Islands government does not have the jurisdiction to lease their land to the US. Kwajalein Negotiation Commission Chairman Christopher Loeak described the US offer as 'insufficient to provide for the people of Kwajalein', and as failing 'to account for population growth and inflation'.[19] This is not a mere quibble over money. The US's taking of the largest island in Kwajalein Atoll for its military base has resulted in the Marshallese being crammed on to the small auxiliary island of Ebeye. The Kwajalein landowners insist that, 'if the US [is] not willing to negotiate a new, fair lease agreement, then the landowners want to discuss repatriation of the base now in preparation for the expiration of the current deal in 2016'.[20] Kwajalein landowners remain determined not to budge: their future depends on it.

The Kwajalein landowners have protested their living conditions on Ebeye since the late 1970s, re-occupying their home islands throughout Kwajalein Atoll through a series of 'sail-ins'.[21] The biggest demonstration was 'Operation Homecoming' in 1982, during which landowners sailed into and set up camp against the fence of the Missile Range on Kwajalein Island. In September 1983, during a plebiscite to decide the Marshallese relationship with the US, the Kwajalein landowners joined the Rongelapese and Bikinians to vote against a Compact of Free Association, which contained clauses granting the US a lease on Kwajalein, and limiting US compensation to those affected by the nuclear testing programme. Of the 60 per cent of the Marshallese population who participated in the vote, 58 per cent were in favour of the terms of the Compact, which meant that only 32 per cent actually voted 'yes'. Of the Kwajalein landowners 70 per cent were against the Compact, as were 90 per cent of the Bikini/Kili people, and 85 per cent of the Rongelap. In fact, ten out of 24 atolls voted against the Compact.[22] In 1985, still unhappy about the US treatment of their people, the Kwajalein landowners again reoccupied their islands. In September 1985, scores of women, men, and children camped outside the Kwajalein base for four months. The US government insisted that its agreement was with the Marshall Islands government, which in turn claimed 'Eminent Domain' over Kwajalein Atoll in the 'national interest'. The protest was broken by the Marshall Islands government arresting women elders, an event without precedence in Marshallese matrilineal society.[23]

Nuclear pollution and cancer deaths

In April 2006, the US Congress noted that the 67 nuclear detonations conducted in the Marshall Islands had released a total force 7,200 times greater than the bomb unleashed on Hiroshima, and 93 times greater than all the tests detonated in Nevada from 1945 to 1992.[24] Congress estimated the explosive force of the bombs as averaging 1.5 Hiroshima sized bombs every day for the full twelve years of the testing programme, 1946 to 1958. The US Centers for Disease Control and Prevention estimates that the tests released 6.3 billion curies of radioactive iodine 131 into the atmosphere – that is, 150 times greater than the 40 million curies released by the Chernobyl nuclear reactor accident. Much of this fallout will have been dispersed by wind to other parts of the global environment.

But the intense nuclearisation of the Marshallese ecosystem combined with displacement from ancestral commons has devastated these island communities. Poisoned soils and water, and thus, loss of traditional island food resources like coconuts and fish; economic dependency created by rapid Westernisation during the tests; and the cultural disturbance from continued US military presence at Kwajalein Atoll; have each led to the disorganisation of an hitherto sustainable humanity–nature relationship. There is now a soaring death rate caused by cancers, malnutrition, diabetes, and mental depression. Infant and child mortality in 1999 was put at 37 per 1,000 live births, increasing to 120 per 1,000 live births in the outer islands.[25] In 2005, the longevity of Marshallese was said to be twelve years less than that of people in the US.[26]

Dr Neal Palafox from the University of Hawaii, Burns Medical School, reported to the American Cancer Society in 1999 that the incidence of cancer among islanders is extreme.[27] Moreover, in 2004, the US National Cancer Institute estimated that only half of the cancers to be expected in the 14,000 Marshallese exposed to the Bravo shot, have developed as yet, or have been diagnosed.[28] The US National Cancer Institute, using records of the Nuclear Claims Tribunal for 470 people who had already died, linked the cancers to lifestyle and environmental factors. This included the US nuclear testing programme in relation to which increases in leukaemia, thyroid and breast cancer were identified, particularly among people exposed to radiation as children. Women have carried the heaviest impacts of nuclear testing, with many dying from breast, cervical, and liver cancers. Breast cancer mortality in the Marshalls is 149 compared to 32 in 100,000 for the US; cervical cancer is 249 compared to 3 in 100,000 for the US.[29] Marshallese breast cancer rates are the highest in the Pacific Ocean region. While some cancers have multiple causes, breast and thyroid cancers are strongly radiogenic. Iodine 131 is a radionuclide (an atom which emits radioactivity) that concentrates in the thyroid. More than two thirds of Rongelap children aged under ten years who were on their home islands at the time of the Bravo shot in 1954 later presented with thyroid nodules.

Many deaths from cancer could have been preventable *if* the Marshallese had had adequate access to medical facilities. Dr Palafox noted that, from 1 October 2005 through 6 June 2006, 26 Marshallese patients with cancer were assessed to see if they would benefit from being referred off-island to hospitals in Hawaii, Guam, or mainland US. Of these patients, eleven were 'denied referral because the cancers were too advanced'.[30] With the Marshall Islands government receiving a mere $2 million annually for the care of 12,259 patients, the Marshallese hospitals do not have adequate facilities to diagnose or treat cancers.

However, other factors would also appear to be implicated in the development of Marshallese cancers, nutrition, for example. Once the islanders could no longer access their fertile farmlands and fish teeming ocean commons, the US encouraged them to rely on purchases of imported canned foods. The shift to non-traditional 'convènience' diets high in fat, salt, and sugar has impoverished their nutrition. Jack Niedenthal, an American legal adviser to the Bikinians, recalled that Emso Leviticus, a Bikini island woman, had told him: 'The Navy men were very kind and gave us big bins filled with all kinds of food we had never eaten before, like C-rations, chocolates, corned beef and other wonderful things.'[31] The Marshall Islands has one of the highest rates of childhood malnutrition in the Pacific Ocean region, with 60 per cent of children aged between one and five years suffering from Vitamin A deficiency and 25 per cent with iron deficiency; and one third of children having both conditions.[32] Vitamin A deficiency is particularly linked to head and neck cancers, but also to lung, liver, cervical, and bladder cancers.[33] Marshall Island communities also have one of the highest diabetes rates in the Pacific. In 2001, 132 Marshallese people were admitted to hospital with diabetes, by 2004 that number had risen to 428.[34] Type II (adult onset, non-insulin dependent) diabetes is one of the nation's most serious health problems. Among the Marshallese, 30 per cent of individuals over 15 years have diabetes, compared to 2 per cent of Americans. This preventable disease was almost absent prior to the arrival of the US military in the country.

Economic, social, and cultural fallout

The Marshallese population has increased rapidly in the past few decades. In 1920 the national population was 9,800; it had reached 43,380 by 1988 and 56,000 by 2005. Two-thirds of the population live in the urban areas of Majuro Atoll and Ebeye Island in Kwajalein Atoll. Ebeye is the most densely populated island in the Pacific Ocean region, with 26,000 people per square kilometre. Numerous social problems have accompanied this growth: overcrowding; inadequate infrastructure for water, electricity, and sanitation; unemployment and poverty, and low education standards. Poverty is extreme, with 20 per cent of households having a cash income of less than $1 a day.[35] With increasing urbanisation, the close bonds of subsistence economies, family and community relationships, are disjointed and children and youth lose the certainty of their customary heritage. Youth to Youth in Health, a non-government organisation of young islanders, attributes the problems to

… westernization and the consequent disintegration of traditional family structures, values and activities. In traditional Marshallese society (which is still very much intact on many Outer Islands), youth were busy with subsistence activities ... [now] families are becoming more nuclear and parents work, leaving youth on their own with nothing to do and little supervision.[36]

The spectrum of youth problems is similar to that found in the so-called developed world: use of alcohol, drugs and cigarettes, high rates of teenage pregnancy and of suicide among young men.[37] Only a fifth of elementary school-age children attend on a regular basis.[38] The government deals with an acute discrepancy between children and desk-spaces by restricting access to high schools through competitive examination. But most schools are so overcrowded and under-resourced that it is remarkable that teachers can teach there, let alone students learn. Many Marshallese youth are said to feel as if life is pointless, or in the words of one young person from Majuro, that they are 'living for nothing'.[39] A recent nationwide survey found that there is a prevalent concern among the Marshallese for their youth: a fear of their becoming 'the lost generation' caused by 'lost cultural identity and weak family and community support'.[40]

In education, girls have higher drop-out rates than boys, particularly at secondary and tertiary levels. This translates into men being more likely to take up employment than women, who then tend to rely on very low-paying jobs or welfare.[41] Traditionally, women in Marshallese matrilineal society were respected as the locus of identity and inheritance. But Westernisation has eroded the old social safeguards designed to protect women and, through them, their children.[42] The social disorganisation that came with US militarisation of the islands has undermined women's status; and young women and girls are particularly at risk of sexual violence. Other social responses to this rapid social change are domestic violence and child sexual abuse. In 2004, over 84 per cent of women surveyed by the local organisation Women United Together, reported having been victims of physical violence. Of those abused women, 92 per cent identified their husbands as the perpetrators. Nearly 40 per cent of women respondents said that they were first abused in their teens, and most felt that abuse was something they just had to accept as women, particularly if going out alone at night in urban areas.[43] These figures are thought to be conservative, as much violence goes unreported.

The capitalist patriarchal economic system introduced through successive waves of German–Japanese–American colonisation has politically and socially disempowered both Marshallese women and men. Traditionally, women were the economic keepers of the family and the conduit through which land rights passed to younger generations. They guided their eldest brothers whom they put into the public domain as their representatives. Their ability to remove them provided a safeguard against the abuse of privilege. But the introduction of the US system turned politics into 'a man's domain'. There have only been two women elected to the 33-member Nitijela since it was established in 1950. Now, more and more Marshallese women point to how their limited representation in local and national politics has seriously hindered the development of the country. Women United Together Marshall Islands is the only women's non-government organisation actively campaigning for their interests.

Crimes against humanity

Many Marshall Island people continue to protest against US militarism and the nuclearisation of their environments and bodies. But these efforts face intense pressure from the US government and interests who benefit commercially from the US military presence. The political determination of the Marshallese is fired by a long history of US testing for its nuclear arsenal. They still suffer the consequences of that era in illness and death, contamination of ancestral commons, cultural displacement, political and economic dependency. The US betrayal of their UN Trusteeship leaves an acute and lingering fear among the island people, for themselves, and for their children's future.

Not all that is bad in the Marshall Islands can be linked to the US military of course, nor was everything the US brought necessarily bad. But there is an undeniable connection between the nuclearised environment and the decay of Marshallese society. All generations have been affected by the bomb tests, including those yet to be born. In 1958, four years after their exposure to the radioactive fallout from the 1954 Bravo shot, Rongelap women began experiencing a rate of stillbirths and miscarriages that was twice that of unexposed Marshallese women.[44] Many became afraid to give birth, afraid of what their baby might be like. One of these mothers is Lijon Eknilang:

> I label myself a nuclear survivor because I am still alive. Yes, I survived, but whenever I think about the seven miscarriages I had I feel empty. I suspect that all my miscarriages were radiation related because several of my stillborns were deformed, and one had only one eye. Each day I ache with pains. The legacy of the nuclear testings will continue to haunt me, and all the other survivor victims in the Marshall Islands.[45]

In 1983, Keju-Johnson, later to die of cancer herself, told the world:

> We have this problem we call 'jelly-fish' babies. These babies are born like jelly-fish. They have no eyes. They have no heads. They have no arms. They have no legs. They do not shape like human-beings at all. But they are born on the labour table. The most colourful, ugly thing you have ever seen. Some of them have hairs on them. And they breathe. This ugly thing only lives for a few hours. When they die they are buried right away. They do not allow the mother to see this kind of baby because she will go crazy. It is too inhumane.[46]

The Marshallese people – women and children in particular – are paying the highest price for the US nuclear arsenal and the ongoing rush to militarise space.

In May 2007 the Republic of the Marshall Islands' government announced that it had approved US$2.65 million from the Kwajalein Compact 'impact' funding to upgrade the power plant, water and sewer systems, and for waste collection and road maintenance on Ebeye. At first glance, this announcement seems to be advantageous for Ebeye islanders, not least because a refurbishment of the Ebeye powerhouse is desperately needed to preserve electricity supply to the island. But the money is tied to the US lease on the missile range. It is part of a larger amount, which the US granted to the Marshallese government three years ago as part of their agreement to extend the lease, but it was put on hold when the Kwajalein landowners refused to agree to an extension. The Kwajalein landowners have rejected the Marshall Island government's latest move as a breach of their Kwajalein Land Use Agreement, which identifies land in the Marshalls as being under the control of its traditional owners. For the Kwajalein landowners to accept the funds would require their agreement to an extension of the US lease until 2086. But, as Kwajalein Senator Tony de Brum has said, the Kwajalein landowners are 'not going to sit idly by and watch the RMI violate one of the most sacred agreements of the Compact'.[47]

By coincidence, but placing added pressure on the Kwajalein landowners to extend the Kwajalein lease, the US Army tripled the ground-handling fee for services by Continental Airlines without notice. Increasing cargo handling charges well beyond the earned revenue, forced the only airline servicing the Marshall Islands to announce a halt to cargo services to and from Kwajalein-Ebeye, starting on 1 June 2007.[48] This abrupt curtailing of the cargo service has the potential to impact severely on the Ebeye hospital's ability to care for its patients. By creating logistical obstacles to sending medical test samples to laboratories in the US, this commercial intervention has further undermined the hospital's diagnostic services, increasing the difficulties for Ebeye and Kwajalein Atoll residents to access care.

It is hard not to agree with the editor of the *Marshall Islands Journal* that: this is 'just one more glaring example of the unfair American pressure being brought to bear on the Marshallese people of Kwajalein'; a further 'case of US arrogance and RMI government acquiescence'.[49] The US ambition to develop security based on a nuclear arsenal has perpetrated one of the world's most horrendous crimes against humanity. Analysts of the Marshallese situation – medical professionals, independent scientists and social researchers – have charged this powerful nation with 'a blend of ignorance, negligence, and intent in the conduct of the tests exposed thousands of Marshallese civilians and several hundred American servicemen to radiation'.[50] When Lijon Eknilang toured

Britain with the Greenham Common Women in 1986 she shared a warning that is just as relevant today as it was then:

> I want you to see your future, what is going to be, through me. I'm living in contaminated land and water but what is your future going to be if this city will fill up with nuclear waste and everything? Where are your children going to live and work? ... There is no choice for us. We don't know what our future is going to be. Maybe there is only the choice to live in our contaminated land and die. But we don't want our friends and neighbours around the world having the same problems that we are facing.[51]

Notes

1. Lijon Eknilang, 'Statement by Lijon Eknilang from Women United Together Marshall Islands', presented to *Health Rights, Women's Lives, Challenges*, Tenth International Women and Health Meeting, New Delhi, September 2005.

2. Zohl dé Ishtar, *Daughters of the Pacific*, Melbourne: Spinifex, 1994, pp. 19–40; Zohl dé Ishtar, *Pacific Women Speak Out for Independence and Denuclearisation*, Christchurch: Women's International League for Peace and Freedom, Aotearoa; Disarmament and Security Centre, Aotearoa; and Pacific Connections, Australia, 1998, pp. 15–26.

3. Paul Jacobs, 'Micronesians Live in Island Ghetto Exile', *Los Angeles Times*, 9 March 1997, p. 9.

4. Giff Johnson, *Collision Course at Kwajalein: Marshall Islanders in the Shadow of the Bomb*, Hawaii: Pacific Concerns Resource Centre – PCRC, 1984, p. 6.

5. David Lilienthal, 'Draft Memorandum for the President, 20 November 1947' in Ann Deines, David Goldman, Ruth Harris, and Laura Kells (eds), *Marshall Islands Chronology*, prepared by History Association Inc. for the US Department of Energy, Rockville, ML, 1990, Online Available HTTP: <www.worf.eh.doe.gov/ihp/chron/> (accessed 20 April 2007).

6. United States of America – USA, 'US Statutes at Large, Vol. 62: 1434–1435' in Deines et al., *Marshall Islands Chronology*.

7. Republic of the Marshall Islands (RMI), *Nuclear Testing in the Marshall Islands: A Chronology of Events, Nuclear Testing in the Marshall Islands: A Brief History*, Micronitor News and Printing Company, 1996, Online Available HTTP: <www.rmiembassyus.org> (accessed 20 February 2004).

8. K.D. Nichols, 'Answer to State Department "List of Possible Questions" Attached to Letter from K.D. Nichols to W. Sterling Cole of Joint Committee on Atomic Energy, 14 September 1954', Online Available HTTP: <www.worf.eh.doe.gov/ihp/chron/A18. PDF> (accessed 17 May 2007).

9. dé Ishtar, *Pacific Women Speak Out*, p. 21.

10. Johnson, *Collision Course at Kwajalein*, p. 12.

11. Sutow Wataru and Robert Conard, 'The Effects of Fallout Radiation on Marshallese Children', Brookhaven National Laboratory 13584, p. 2, Doc. 19247' in Deines et al., *Marshall Islands Chronology* (accessed 20 April 2007).

12. Deines et al., *Marshall Islands Chronology*, p. 12.

13. Robert Conard (1958), *Medical Survey of Rongelap and Utirik People Three Years After Exposure to Radioactive Fallout*, Brookhaven National Laboratory, quoted in Johnson, *Collision Course at Kwajalein*, p. 13 (emphasis added).

14. Women Working for a Nuclear Free and Independent Pacific – WWNFIP, *Pacific Women Speak Out: Why Haven't You Known?* Oxford: Greenline, 1987, p. 10.

15. Johnson, *Collision Course at Kwajalein*, p. 40.

16. Nic Maclellan, 'Kwajalein Army and the New Arms Race', Peace Movement Aotearoa, 2000, Online Available HTTP: <www.converge.org.nz> (accessed 14 March 2001).

17. Ibid.

18. Floyd Takeuchi and Scott Whitney, 'US Locks In Kwajalein Through 2066 Breakthrough Takes Place at Hawaii Talks', *Pacific Magazine*, 1 February 2003, Online Available HTTP: <www.pacificmagazine. net> (accessed 19 June 2005).

19. Ema Tagicakibau and Nic Maclellan, 'Australia's Missile Involvement Will Alienate Pacific', NFIP and Pacific Concerns Resource Centre, Media Release, 28 February 2003, Online Available HTTP: <www.pcrc.org.fj/Media_releases/austmissille.html.doc> (accessed 15 March 2003).

20. Giff Johnson, 'A Deal by Summer', *Pacific Magazine*, February 2002, Online Available HTTP: <www.pacificislands.cc> (accessed 4 July 2003).

21. Johnson, *Collision Course at Kwajalein*, pp. 27–38.

22. Jane Dibblin, *Day of Two Suns: US Nuclear Testing and the Pacific Islanders*, London: Virago Press, 1988, p. 180.

23. dé Ishtar, *Daughters of the Pacific*, pp. 29–31.

24. 'US Congress Confirms Nuclear Testing Cover-up', *Marshall Islands Journal*, 21 April 2006, p. 3.

25. Asian Development Bank (ADB), *Juumemmemj: Republic of the Marshall Islands Social and Economic Report 2005*, Manila: ADB, 2006, p. 115.

26. Neal Palafox, 'Statement to the US Senate Energy and Natural Resources Committee, 19 July 2005' in *Nuclear Fallout: Testimony of Dr Palafox, Senate Hearing*, Online Available HTTP: <www.yokwe.net> (accessed 14 December 2006). See also: Committee on the Biological Effects of Ionizing Radiation, *BEIR-IV: Health Risks of Radon and Other Internally Deposited Alpha-Emitters*, Washington, DC: National Research Council, 1988.

27. Giff Johnson, 'Study Calls Marshall Islands' Cancer Rate Extreme', *Pacific Islands Report*, 22 March 1999, Pacific Islands Development Program, East-West Center for Pacific Island Studies, University of Hawaii.

28. National Cancer Institute, *Estimation of the Baseline Number of Cancers among Marshallese and the Number of Cancers Attributable to Exposure to Fallout from Nuclear Weapons Testing Conducted in the Marshall Islands*, prepared for the Senate Committee on Energy and Natural Resources, Washington, DC: 2004; Gemma Casas, 'Expert Notes Rise of Cancer in Pacific: Spending is Down Near Former Nuclear Test Sites with a High Rate of Disease', *Star Bulletin*, 11 October 2006.

29. Johnson, 'Study Calls Marshall Islands' Cancer Rate Extreme'; Frank Roylance, 'Struggle: US Nuclear Tests and Westernization have Crippled the Marshall Islands', *The Baltimore Sun*, 26 October 1997, p. 1.

30. Palafox, 'Statement to the US Senate Energy and Natural Resources Committee, 19 July 2005'.

31. Roylance, 'Struggle', p. 1.

32. World Bank, 'Opportunities that Change People's Lives: Human Development Review of the Pacific Islands: Country Case Study Marshall Islands', Washington DC: draft report, 2005. The World Bank has not published a final report.

33. Johnson, 'Study Calls Marshall Islands' Cancer Rate Extreme'.

34. ADB, *Juumemmemj*.

35. Republic of the Marshall Islands (RMI), *Census of Population and Housing*, Majuro, RMI Printer, 1999, Online Available HTTP: <www.rmiembassyus.org/nuclear/chronology.html> (accessed 10 June 2005).

36. Kathryn Braun, *Jodrikdrik Nan Jodrikdrik Ilo Ejmour: An Assessment of Youth to Youth in Health: A Peer Education Program for Primary Health Care in the Marshall Islands*, prepared by the School of Public Health, University of Hawaii, for the Minister of

Health and Environment, Republic of the Marshall Islands, April 1994, p. 5.

37. ADB, *Juumemmemj*, p. 118.

38. United States Department of State, *Country Reports on Human Rights Practices*, Bureau of Democracy, Human Rights, and Labor, 2005, Online Available HTTP: <www.state.gov> (accessed 10 November 2006).

39. Braun, *Jodrikdrik Nan Jodrikdrik Ilo Ejmour*, p. 5.

40. ADB, *Juumemmemj*, pp. 79–80.

41. Ibid., p. 81.

42. Ibid., p. 36.

43. Shamina Ali, *Violence Against the Girl Child in the Pacific Islands*, Rome: UNICEF, 2006.

44. Suliana Siwatibau and David Williams, *A Call to a New Exodus: An Anti-Nuclear Primer for Pacific People*, Suva: Pacific Conference of Churches, 1982, p. 54.

45. Zohl dé Ishtar, 'A Survivor's Warning on Nuclear Contamination: Sustainable Security for the 21st Century', *Pacific Ecologist*, 2007, No. 13, 50–3.

46. dé Ishtar, *Daughters of the Pacific*, p. 24.

47. Anon., 'RMI: $2.4m for KAJUR', *Marshall Islands Journal*, 2007, Vol. 38, No. 20, p. 1.

48. Giff Johnson, 'USAKA Hike to Hit Ebeye', *Marshall Islands Journal*, 2007, Vol. 38, No. 20, p. 1.

49. 'Hard to Believe', *Marshall Islands Journal*, 2007, Vol. 38, No. 20, p. 8.

50. ADB, *Juumemmemj*, p. 4.

51. Frances Connelly, Joan Grant, Susie Cohn, and Fran Willard, *Pacific Paradise: Nuclear Nightmare*, London: Women Working for a Nuclear Free and Independent Pacific and CND Publications, 1987, p. 52.

7

DELIBERATIVE WATER MANAGEMENT
Women's Experience in Brazil

Andrea Moraes and Patricia E. Perkins

In January 2005, on a research exchange from Canada, we visited Brazilian partners in the Sister Watersheds, a project which does community environmental education in conjunction with the Ecoar Institute for Citizenship.[1] We were shown the Pirajussara Creek upstream from where it empties into the Pinheiros River on the campus of the University of São Paulo. This is a poor neighbourhood where informally built houses push up against a dirty watercourse carrying raw sewage from a big housing block up, the hill. The stream bed was littered with plastic bags, food waste, tin cans, and other garbage. Bridges over the stream, some of them quite wide, were in places topped by a porch or entire room. When we asked the women who came out to greet us to talk about this stream, they said they were concerned about children playing there, and that every time it rained the filthy water flooded into their houses. 'Why do we have to cover it over ourselves, and pay for the cement and beams? Why doesn't the government come to build a covered channel, as it should?' They saw the stream as an open sewer, which needed to be enclosed to protect them and their families from the dirty water. And yet, across the street from the stream was a house with a big metal gate decorated with a lovely painted mural of an idyllic lake with a waterfall, swimming swans, green grass and trees all around. The contrast between the idealised vision of nature depicted in the mural and the reality of the polluted stream could not be starker. Clearly, people in that Brazilian community imagined water as a source of peace, pleasure, health, and beauty – yet in their own surroundings water was nothing but a hazard.

In this chapter we consider the question of gender in relation to the evolution of water management in Brazil. In this work on women and water, we have been inspired by ecofeminist philosophy and the concept of 'feminist transformative leadership' as developed by Brazilian activists. Our chapter calls attention to the political under-participation of poor and racialised women in Brazil's new national system for water management, and it looks at what changes might facilitate women's involvement in watershed management. Today, as in the past, and as in many other countries, water-related problems in Brazil most seriously affect the underprivileged, whose water problems take several forms: first, people living in informal and irregular settlements often do not have access to clean water and sewer services. Second, floods and rainfall-induced landslides can cause residents of informal settlements to lose their houses, belongings, and sometimes even their lives. Third, the health of people in poor communities is damaged by pollution in the rivers and streams that they must draw on.

As traditionally ascribed gender roles make poor women the main caregivers and cleaners for society at large, they are the ones most concerned by this complex of interrelated water problems. In fact, United Nations surveys report that throughout the world, whatever the details of water access, technology, or gendered labour, water has a different meaning for women than for men.[2] In the case of Brazil, almost one-third of employed women are domestic workers, for whom water is an important tool, input, and determinant of work conditions.[3] This is so, despite the fact that women have higher average levels of education than men.[4] But poverty notwithstanding, Brazilian homes headed by women have better access to clean water than homes headed by men.[5] The same is true for sanitation services and public waste collection. The Brazilian national statistical agency concludes that 'a possible explanation for why households headed by women have better sanitation conditions is the fact that women are more careful in relation to aspects that relate to conditions of health and hygiene of the family'.[6]

Unfortunately, access to clean water is not the only water-related problem for poor women and men. In the biggest cities of southeastern Brazil, where new informal settlements are constantly appearing, slum houses are often built too close to streams or too high on slope land that is undesirable and risky. Floods and landslides caused by rain, tree cutting, and general environmental degradation, compounded by inadequate water infrastructure, are regular events. Every year, mostly in summer when rains are heaviest, the newspapers are full of images of people who have lost everything they own, or even loved ones. The water from heavy rains often mixes with water from open sewers or polluted rivers, bringing additional health problems and cleanup work, especially for mothers. But, according to Monica Porto, a professor at the University of São Paulo, 'What has been constantly disregarded when political decisions related to water are to be taken is the country's poor, who have no access to safe water, and who have high infant mortality rates, and a very weak and usually unheard voice in asking for change.'[7] At present, poor women's role in water management is very limited. Does the feminist movement offer hope of advancing their political agency?

Women, feminism, and NGOs

Full political participation is central to the feminist agenda in Brazil, as elsewhere. Jacqueline Pitanguy writes that initially, during the dark days of dictatorial government in the 1960s–70s, civil society in Brazil was organised around 'survival and resistance' where people 'in political terms had no sex, race, ethnicity, or sexual orientation'.[8] Around the mid 1970s–80s, the feminist movement appeared in Brazil as a political force fighting for the visibility of women and simultaneously working 'to re-establish democracy and to widen the democratic agenda beyond classical civil and political rights to include gender inequality as a central democratic theme'.[9] Between 1975 and 1978, during the political *abertura*, the politics of gender discrimination was raised in many different spaces, and the first explicitly feminist organisation, the Brazilian Women's Centre, was created in Rio de Janeiro.

A second phase of the feminist movement in Brazil took place in the 1980s during the national transition to democracy. In 1985, the country had the chance to vote directly for a civilian president and for a new Congress, which was in charge of writing the democratic constitution of Brazil. This was a time of incredible growth in social movements and black, gay, landless, indigenous, and ecological, as well as feminist groups, were expanding the definitions of citizenship, democracy, equality, and participation – movements influencing the constitution, launched in 1988. This period saw ambitious feminist public action strategies where the goal was to penetrate state power and use it to implement large-scale change affecting legislation and public policies. The National Council for Women's Rights (CNDM), a federal body reporting directly to the President of Brazil, was created by Congress in 1985.[10] Also in 1985, the state of São Paulo established the first Police Stations for the Defence of Women (DDM).[11] These were designed to create a supportive environment for women where they could make complaints about sexual and domestic violence to an almost exclusively female police staff. The Brazilian Constitution of 1988 incorporated many feminist proposals regarding labour and social rights, social security, family life, reproductive rights, and domestic violence.[12]

However, political scientist Mala Htun notes that while Brazil has had more policy changes advancing women's rights than any other country in Latin America, it has the lowest levels of representation in national politics. If Brazilian women are advancing in other areas, why not in politics? Htun considers that Brazil's gender quota law, electoral rules, and clientelistic political parties are all partly to blame.[13] In 1996, Brazil approved a quota law to the effect that 'parties must reserve a minimum of 30 per cent and a maximum of 70 per cent of slots for candidates of one sex'.[14] The problem is that the law requires that 30 per cent of slots be reserved for women, but it does not force parties to actually fill these slots. And even if congressional seats are occupied by women, what is to ensure that the interests of poor or racialised women are effectively expressed? This question highlights the shortcomings of representative democratic politics resulting from class, race, and gender based barriers to women's effective political participation.[15]

A third phase of the Brazilian feminist movement began in the 1990s, when

> ... the feminist agenda in Brazil was carried forward ... mainly by non-governmental organizations (NGOs). The significant role played by women's NGOs in the national arena and the efficacy of the advocacy strategies developed by regional and international networks and coalitions of NGOs characterize this third moment.[16]

At the time of the 1992 Earth Summit in Rio de Janeiro, Brazilian feminism also took an ecological turn, as middle- and upper-class women interested in ecofeminism began networking internationally, while also making opportunities for indigenous and working-class women to speak out about their realities.[17] The international NGO Women's Environment and Development Organisation (WEDO), convened by former US Congresswoman Bella Abzug, mobilised women from the global North and South to come together at the Earth Summit and speak out about environment and health matters and about the problem of getting women's voices heard in the political arena.

Today, many of the people working through NGOs in Brazil are middle-class and well educated. For example, in the Embú neighbourhood, whose stream pollution was described at the beginning of this chapter, the Ecoar Institute for Citizenship and the Sister Watersheds project organise environmental education meetings for poor women, who are demanding sewer construction and containment of the polluted stream on health grounds.[18] Such NGOs provide meeting points for intersecting interests and problems such as gender, environment, poverty, race, and health.[19] As Brazilian ecofeminist Regina di Ciommo writes: 'The participation of women in NGOs connected in networks gives them the experience (and the challenge) of working in a non-hierarchical way.'[20] The informal and supportive structures characteristic of NGOs allow people of different backgrounds to share information and work together across gender, race, and class lines more effectively than highly-structured and formalistic business or government committees do. Moreover, transnational and lateral networking of women across borders – as exemplified by both the Sister Watersheds project and the earlier WEDO initiative – is a way of destabilising vertical power structures within capitalist patriarchal nation states.

Ecofeminist and transformative leadership

Our reading of these issues is based on the ecofeminist principle that there is an integral material link or 'connection between the exploitation and degradation of the natural world and the subordination and oppression of women ...' and Mary Mellor adds that 'Humanity is not just reliant on its physical environment, but the natural world, including humanity, should be seen as an interconnected and interdependent whole.'[21] Vandana Shiva spells out this understanding in her analysis of global water politics and we see it as a vital basis for political action.[22] When there is a flood in a big *favela* in São Paulo, a number of environmental and social justice problems are interconnected: climate change, structural adjustment, global financial inequities and debt, inadequate technocratically designed urban infrastructure, unplanned urbanisation, erosion of hillsides, channelisation and enclosure of rivers. But the fact is that in Brazil as elsewhere, poor women's problems are not a public priority. On the contrary, lower-class and racialised women are forced to bear the brunt of water-related problems created by the whole economy.

But economies and social institutions are also subject to destabilisation and change.[23] We contend that the best way to construct successful movements is to begin locally, rely on democratic pluralism, and take advantage of opportunities that can help shape new forms of governance.[24] In this instance, we explore the locally transformative potential of new deliberative structures ushered in by the Brazilian government's new Water Law. Even so, ecofeminist Moema Viezzer describes social change through 'transformative leadership' as being about much more than getting women into positions of power. Rather, it is

> ... transformative in the sense that it challenges the existing structures of power; it is inclusive, in the sense that it takes into account the needs, interests and points of view of the majority of the marginalized and poor in society; it is integral, in the sense that it attends to all forms of social injustice ... Feminist transformative leadership can be exercised, advanced or defended by women and men, young or old.[25]

Addressing interconnected water problems successfully requires the leadership and participation of those whose knowledge is locally informed and specific to the experience of their gender, race, and class positions. As ecofeminists argue, it is this groundedness that best equips them to understand these problems in all their complexity. But does this transformative vision get to be expressed in practice?

In international sustainable development circles, the current approach to water management is to engage civil society by establishing watershed committees with substantial public involvement, as well as support from various levels of government. In principle, this means that water users collectively can help decide on allocation, infrastructure, and regulation at the watershed level.[26] The assumption is that watershed committees supplement and strengthen democratically elected government bodies by emphasising local environmental conditions.[27] These grounded community based deliberations should allow people jointly to reach more sustainable solutions to complex ecological problems than is possible otherwise. In the social sciences, 'empirical backing is beginning to emerge for the theoretical claims made for the transformative and educative power of democratic deliberation'.[28] The approach has strong theoretical justification and potential in bioregional, ecological, and political terms, and it is being implemented in a growing number of countries worldwide.[29]

Since 1997, Brazil has had one of the most participatory water management regimes in the world.[30] It has established watershed committees composed of representatives from government agencies and civil society representatives, and poor women can, in principle, sit as representatives on the watershed committee for the river close to their houses. As members of the committee, they can help decide 'how to manage water and its allocation, new development projects, pollution abatement and control restrictions, indeed all subjects dealing with water use'.[31] They can use their knowledge of the seriousness and interlinked nature of water-related problems to seek solutions, working with government officials and other water users.

Deliberative democracy in practice

To some degree, women are present at all levels of the Brazilian water management system. The National Council of Water Resources, for instance, which is a consultative and deliberative body representing water users, government and civil society, coordinates federal, state, and regional planning and arbitrates conflicts. It is chaired by the Federal Environment Minister, currently Marina Silva, and includes a seat for the Special Secretary for Women's Policies.[32] The Council's approval of the National Water Plan in 2006 notes the importance of gender differences in its Base Reference Document. However, at this point in time, women make up only 20 per cent or less of the membership of all watershed committees studied.[33] This under-representation of women reveals that the current system, while intended to be 'participatory', is not democratically inclusive in practice. In part, this problem results from the fact that water management committees are more technical and specialised than other government bodies, and thus harder for grassroots women to enter. Water in Brazil has historically been linked with energy and hydroelectric dams – a subject area for the engineering profession still dominated by men. Although the new Water Law emphasises that water management involves multidisciplinary questions, changing the culture of water management will take time.[34]

As an expert on Brazilian water management, Porto maintains that women's participation as educated professionals in the water sector is growing very fast and, in consequence, gender equity is not a problem. In her view, the need for a sufficient number of trained and competent professionals is more important than gender balance *per se*.[35] Porto believes that successful implementation of the Water Law in Brazil depends on the ability of the watershed committees to: (a) use a transdisciplinary approach, (b) raise awareness about water issues among the public and policy makers, (c) educate the population, (d) prepare communities to participate, and (e) build technical capacity.[36]

However, while women's contributions to water management as professionals may be increasing, there remain serious class and race barriers to the active involvement of poor and racialised women. Yet their daily work, and often their family income, is so heavily dependent on water. In our observation, these barriers to women's engagement in deliberative politics are:

- limited time for participation,
- times and location of meetings,
- lack of childcare or transport subsidies,
- the open prejudice of some committee members,
- internalised oppression,
- lack of education,
- technocratic language in reports and minutes,
- frustrating bureaucracies, and
- the near-absence of organised constituency groups for local political representation on water questions.

Since Brazil's water management structure has a ten-year history now, it is timely to document the nature and direction of community contributions to water policy. One preliminary study of the participation of civil society representatives on watershed committees – women and men – notes a difference in the capacity of government and civil society representatives to follow the technical aspects of committee work.[37] This results in the domination of citizen voices by government voices. But the study also points to real advances in the mutual education of committee members and the general public. This involves an exchange, with grassroots members learning about technological questions, on the one hand, and government agencies learning about gender based problems, on the other. It indicates that practicalities such as committee meeting times and locations, the need for transportation subsidies and administrative backup for civil society representatives, and the diverse interests of civil society groups, all limit the capacity of local representatives to participate equally alongside government officials. Documenting the practical disadvantages faced by grassroots participants in the deliberative process, allows them to be addressed as part of the implementation process for participatory management structures. In this respect, ecofeminist research and feminist transformative leadership have important roles to play.

Ecofeminist claims relate to basic survival, and indeed, the Brazilian Federal Government has begun to take note of women's call for more voice in ecological issues. This is especially apparent in rural areas, where the country has seen a rise in social policies that include poor women of colour as beneficiaries.[38] Many new feminist voices are emerging in Brazil. Women in the *quilombo* movement of separate black communities, feminist activists within the Landless Workers' Movement (MST), poor women struggling for reproductive rights and health care in the era of HIV/AIDS, and others whose basic needs remain unmet as Brazil moves from 'developing' to 'newly-industrialised country', are all part of this growing diversity of Brazilian feminisms. While the established movement works to advance its transformative agenda based in democratic politics and efforts to advance women's political rights and leadership, the basic needs agenda of lower-class Brazilian feminists is also surging forward. As the political forces of liberal feminism and ecofeminism converge in advancing their objectives, NGOs like WEDO and Ecoar are instruments of this convergence.

The history and strength of feminist NGOs in Brazil, formed as they were in struggles against the military dictatorship, suggest that movement organising will overcome practical and political barriers faced by poor and racialised women. Commonalities among people – especially around environmental issues like water – have the potential to deepen political understanding and create new alliances as the global ecological crisis deepens. Brazil is already leading the way in such alliance building, for example with participatory municipal budgeting, Local Agenda 21 initiatives, and at the transnational level the World Social Forum. In the words of ecofeminist theologian Ivone Gebara:

> In Latin America we want to be part of a national and international movement for the globalization of social justice ... A new national and international order is our goal. An ecofeminism as an echo of feminism takes this as its goal without forgetting the special commitment for all women, without forgetting the importance of local education for a better world for everybody. It is the first time in our history that international civil society is uniting to form a new social and political order. It is the first time that together we are asking for a new qualitative daily life. In this perspective there is a new hope for all of us.[39]

Notes

1. Sister Watersheds is a North–South exchange project linking universities and NGOs, funded by the Canadian International Development Agency through the Association of Universities and Colleges of Canada. It seeks innovative ways of broadening public involvement in water basin committees in São Paulo State. The exchange also includes environmental education initiatives in the watershed around York University in Toronto. The *Ecoar* Institute for Citizenship was founded by professional people in São Paulo following Earth Summit in 1992.

2. United Nations, *International Year of Fresh Water 2003*, Online Available HTTP: <www.wateryear2003.org/en/ev.php-URL_ID=2543&URL_DO=DO_TOPIC&URL_SECTION=201.html> (accessed 18 June 2007). On the goals of the Beijing Declaration and Programme for Action, see: United Nations, *Women 2000 and Beyond*, New York: UN Department of Economic and Social Affairs, 2005, Online Available HTTP: <www.un.org/womenwatch/daw/public/Feb05.pdf> (accessed 18 June 2007).

3. Hildete Pereira de Melo, *Gênero e Pobreza no Brasil: Relatório Final do Projeto 'Governabilidad Democrática de Género en America Latina y el Caribe'*, Brasilia: Convênio Comissão Econômica para América Latina e Caribe e Secretaria Especial de Políticas para as Mulheres, 2005.

4. In most countries, women earn significantly less than men, so homes headed by women tend to be poor, and race compounds the problem. In 2000, women identified as 'black or brown' received only 51 per cent of the average income of white women.

The government statistical agency uses the Portuguese word *pardo*, translated as brown, for people of mixed European and African or Indigenous ancestry. See: Ricardo Franklin Ferreira, *Afro-descendente, uma Identidade em Construção*, Rio de Janeiro: Pallas/EDUC/FAPESP, 2004.

5. *Instituto Brasileiro de Geografia e Estatística*, 'As mulheres como alvo das políticas públicas brasileiras,' 2006, p. 3, Online Available HTTP: <www.ibge.gov.br/home/presidencia/noticias/noticia_visualiza.php?id_noticia=605&id_pagina=1> (accessed 10 June 2006).

6. Interestingly, despite their economic disadvantage, 82 per cent of homes headed by women have direct waste collection, whereas for households headed by men the figure is 72 per cent: ibid., p. 3.

7. Monica Porto, 'Women and Water Resources Research in Brazil' in Cecilia Tortajada (ed.), *Women and Water Management: The Latin American Experience*, Oxford University Press, 2000, p. 90.

8. Jacqueline Pitanguy, 'Bridging the Local and the Global: Feminism in Brazil and the International Human Rights Agenda', *Social Research*, 2002, Vol. 69, No. 3, 805–20, p. 807.

9. Ibid., p. 807.

10. Ibid., p. 810.

11. As of May 2006, there were more than 300 such *Delegacias de Defesa da Mulher* all over Brazil; but some commentators believe they have become a way to sideline women's issues in relation to law enforcement, a sort of 'police station kitchen'.

12. Pitanguy, 'Bridging the Local and the Global', p. 811.

13. Mala Htun, 'Puzzles of Women's Rights in Brazil', *Social Research*, 2002, Vol. 69, No. 3, 733–51.

14. Ibid., p. 734.

15. See the extensive discussion in Jane Mansbridge, 'Should Blacks Represent Blacks and Women Represent Women? A Contingent "Yes"', *Journal of Politics*, 1999, Vol. 61, No. 3, 628–57.

16. Pitanguy, 'Bridging the Local and the Global', p. 811.

17. Maria Inacia d'Avila and Naumi de Vasconcelos (eds), *Ecologia, Feminismo, Desenvolvimento*, Rio de Janeiro: EICOS/Universidade Federal do Rio de Janeiro, 1993.

18. Another initiative for women is the *Programa Um Milhão de Cisternas* (P1MC), or One Million Cisterns. Coordinated by the *Articulação do Semi-Árido*, this is a coalition of some 750 civil society organisations, Catholic and Evangelical churches, rural and urban workers' unions and federations, community associations, social movements, national and international cooperation organisations, public and private institutions – across eleven Brazilian states. The programme provides training and material

assistance for families to build and maintain cisterns cooperatively in semi-arid regions, and it prioritises poor women in northeastern Brazil, see: P1MC, 'Programa um Milhão de Cisternas'. *Universia* online newsletter, 1 November 2003, Online Available HTTP: <www.universia.com.br/html/materia/materia_dibg.html> (accessed 6 June 2007). Also, on the *cisterneiras* in the state of Rio Grande do Norte, Online Available HTTP: <www.semarh.rn.gov.br/detalhe. asp?IdPublicacao=4505> (accessed 6 June 2007).

19. Vanessa Campagnac, 'As organizações não-governamentais (ONGs) e o mercado de trabalho', *Rede de Informações para o Terceiro Setor (RITS)*, 2006, Online Available HTTP: <www.rits.org.br/ estudos_teste/ce_testes/ce_paraler2.cfm> (accessed 30 May 2006); Gwyn Kirk, 'Ecofeminism and Environmental Justice: Bridges Across Gender, Race, and Class', *Frontiers*, 1997, Vol. 18, No. 1, 2–20; Salete Silva, 'Avanço Lento: Participação feminina na política brasileira é pequena e cresce com muita timidez', *Revista Problemas Brasileiras*, 2000, No. 341, Online Available HTTP: <www.sescsp.org.br/sesc/revistas_sesc/pb/artigo.cfm?Edicao_Id=87 &breadcrumb=1&Artigo_ID=927&IDCategoria=1090&reftype= 1> (accessed 30 May 2006); Andrea Cornwall, Elizabeth Harrison, and Ann Whitehead, 'Repositioning Feminisms in Gender and Development', *IDS Bulletin*, 2004, Vol. 35, No. 4, 1–10; Sonia Alvarez, 'Advocating Feminism: The Latin American Feminist NGO "Boom"', *International Feminist Journal of Politics*, 1999, Vol. 1, No. 2, 181–209.

20. Regina di Ciommo, *Ecofeminismo e Educação Ambiental*, São Paulo: Editoral Cone Sul / Editora UNIUBE, 1999, p. 15; Regina di Ciommo, 'Ser Rede: Vida Pessoal e Participação Política nas Redes Eco-feministas', *MultiCiência: Revista Interdisciplinar dos Núcleos e Centros da Unicampo. A Linguagem da Ciência*, 2005, No. 4; Regina di Ciommo, 'Being a Network: Personal Life and Political Participation Within Ecofeminist Networks', *Multiciencia: Revista Interdisciplinar dos Centros e Nucleos da Unicampo*, 4 May, Online Available HTTP: <www.multiciencia.unicamp.br/rede_2_4_i.htm> (accessed 29 May 2006).

21. Mary Mellor, *Feminism and Ecology*, Cambridge: Polity, 1997, p. 1.

22. Vandana Shiva, *Water Wars*, Cambridge, MA: South End, 2002.

23. See Anthony Bebbington, 'Re-encountering Development: Livelihood Transitions and Place Transformations in the Andes', *Annals of the Association of American Geographers*, 2000, Vol. 90, No. 3, 495–520, p. 514.

24. Graham Smith, *Deliberative Democracy and the Environment*, London: Routledge, 2003, pp. 128–30; Graham Smith, 'Liberal

Democracy and the Shaping of Environmentally Enlightened Citizens' in Marcel Wissenburg (ed.), *Liberal Democracy and Environmentalism*, London: Routledge, 2004.

25. Moema Viezzer, 'Feminist Transformative Leadership: A Learning Experience with Peasant and Gatherer Women in Brazil', Annual Dame Nita Barrow Lecture, 4th International Conference on Transformative Learning, University of Toronto, 2001, p. 11.

26. Fiona Hinchcliffe, John Thompson, Jules N. Pretty, Irene Guijt, and Parmesh Shah, *Fertile Ground: The Impacts of Participatory Watershed Management*, London: Earthscan/IT Publications, 1999; Patricia E. Perkins, 'Participation and Watershed Management: Experiences From Brazil', paper presented at the International Society for Ecological Economics Conference, Montreal, 2004.

27. Mansbridge, 'Should Blacks Represent Blacks and Women Represent Women?'

28. Smith, 'Liberal Democracy and the Shaping of Environmentally Enlightened Citizens', p. 150.

29. UNESCO (2003) World Water Report, Chs 1 and 4 Online Available HTTP: <www.unesco.org/water/wwap/wwdr/index.shtml> (accessed 10 June 2006). Also: Smith, *Deliberative Democracy and the Environment*; Shiva, *Water Wars*; Perkins, 'Participation and Watershed Management'.

30. Margaret Keck and Rebecca Abers, 'Running Water: Participatory Management in Brazil', *NACLA Report on the Americas*, 2004, Vol. 38, No. 1, 29–34; Agência Nacional das Aguas, 'The Evolution of Water Resources Management in Brazil', 2006, Online Available HTTP: <www.ana.gov.br/ingles/Portais/06-General_Aspects. html#3> (accessed 29 May 2006); Ministério do Meio Ambiente, *Documento de Introdução: Plano Nacional de recursos Hídricos – Iniciado um processo de debate nacional*, 2005, Online Available HTTP: <www.pnrh.cnrh-srh.gov.br/> (accessed 29 May 2006); Rebecca Anders and Karina Dino Jorge, 'Decentralização da Gestão da Água. Por que os Comitês de Bacias estão sendo criados?' *Ambiente e Sociedade*, 2005, Vol. 8, No. 2, 99–124; World Wildlife Fund, 'Successes: Brazil Approves National Water Plan', Media Release, 8 February 2006, Online Available HTTP: <www. panda.org/about_wwf/what_we_do/freshwater/news/successes/ index.cfm?uNewsID=60120> (accessed 29 May 2006); Ramy Hanna, 'Democracy, Citizenship and Civil Society Participation in Watershed Management: The Case of the Piracicaba, Capivari, and Jundiai Watershed Committee, São Paulo State, Brazil', Unpublished manuscript, Environmental Studies, York University, Toronto, 2005.

31. Monica Porto, 'The Brazilian Water Law: A New Level of Participation and Decision Making', *Water Resources Development*, 1998, Vol. 14, No. 2, 175–82, p. 177.

32. Even in the progressive Labor Party government in Brazil, there are only four women ministers, and they carry the less influential social and environmental portfolios: Nilceia Freire (Women's Policies), Matilde Ribeiro (Policy for the Promotion of Racial Equality), Dilma Roussef ('Casa Civil' or Domestic Affairs), and Marina Silva (Environment). As this book went to press, Marina Silva resigned her position in protest against cabinet policies. Chile, under President Michelle Bachelet, is the only Latin American country to have a cabinet with 50 per cent of women members.

33. Mariana Sell and Ninon Machado, 'Gênero na Gestão de Águas no Brasil', paper presented at the *Encontro Ibero-Americano por uma Nova Cultura da Água*, Rio de Janeiro, 2005; Andrea Moraes and Patricia E. Perkins (forthcoming), 'A Bucket of Water and Daily Bread', *International Feminist Journal of Politics*.

34. Christine van Wijk-Sijbesma, *Gender and Water Resources Management, Water Supply and Sanitation: Roles and Realities Revisited*, The Hague: International Water and Sanitation Centre, 1998; Patricia E. Perkins, 'Public Participation and Ecological Valuation: Inclusive = Radical', paper presented at the Capitalism Nature Socialism Conference, York University, Toronto, 2005; Cap-Net International Network for Capacity Building in Integrated Water Resources Management, *Why Gender Matters: A Tutorial for Water Managers*, Multimedia CD and booklet, Delft, NL, 2006.

35. Porto, 'Women and Water Resources Research in Brazil', p. 91.

36. Ibid.

37. Marcia Chandra, *Participation and Watershed Management: Experiences from Brazil*, Environmental Studies, York University, Toronto, 2004, Online Available HTTP: <www.baciasirmas.org.br/english/doc/article03.pdf> (accessed 6 June 2007).

38. The national programme *Fome Zero*, or Zero Hunger, for example, gives poor families the equivalent of US$30 dollars a month to buy food. In contrast with earlier federal policy, this money is given to women in the household, see: Walter Belik and Mauro Del Grossi, 'O programa Fome Zero no Contexto das Políticas Sociais no Brasil', paper presented at the XLI Congress, Sociedade Brasileira de Economia e SociologiaRural (SOBER), Juiz de Fora, Brazil, 30 July 2003, Online Available HTTP: <www.fomezero.gov.br> (accessed 1 June 2007).

39. Ivone Gebara, 'Ecofeminism: A Latin American Perspective', *Cross Currents*, 2003, Vol. 53, No. 1, 93–103, p. 97.

Part III

Governance

The whole human economy should be seen from a subsistence perspective, where 'cultivation' takes precedence over 'extraction', and the household is at the centre. The household has always been the basic unit of the economy ... By recognising this, we turn conventional governance right side up. The commodity economy – industrial production and trade – should operate with a view to serving human needs and preserving natural resources ... The real 'bottom line' is that living nature is the absolute condition for survival ...

Hilkka Pietila,
'Some Ontological Presuppositions of Economics',
International Society for Ecological Economics Conference,
New Delhi, December 2006

8

MAINSTREAMING TRADE AND MILLENNIUM DEVELOPMENT GOALS?

Gigi Francisco and Peggy Antrobus

Gigi Francisco, to the Financing for Development Summit side event organised by the Institute for Agriculture and Trade Policy, Monterrey, Mexico, March 2002:

In response to the activism of women's movements worldwide, the buzzword in international conferences since the 1990s has been to 'engender' policies and programmes through gender analysis and mainstreaming. This is true of current efforts around the Millennium Development Goals (MDGs). It is crucial to assess how gender mainstreaming has been carried out, as well as to place the MDGs in the broader context of trade and liberalisation policies. There are two ways in which gender mainstreaming continues to be officially interpreted. The first is to integrate textual references to the principles of gender equality and equity, usually in the preambular section of agreements and declarations while the key policy thrusts and elements remain gender blind. The second is to ensure that the implementation of programmes, processes, and mechanisms are inclusive of women's participation and responsive to poor women's needs only in so far as to encourage and sustain their involvement without any real policy impact.

Engendering neoliberal policies

The call for gender analysis and mainstreaming also reverberates on the trade front within the World Trade Organisation (WTO) and other trade fora. Official efforts to engender trade rules and reforms in general, whether at the global or regional levels, have so far resulted in two near universal outcomes. Either gender analysis and mainstreaming end up softening the impact of destabilising trade liberalisation policies through targeted social safety nets, or they lead to interventions that make poor women more efficient contributors to – and women in politics more effective policymakers for – the systematic expansion and deepening of trade liberalisation reforms. Very often, these are inter-linked objectives. Such interpretations and outcomes emerge out of a narrow instrumentalist and managerial understanding of gender by governments and multilateral bodies. For them it is a simple matter of women getting their share of benefits from – while uncritically participating in – policies and programmes, just like men.

This prevalent official interpretation is a subversion of the real meaning of what a gender perspective is, and enables a 'gender agenda' to be co-opted and squarely fitted into the dominant neoliberalist regime for trade, development, and governance. A critical gender perspective applied to trade, development, and governance cannot but fundamentally challenge paradigms and models that continue to promote in an inter-linked fashion the following trends:

- invisibility of social reproduction in the economy;
- re-creation and consolidation of processes of accumulation that result in massive poverty; and,
- instrumentalisation of democracy and human rights.

A set of rules for trade, development, and governance that insists on the centrality of market forces above persons, communities, and governments, that promotes the rights of the business sector over those of people, communities and states, and that continues to overlook the structural, institutional, and cultural barriers to women's self autonomy, is immediately and fundamentally in discord with the visions and politics of gender transformation. To embark on gender mainstreaming in such a context is at once artificial and leads to the transmogrification of 'gender', something we are now witnessing in many places. The alternative is to reclaim, 'gender', and reposition it as a source of sound analysis and sharp critique of the mainstream's politics, perspectives, documents, rules, and programmes.

For example, a gender analysis of the impact on poor women's workload and social conditions of rapid liberalisation in the agricultural and manufacturing sectors provides us with enough evidence for demanding that the WTO immediately act on more than 100 cases of implementation issues lodged by developing countries. Such a gender analysis and critique inter-connect women's organisations and networks to a broader range of civil society groups and social movements that continue to challenge and resist unfair and undemocratic WTO rules and processes, and to explore alternative trade, development, and governance arrangements. This – and not the mainstream – is the genuine place of gender, if it is to be a truly transformative project and process.

Peggy Antrobus, to the UNDP Caribbean Regional MDGs Conference, Barbados, July 2003:

I first heard of the Millennium Development Goals in the outraged response of the global feminist community when the hard-won goal of women's sexual and reproductive rights was excluded from the list. This is even more inexcusable given that women's sexual and reproductive rights is a crucial Target and/or Indicator of progress under at least four goals – MDG3 (women's equality and empowerment), MDG4 (child mortality), MDG5 (maternal health), and MDG6 (combating HIV/AIDS). The deliberate exclusion of this fundamental indicator of women's human rights and empowerment from the MDGs symbolises the struggle that lies ahead for anyone who seriously seeks equality, equity, and empowerment for women. In fact, a major problem of the MDGs is their abstraction from the social, political, and economic context in which they are to be implemented – the 'political economy' of the MDGs.

Between religious and economic fundamentalism

Specifically, the exclusion of the goal of women's sexual and reproductive rights reflects the power of the forces of religious fundamentalism that emerged in the processes surrounding the 1994 International Conference on Population and Development, that continued to gain strength in the context of the ongoing economic struggles of the South against the spread of neoliberalism in the late 1990s, and that have received a boost with the right-wing control of the current US administration. In addition to the spread of religious fundamentalism and the male backlash against women's rights, there is the spread of economic 'fundamentalism' in the form of the neoliberal agenda through WTO-enforced trade liberalisation. In fact, the major limitation of the MDGs lies in the fact that, in the official literature on these goals, I can find almost no acknowledgement of the extent to which the neoliberal policy framework, starting with the 1980s macro-economic policy framework of the Washington Consensus, served to halt and reverse progress toward the achievement of these goals.

This policy framework – with its 'marketisation of the state' through the substitution of the profit-driven market for a democratically elected state accountable to the electorate – and its emphasis on privatisation and reforms that diminish the role of the state – has been reinforced by trade liberalisation and the new trade agreements enforced by the WTO. A consequence of trade liberalisation that has immediate relevance for the implementation of the MDGs in the Caribbean is the loss of government revenues resulting from the reduction in tariffs and the sale of profitable government assets. How are governments to finance primary health care and basic education when they are under pressure to reduce their sources of public finance?

To the extent that all the goals relate to the role of the state, one must ask: How feasible is it that states weakened by the requirements of policy frameworks of neoliberalism and whose revenues are reduced by privatisation and trade liberalism can be expected to achieve the goals and targets of the MDGs? From the perspective of women, the current macro context in which these Goals have emerged contains the twin demons of religious and economic fundamentalism. Both have at their core the subordination and exploitation of women's time, labour, and sexuality for the benefit of patriarchal power on the one hand, and capitalism on the other. I cannot imagine a less 'enabling environment' for the promotion of policies and programmes for the achievement of women's equality and empowerment – as well as for all MDGs, dependent as they are on this central goal.

On the other hand, since all MDGs (with the exception of the last) relate to biological and social reproduction, women's equality and empowerment are critical to their achievement. This provides women with a strategic opportunity for engaging in the policy dialogue around goals that have come to occupy a privileged position in the processes of socio-economic planning and in the policy dialogue between governments and donors. The inclusion of MDGs and Targets of major interest to women provides a strategic talking point for assessing the barriers to the achievement of goals. To the extent that women's subordination and exploitation represent a major barrier to the achievement of most of the goals and targets, the MDGs can provide a tool with which to hold both donor agencies and governments accountable.

Equality and women's empowerment

MDG3, gender equality and women's empowerment, is the goal to which women are expected to pay the most attention. Yet it has many problems, in particular its totally inadequate Target 4 of 'eliminating gender disparity in primary and secondary education' and its accompanying Indicators. While the Indicators on education and literacy represent major achievements for women everywhere, the Caribbean experience shows how inadequate they are as indications of empowerment, where they have certainly not translated into higher access to employment, incomes, decision-making positions in the public domain, or political office. Women in CARICOM countries have already achieved the Target, yet can hardly speak of equality, equity, or empowerment in a situation where

- poverty persists;
- violence against women continues unabated;
- there is increasing hostility against women (possibly generated by these very achievements in education and employment);
- the spread of HIV/AIDS is the second highest after Sub-Saharan Africa and spreading most rapidly among women;
- only two CARICOM countries (Barbados and Guyana) provide for abortion services that are accessible, safe, and affordable.

Moreover, despite efforts to change this, there is still a great deal of sex-role stereotyping in the school curriculum that limits the options of girls.

Regarding the Indicator on the number of women in parliaments as an indication of women's empowerment, it depends on the circumstances under which women candidates take part in elections. In CARICOM, with few exceptions, the small number of women who run for and win seats owe their preferment to the men who make decisions within the political parties: women who challenge male privilege are not likely to be among these. Once in office, women (and men) tend to cede their own power to that of their government and are unlikely to have the freedom to demonstrate empowerment and agency, especially in relation to gender issues.

UNIFEM has proposed additional Indicators including on women's wages and economic equality but they are still inadequate and would have to include others such as access to and control of land, equality before the law, incidence of domestic violence and rape, and access to health services that embody the ICPD Programme of Action principles. There is much more to gain from paying as much attention to the gender dimensions of the other goals as that of MDG3 on Gender Equality. Particularly for women in CARICOM countries, MDG1 (eradication of extreme poverty) and MDG6 (combating HIV/AIDS) should be of much greater concern. *One obvious problem with the Targets and*

Indicators of these Goals is that they are not disaggregated by gender, although the gender dimensions of all are clear.

Poverty is embedded in gender relations

Poverty reduction programmes must take into account that outcomes of poverty are embedded in processes and relations of gender. For example, programmes must provide low income housing; access to water and sanitation; health services that integrate primary health care, maternal and child health, family planning, cancer detection, and services for the detection and treatment of sexually transmitted diseases and HIV/AIDS; free and compulsory primary education, day care programmes; women's access to credit, land, and skills training. They must also ensure that the minimum wage legislation extends to domestic workers and other categories of low-income work. Because of the primary responsibility that women have for the care of children, the elderly, and the sick and disabled, women's income-earning capacity is more limited than that of men. Women's poverty is therefore more severe than men's poverty, and carries more serious consequences.

The tendency of governments and donors alike to 'collapse gender concerns within the wider category of poverty' tends to depoliticise the issue and masks the uneven distribution of power and resources within households. Caribbean women know that when a man is present he receives the major share of food in the household, and his needs take priority. The link between gender equality, women's empowerment, and food security is critical in poor households: while Caribbean men can (and do) walk away from household responsibilities when they are not in a position to offer financial support, women stay and will do whatever it takes to 'put food on the table'.

Central to the spread of HIV/AIDS is the issue of sexuality and women's sexual and reproductive rights: no amount of education can protect a woman from exposure to the virus if she cannot negotiate safe sex. Young women and girls are particularly vulnerable when they engage in sex with older men, especially those in positions of authority, such as clergymen, teachers, and employers. According to a UNAIDS Fact Sheet of February 2001, HIV rates in Trinidad & Tobago are reported to be five times higher for girls than for boys aged 15–18 years; this is probably true of other countries in the region. Women's sexual and reproductive rights must be the cornerstones to any effective programme for combating the spread of HIV/AIDS, even if this is presently excluded from the Goals and Targets and Indicators. What is needed are – strategies to ensure that gender inequalities are identified and addressed in the MDG process, and that national government policy responses include better statistics. We also need a strong women's movement to monitor the officials who are mandated to link MDG work with gender budgets.

Given that the MDGs are weak on the goal of gender equality and that the gender dimensions of other more general MDGs are almost invisible, those committed to the advancement of women's equality and empowerment need to consider putting their efforts into developing strategies for monitoring and measuring progress toward the achievement of the Beijing Platform of Action, rather than abandoning the MDGs. After all, the BPA is theoretically consistent (which the MDGs are not); it includes all of the MDGs; and it already has a constituency of support. Work will have to be done to spell out links between the MDGs and BPA in terms of Targets and Indicators, and new Indicators, such as violence and time use, may have to be added.

When others talk MDG, we must think BPA, and substitute the Best Plan of Action (BPA) for the Most Distracting Gimmick (MDG).

9

POLICY AND THE MEASURE OF WOMAN
Revisiting UNSNA, ISEW, HDI, and GPI

Marilyn Waring

The United Nations Decade for Women ran from 1975 to 1985. Since the Second United Nations Women's Conference in Copenhagen in 1980, feminists have strategised to force global and national accounting bodies to make women's economic contribution visible in their data. A main focus for attention has been the United Nations System of National Accounts (UNSNA).[1] UNSNA was instigated in 1953, with the aim of enabling comparisons to be made between national economies, and serving as a guide to countries developing their own accounting systems. In the UNSNA, national economies are defined in terms of market transactions; consumption, investment, and saving measures are given in addition to income and production totals. A vast amount of work performed by women is for household consumption or unpaid work in the informal economy. This work is not counted in UNSNA. The lack of visibility of women's contribution to the economy results in policies which perpetuate economic, social, and political inequality between women and men. There is a very simple equation operating here: if you are invisible as a producer in a nation's economy, you are invisible in the distribution of benefits (unless they label you a welfare 'problem' or burden').

In 1993, the rules of the UNSNA were changed.[2] This was an opportunity to address feminist concerns, and incorporate essential work performed for home consumption into the accounting system. However, this chance was missed. Paragraph 1.25 of the 1993 UNSNA establishes the 'consumption boundary', enumerating the many domestic and personal services which do not 'count' when they are produced and consumed within the same household. Women all over the planet perform the bulk of these tasks. They are the cleaning, decoration, and maintenance of the dwelling occupied by the household; cleaning, servicing, and repair of household goods; the preparation and serving of meals; the care of the sick, infirm, or old people; and the transportation of members of the household or their goods. These services do count in the UNSNA when they are supplied by government or voluntary agencies, and when they are paid for. The 'uncounted' tasks are termed 'indicators of welfare'.

Do women count for nothing?

Out of a breathtaking conceptual ignorance, and undoubted Western bias, the UNSNA fails to grasp there is no demarcation for women in the subsistence household between production inside or outside the consumption boundaries. Just picture the following. A woman wakes; she breastfeeds her four-month-old child (unproductive inactive primary production, consumed by a member of the household). There is no accurate way of ascribing value to this activity, even in the proposed 'satellite accounts'. (The satellite accounts are the 'add on' compromise that will include unpaid work. They have to be separate so as not to disturb what the experts call the 'internal integrity and international comparability of the current accounting framework'.) There is no market price for breast milk, so the satellite accounts will price that food at its nearest replacement equivalent. But infant formula, whatever cost is ascribed to it, cannot compete with the quality of breast milk, which means that its use will have a cost impact on the future health and education of the child.

Let's continue with the picture. The woman goes to collect water. She uses some to wash dishes from the family evening meal (unproductive work) and the pots in which she previously cooked a little food for sale (informal work). Next, she goes to the nearby grove to collect bark for dye for materials to be woven for sale (informal work), which she mixes with half a bucket of water (informal work). She also collects some roots and leaves to make a herbal medicine for her child (inactivity). She uses the other half of the bucket of water to make this concoction (inactivity). She will also collect some dry wood to build the fire to boil the water to make both the medicine and the dye (active and inactive labour). All this time she will carry the baby on her back (inactive work).

Of particular importance to feminists is paragraph 1.22 of the 1993 UNSNA, which describes the UNSNA as a 'multi-purpose system ... designed to meet a wide range of analytical and policy needs'. It states that 'a balance has to be struck between the desire for the accounts to be as comprehensive as possible', and their being swamped with non-monetary values. The revised system excludes all

> ... production of services for own final consumption within households ... The location of the production boundary ... *is a compromise, but a deliberate one that takes account of most users* [it is difficult to make extensive use of statistics in which you are invisible] ... If the production boundary were extended to include production of personal and domestic services by members of households for their own final consumption, all persons engaged in such activities would become self-employed, making unemployment virtually impossible by definition.[3]

Rather than justifying leaving most of the work done by most women out of the equation, this statement surely demonstrates that the current definition of unemployment is inappropriate.

The International Labour Organisation (ILO) specifies that the production of economic goods and services includes all production and processing of primary products, including that for home consumption, with the proviso that such production must be 'an important contribution' to the total consumption of the household.[4] In a 1992 resolution concerning the international classification of status in employment, the International Conference of Labour Statisticians defined subsistence workers as those 'who hold a self-employment' job and in this capacity 'produce goods and services which are predominantly consumed by their own household and constitute an important basis for its livelihood'.[5]

Compare the concepts of 'an important basis for livelihood', and 'an important contribution' to the total consumption of the household, with the specific exclusions from production in the 1993 UNSNA.

The distinctions made in terms of the boundary of production and consumption, and the definitions of the informal sector worked on so earnestly for the last ten years, are in these few sentences revealed as a load of patriarchal nonsense. As the example above shows, women's lives are not so meaninglessly divided. All tasks of survival in such circumstances are related. The UN Statistical Commission reported: 'As far as household production is concerned, the central framework includes for the first time all production of goods in households, whether sold or not, and services *if they are supplied to units other than their producers*.'[6] As concerned as they have been with conceptual and measurement difficulties, and boundaries of consumption or production, the designers of the new UNSNA just miss the point, and in so doing fail to reflect the reality of the majority of women on the planet.

The problem is systemic, and encompasses issues other than gender inequality. There are other significant measurement problems in the current UNSNA framework. Among the research topics of the Inter-Secretarial Working Group on national accounts, coordinated by the UN Statistical Commission, have been the indirect measurement of financial intermediation services; services in the informal sector; the classification of the purposes of non-profit institutions serving households; a workshop on intangible assets; the issue of measuring e-commerce; and more on counting the hidden economy. All of these pose significant technical, measurement, and valuation problems. Wild, speculative abstractions regarding these concerns have resulted in the figures produced being absolutely meaningless for the purposes of public policy, yet the framework of the UNSNA remains intact. However far removed from reality the UNSNA becomes, governments, business and multilaterals are committed to it, in the misguided conception that it accurately measures the thing which matters most: economic 'growth'.

John Ralston Saul opined in his CBC Massey Lecture Series:

I would suggest that we are in desperate need of a reformulation of the idea of growth ... It is difficult to imagine how we might escape our ongoing economic crisis unless we can reconsider [its] nature ... By reconsideration, I mean that we must attempt to draw back far enough to see where value lies in society.[7]

In the next section, I look at some work which has resulted from such attempts.

Real life: alternative models

In the past twelve years, some very fine work has resulted from the consideration of such issues. The figures feminists needed, to ensure that the realities of women's and children's lives are made visible to economists and politicians, are finally starting to be produced. Data on the ways in which we survive in a context of resource exploitation and environmental degradation are emerging. What alternative models have been developed which yield such material, and render it useful for public policy purposes? The new feminist challenge is to identify and use these models.

The Index of Sustainable Economic Welfare (ISEW)

The authors of this model, Herman Daly and John Cobb, share a concern that 'what is needed is *a* new measure'.[8] They are particularly concerned that 'costs' should be registered as deficits or depletions, not as 'goods' or 'benefits' in production and consumption, as in the UNSNA.

Daly and Cobb propose the Index of Sustainable Economic Welfare (ISEW). In this method of data collection and analysis, growth is no longer God; the emphasis is now on sustainability. The characteristics used in the ISEW are personal consumption, distributional inequality, household labour services, consumer durables, services provided by highways and streets, improvement in health and education by way of public expenditures, expenditures on consumer durables, and defensive private expenditures on health and education. Costs included are the costs of commuting, the costs of personal pollution control, costs of automobile accidents, costs of water pollution, air pollution, noise pollution, losses of wetlands, losses of farm land, depletion of non-renewable resources, long-term environmental damage, cost of ozone depletion, net capital growth (that is, the growth in the stock of goods used to produce other goods), and a change in net international position (indebtedness).

Attempts to ascribe a value to leisure were omitted from the ISEW, because 'the rather arbitrary assumptions upon which such a calculation is based ... are particularly problematic'.[9] However, Daly and Cobb include 'a rather speculative estimate of long-term environmental damage, particularly from climate modification'. They admit to being forced to make 'heroic assumptions' in compiling the ISEW, such as the cost imposed on future generations by the depletion of natural resources.

The ISEW falls down on the issue of unpaid work. While it shows evidence of new thinking, it remains patronising. 'Which of the activities within the household should be classified as work as opposed to leisure or an intrinsically satisfying activity?', they ask.[10] There is an easy response to this point: members of the paid workforce also take time for leisure in paid time, and find elements of their employment intrinsically satisfying. We still count all their activities as work.

In addition, Daly and Cobb's valuations are based on old inequalities. In ascribing a value to unpaid work, they adopt Robert Eisner's method of estimating the value of time spent on unpaid household work on the basis of the average wage rate for household domestic workers.[11] This, they say, avoids the problem of using differential market wage rates for men and women. However, this does not avoid the problems thrown up by using traditional low wage rates from a female occupation to estimate the value of the work of domestic workers, especially when much of that work is in the management of a small business, even if there is no market exchange!

The results of the ISEW are measured in per capita dollars. They have been calculated in the USA for the years 1950–90, and show variations when measured against the GDP in each of the four decades, and a decline in the 1980s. In retrospect, these studies can demonstrate that improvements in car safety and reductions in air pollution have made contributions to raising the level of economic welfare. So have social policies to reduce income inequality.[12] The categories included in the ISEW make this method of data collection yield a far more recognisable picture of reality. But the ISEW still remains one conglomerate, a single new measure, and the dollar is the measurement tool.

The Human Development Index (HDI)

Since its inception in 1990, the United Nations Human Development Report series has been dedicated to ending the mis-measurement of human progress by economic growth alone. 'To be valuable and legitimate, development progress, both nationally and internationally, must be people-centred, equitably distributed and environmentally and socially sustainable ... If present trends continue economic disparities between the industrial and developing nations will move from inequitable to inhumane.'[13]

To make the HDI capture gender-related inequalities, life expectancy, adult literacy and education are disaggregated by sex, as are data on share of earned income. A 'Gender Empowerment Measure' (GEM) includes data on the proportion of seats in parliament occupied by women, data on women as a percentage of administrators and managers, professional and technical workers, and women's percentage of earned income. The Human Development Reports are augmented with other data relevant to gender-based poverty and inequality. Despite the data limitations of timeliness and availability, the problems of currency conversions to the USD baseline, differing concepts, classifications and methods, and charges that there are too many data with too many different indicators, the HDI begins to approach approximate accurate input for the purpose of policy making.

The Genuine Progress Indicator (GPI)

One key indicator that is missing from the UN HDI is time-use. Time-use has figured prominently in the work to establish a Genuine Progress Indicator (GPI) in Nova Scotia. Prepared by Dr Ronald Coleman, the Nova Scotia GPI project has been designated as a pilot with Statistics Canada, which is providing ongoing assistance in data collection and analysis, and staff support. In addition to the national census, the GPI uses data from the Canadian System of Environmental and Resource Accounts. The index consists of 20 components with a sectoral approach and an emphasis on policy relevance.

The GPI indices distinguish direct contributions to economic welfare from defensive and intermediate expenditures, and from activities that produce an actual decline in wellbeing. Natural resource accounts include fisheries, soil and agriculture, forestry, wildlife, and greenhouse gas emissions. There are data on the costs of crime, income distribution, and transportation cost analysis. Monetary values are estimated where possible, but in the GPI it is not necessary that all components should have a financial value attributed to them.

The indicators of the GPI include statistics on unpaid work, divided into voluntary and community work, unpaid housework and parenting, and the value of unpaid overtime and under-employment. These figures can be gender-disaggregated. The monetary valuation method used in this study for calculating the economic value of unpaid work is the replacement cost (specialist) method. This reflects the hourly wage rate that would be paid in Nova Scotia to replace existing activities at market prices for the same kind of work. While this financial valuation is used to demonstrate linkages between the market and non-market sectors of the economy, a clear focus of the analysis is on time. In 1997 Nova Scotians contributed an estimated 134 million hours of their time to civic and voluntary work, and more than 940 million hours to unpaid household work. Their unpaid work in these two categories was the equivalent of 571,000 full-year full-time jobs!

The GPI work in Nova Scotia is the most sophisticated measurement work for policy outcomes anywhere. I recommend it to you. Of particular use are the crosscutting sectoral work in the forestry accounts, the water accounts, and the unpaid work accounts in both the household, and voluntary and community sectors. Only the key points and press statements in each area appear on the GPI website, but full reports can be purchased.[14]

The original aim of the GPI for Nova Scotia was to create an economic data set in which all activities had an estimated monetary value – obviously, the involvement of Stats Canada and the Nova Scotia Provincial Government had to be appeased. But it is the ground breaking work in the policy field that has saved this from being just another data set, and moved it on inestimably from the Cobb and Daly work, which continued to 'redefine progress'.[15] Rather than producing pages of retrospective alternative data sets with alternative explanations for policy outcomes, GPI Nova Scotia's publications look forward to raising the key questions for policy decisions today and tomorrow, and with cross-sectoral trade-offs explicit in the equations. It is superb work. It is also written in totally accessible language, for non-economists. The ongoing engagement of the Nova Scotia community in the analysis of the GPI has also been a breakthrough in all the projects on alternative indicator sets of which I am aware.

People setting their own indicators

The process in Nova Scotia partially solves two of the key problems that remained (at that point) with the GPI approach (which was originally Daly and Cobb's successor to the ISEW).

The first of these partial solutions is that while the indices seek to measure the wellbeing or development of a people or peoples, community, nation state or region, it is not usual for anyone to ask people themselves what indicators they would use to describe their wellbeing, and how they would measure outcomes of policies based on this data. Instead, the indicator sets are either what the authorities determine as being the figures they will collect (because the World Bank or IMF says so; because you can get a lot of software and hardware and vehicles if you collect particular data in a development assistance programme; because they support a corrupt government and can be easily manipulated; or just because they are the ones that have always been collected and there is comparability over time), or the figures that can be collected, from a logistical and technical standpoint, with a so-called reasonable degree of accuracy. Sometimes the choice of what data to collect depends simply on what is on the UN agenda for that year.

Interpreting data in non-monetary terms

The fine policy work in Nova Scotia also mitigates the second problem of data which cannot be presented and interpreted other than in monetary terms. This means that all sections of the population, not just academic statisticians and economists, can participate in debates about the research. It is expressed in the way that people might talk about it in a community meeting, in 'real world' terms. It is also important that data can be debated in terms of its own integrity, instead of the somewhat farfetched abstractions that result when everything is given a monetary value. For example, if we think of gender inequality and the potential users and objectives of time-use data relating to women's and men's workloads, we know that it is not necessary for policy discussions to ascribe monetary values to that work. For example, awareness of unequal time-use may spark off discussions about the need for day nurseries to offer more flexible services so that women's need for child-care can be met. These discussions do not require information about the value of the work which women are undertaking for such long hours. Nor do debates about policy regarding assistance to private businesses, or the planning and production of goods and services for home care. The need for monetary values to be ascribed occasionally is not a reason to abstract all time-use data to the economic model. Far more rigorous planning can be achieved by retaining the time-use framework, and it makes much more sense.

Ascribing monetary values to labour results in a loss of detail and specificity in policy analysis. Nowhere can the consequences of this be more starkly seen than in the case of children who work. Stories in the *State of the World's Children 1997* illustrate this. The ILO Minimum Age Convention allows light work at age 12 or 13, but prohibits hazardous work before 18. It also establishes a general minimum age of 15 years for paid work, provided 15 is not less than the age of completion of compulsory schooling. Yet, of the projected 190 million working children in the 10–14 age group in the developing world, three-quarters work six days a week or more, and one half work nine hours a day or more.[16] In a 1993 study in Malawi, 78 per cent of the 10–14 year olds, and 55 per cent of the 7–9 year olds living on tobacco estates were working full- or part-time. One quarter of the workforce – around 50,000 – in the glass bangle industry of Firozabad in India are children under 14, working in indescribably unsafe and inhumane conditions. Haiti has an estimated 25,000 child domestics, 20 per cent of whom are 7–10 years old. In the United States, at least 100,000 children are believed to be involved in child prostitution. As many as 3 million children aged 10–14 are estimated to work in Brazil's sisal, tea, sugar cane, and tobacco plantations. The most reliable estimates available for the United Kingdom show that between 15 and 26 per cent of 11 year olds are working.[17]

Do we want to lose the detail of what we do to children by ascribing monetary values to their production? I certainly do not, but that would be the result of including their labour and its outcome under a generic 'producer' category. Similarly, I do not want to lose the complexity of the impact of human activity on our ecosystem behind dollar signs. Yet that is the direction being pursued to give 'visibility' to environmental issues. To establish the United Nations satellite system of integrated economic and environmental accounting, the first step for each country is to draw up a comprehensive balance sheet of natural resources, measured in physical quantities. That ought to be sufficient for effective policy planning. Different units yes, but with judgement exercised. Yet the economists want one baseline, so that depletion of capital could include not just depreciation of physical capital, but depletion of natural resources along with deterioration of environmental quality. The problem is, they say, that so much expenditure for environmental protection compensates for the negative impact of economic growth, so it should be a cost to be deducted from national income.

There's an attractive logic here, and it parallels the 'costs' component of Daly and Cobb's ISEW system. The UN satellite system has been tested in several countries. For Mexico between 1986 and 1990, it was found that the environmentally-adjusted domestic product was 13 per cent less than the conventionally measured net domestic product. The new accounting measures also showed that net investment, which conventional measures showed as positive at 4.6 billion pesos, was a negative 700 million pesos. Net savings, also assumed to be positives, were actually close to zero. A case study for Papua New Guinea over the same period produced similar results. There, consumption exceeded output so net savings were negative.[18] But there had to be a better way.

The Alberta GPI

The latest work in which I have been involved as an adviser appears to have addressed both these major impediments to using the GPI in a major tool for policy planning. My challenge to the Alberta GPI Project Director, Mark Anielski at the Pembina Institute, was that the characteristics of wellbeing to be utilised in the Alberta GPI should reflect the values seen as indicative of wellbeing by Albertans themselves. The values held by Albertans should also determine how a characteristic in the GPI approach is treated. For example, in some communities, divorce is seen as a negative social cost. We know it usually leads to the economic downward mobility of women. Most governments focus on single-parent-headed households as a negative phenomenon. Yet we all know cases where the separation or divorce brings about an end to prolonged violence, and the wellbeing of children and mothers improves substantially. Divorce can therefore, in some contexts, be seen as positive. Similarly, some communities would see the rate of oil extraction in Alberta as a positive contribution to wellbeing;

others might see such extraction as a cost, particularly in terms of intergenerational equity.

In the time available, the Alberta GPI team was not able to conduct new research, but it was able to undertake a meta-data analysis of the Canadian and Albertan research on community values as reflected in the past five to ten years. This had the immediate effect of increasing the characteristics to be included to over 50, as opposed to the 26 in the original GPI or the 20 used in Nova Scotia.

The next challenge was to find a way of presenting all the data without ascribing notional monetary values, in such a way that all characteristics were measured in terms of their own integrity. It would obviously be useful if the system or model could also make trade-offs visible, and could be accessible for communities to understand and to participate in the analysis and planning that flows from the presentation of data. It would also be a vast improvement if the system could have 'open architecture' – that is, when a community or nation state demonstrated that a particular characteristic was no longer important to them, it could drop out of the system. Similarly, whenever a new measurement deemed important presented itself, it too could be introduced, without the tedium of 'not disturbing the comparability of the model over time', which is the outdated approach of the UNSNA and its policy of satellites.

I believe there is now this model. It is based on the healing circle used by the First Nations People of North America. It requires no expensive software: it can be downloaded as a simple radar diagram in Microsoft Excel format.[19]

I believe this approach offers enormous possibilities, but it must not be abused. (I dread to think of it as a tool in the hands of unethical postgraduate students who need a thesis.) In the first place, users should know the origins of opposition to the UNSNA approach, and how and why this alternative approach evolved. It must come as a whole piece of work, which is initiated by the communities whose wellbeing (or level of poverty, or development indicators) is or are being determined. These people themselves should determine the indicators to be included, and this list should be revisited with them every five to ten years. You can see immediately that the open architecture could deal with all the following: inflation rate, daily caloric intake, maternal mortality, the cost of a litre of water, last year's rainfall, notifiable and contagious disease levels, levels of education or literacy or school attendance, access to and use of family planning, agricultural extension programmes, micro-credit schemes, the retention of indigenous languages, natural disasters, pollution of air and water, deforestation – the list can be as long as a community determines. They should also be party to the interpretation of the radar diagram, which would determine the policy inputs required for desired outcomes, with trade-offs being very explicit.

I believe this model can be rigorous, ethical and accessible in our hands as a real breakthrough for policy work, with and for women and their communities.

In conclusion: the UNSNA is still the most influential model being used universally, but it is failing women miserably as a policy instrument, regardless of all its other problems. The feminist agenda in reinventing globalisation sees the removal of this pathological arbiter of 'wellbeing' as a critical focus. The satellite alternative is a co-option. The Alberta model is the most exciting alternative development in my lifetime – and one we can begin to use in our own nations and communities.

Notes

1. For a detailed analysis of the UNSNA: Marilyn Waring, *Counting for Nothing: What Men Value and What Women are Worth*, University of Toronto Press, 1999.
2. United Nations, *A System of National Accounts*, New York: UN, 1993.
3. Ibid., para. 1.22 [Waring's italics and insert].
4. International Labour Organisation, *Fifteenth International Conference of Labour Statisticians: Report II, Labour Force, Employment, Unemployment and Underemployment*, Geneva: ILO, 1982.
5. International Labour Organisation, *Fifteenth International Conference of Labour Statisticians: Report IV, Revision of the*

International Classification of Status in Employment, Geneva: ILO, 1992.

6. United Nations Statistical Commission [Waring's italics], Online Available HTTP: <unstats.un.org/unsd/commission.htm> (accessed 8 March 2008).

7. John Ralston Saul, *The Unconscious Civilization*, Ringwood, VIC: Penguin, 1997, pp. 156–7.

8. Herman Daly and John Cobb, *For the Common Good: Redirecting the Economy Towards Community, the Environment and a Sustainable Future*, Boston: Beacon Press, 1994, p. 378.

9. Ibid., p. 455.

10. Ibid., p. 457.

11. Robert Eisner, *The Total Incomes System of Accounts*, University of Chicago Press, 1989.

12. Daly and Cobb, *For the Common Good*, p. 507.

13. United Nations, *Human Development Report*, New York: UN, 1996, p. iii.

14. The Genuine Progress Indicator, Online Available HTTP: <www.gpiatlantic.org> (accessed 8 March 2008).

15. Redefining Progress, Online Available HTTP: <www.rprogress.org/sustainability_indicators/genuine_progress_indicator.htm> (accessed 8 March 2008).

16. UNICEF, *The State of the World's Children*, New York: UN, 1997, p. 25.

17. Ibid., pp. 20–38.

18. United Nations, *Human Development Report*, p. 63.

19. The Alberta GPI, Online Available HTTP: <www.pembina.org> (accessed 8 March 2008).

10

FEMINIST ECOLOGICAL ECONOMICS IN THEORY AND PRACTICE

Sabine U. O'Hara

The word 'economics' stems from the Greek *oikos nomos*, management of the household. Ecology too carries this idea: *oikos logos* refers to the law or the working of nature's household. Economics is concerned with the ways in which human households are managed and with the systems, institutions, and policy measures devised to accomplish household management goals. These goals have generally been summarised under three economic management questions, namely: what to produce (production), how to produce it (resource allocation), and for whom to produce (distribution). A far broader philosophical question has also been part of the economic management question, namely – what makes for the good life and how do humans determine its goodness or value?

Ecology, the law or workings of the natural household, offers a less anthropocentric perspective on household management. It is concerned with the interrelations and workings of systems of organisms and their environments. Ecosystems offer fascinating examples of the interaction of vast arrays of natural household members that sustain the productive capacities of human agricultural systems, maintain biological diversity, contribute to water purification, enhance resilience to droughts and other extreme climate conditions and much, much more. At the same time, ecosystems evolve and change and adjust to new humanly created conditions and challenges, unless of course, they reach the limits of their adaptability and simply collapse.

Yet how does human household management – the economy – account for the critical, non-human made context systems and conditions described as the laws of the natural household – ecology? The answer is, not well. What follows is a review of the limited scope of economic household management functions in mainstream economics. This chapter will then review several innovative perspectives for broadening its scope; approaches introduced by ecological economics, feminist economics, and the relatively new field of feminist ecological economics.

Reclaiming neglected contexts

Ecological economics or the science of sustainability, seeks to connect the two perspectives of household management and household systems functioning.[1] The economic side of ecological economics acknowledges that ecosystem functions, that is the contributions of the non-human household, have significant value for the human household. Humans would not be able to exist without clean water, clean air, and plants to supply food, medicine and building materials. In addition, there are aesthetic and recreational benefits of the natural environment that sustain and restore physical, emotional, and spiritual dimensions of human life. However, assigning economic value to these environmental contributions is no easy task. The management systems developed to organise the human household do not easily capture the value of ecosystem functions. In fact, these management systems are not only inconsiderate of non-human ecosystems, but may undermine their viability and functioning. One central question for ecological economists therefore, is how to adequately reflect the value of ecosystem functions and services to the human-made systems of household management called the economy.

The ecological side of ecological economics raises a somewhat different question. Here, the focus on ecosystem functions is about managing the tasks of production, resource allocation, and distribution in ways that are more aligned with ecosystem functions and therefore, less destructive of them. If ecological economists place the economy as an open sub-system within a wider environmental context system that is materially limited and thermodynamically constrained, then management rules change dramatically. Thus the deeper philosophical dimension of ecological economics comes into view, with its fundamental focus on the overall 'scale' of the economy and its ethical implications.

- How much is enough?
- What satisfies our needs and makes for the good life?

These questions as posed by ecological economists Herman Daly, Robert Costanza, and myself, among others, point beyond conventional economic valuation and systems approaches to the natural context of the economic household.[2]

Feminist ecological economics adds a further perspective.[3] Given women's long history of primary responsibility for the management of households in virtually every culture, it is surprising that women's voices have been largely absent in economics, as well as in ecological economics. However, if few women are being heard in economics and in ecological economics, the parallel field of feminist economics is well developed. Feminist economists such as Marianne Ferber, Julie Nelson, and Edith Kuiper are re-defining its scope beyond consumer choice and raising the 'what' and 'for whom' questions in relation to human household management.[4] They argue that economics should be about 'provisioning' including the provision of productive and reproductive needs and wants. Feminist economists point out that household production, human and social reproduction, and 'free' transfers of goods and services lie outside the scope of neoclassical economics, unless they can be assigned monetary value. Yet unlike environmental factors, the free contributions of women's labour are often not even recognised as 'externalities', they simply remain invisible.

The pathbreaking work of Hazel Henderson, Susan Himmelweit, Adelheid Biesecker, and other women economists has highlighted the centrality of valuation in both feminist economics and ecological economics.[5] Feminist ecological economists must straddle both sets of concern. Humans interact not only within an environmental context of physical, biological, and ecological systems but also within a social context of families and communities. As I argued a decade ago in the first feminist issue of the journal *Ecological Economics*, these relationships too, are often undermined by the very economic management systems devised to meet human material needs and to improve wellbeing.[6] This neglect of the value of social contexts and relationships is decidedly gendered, for it is particularly women's contributions that are unvalued. Women undertake the majority of reproductive, recreative, and restorative work in most societies. They birth children, teach, and nurture them, they care for the elderly, for spouses and extended family members, they volunteer in communities and neighbourhood organisations, they grow and protect shade plants that make their communities liveable, and much, much more. In doing so, women experience a different household management logic from that on which mainstream economics is based. Yet their experience remains excluded, as women are notoriously invisible as economic actors. *Homo oeconomicus*, the standard designated head of the household, is decidedly a man and unburdened by tasks that would infringe on standard economic rationality.

So how did this dual neglect of nature's ecological household and women's nurturing and reproductive contributions come about? One answer might be that economic systems are exceedingly complex. The processes, functions and relationships that determine production, allocation and distribution decisions, and which define welfare, are not easily explained, much less predicted. Economic models, like all models, must reduce real life complexity and simplify the ways in which economic functions and relationships are described. Modelling requires short-hand assumptions about human behaviour, motivations, and values. Ecological economist John Gowdy and I, have identified the main taken-for-granted assumptions of the dominant economic model as: the utility and profit maximising behaviour of consumers and producers, non-satiation, substitutability, value assigned via prices in interactive, ideally perfectly competitive markets.[7] These short-hand assumptions of economic theory are not simply value neutral. They discriminate disproportionately against women and against the natural environment. Moreover, their application can undermine the long-term sustainability of the economic process itself, by undervaluing the social and environmental inputs and context conditions, which underpin the economy. Ecological destruction and escalating environmental crises, poverty, stress, and the loss of restorative and recreative capacity are the result. Despite common concerns with issues of valuation, exclusion, and ethics, ecological economists have rarely focused on feminist economics and on the role of women's work in sustaining essential economic, ecological, and social systems.[8] To recover the complexities of the whole household – *oikos nomos* and *oikos logos* – the practitioners of ecological economics will need to address both – the contexts of economics and its valuation biases.

Making the invisible visible

Feminist ecological economics is context conscious economics and its main task is making hidden ecosystem and social functions visible. Consequently, feminist ecological economists identify indicators of the health, resilience, and long-term sustainability of supportive social and environmental systems. The impact of 'scale' on sustaining environmental and social realities is critical. Yet adding scale and appropriate indicators of social, environmental, and economic wellbeing adds complexity to the economic model. The observations that individuals do not always want more things, as assumed in the principle of non-satiation; that value has many dimensions and is not necessarily well-measured by monetary value; that biological time does not function in a mechanistic way; and that ecological health is an evolving proposition; each requires new measures and new models. The fact that mainstream economics treats most environmental factors as 'externalities', because there are no markets in which their prices can be set, does not solve the measurement problem. Valuation techniques like hedonic pricing, travel costs assessment, and various types of survey based contingent valuation, simply internalise unaccounted for environmental services into economic valuation categories of use value, option value, or existence value.

These techniques, however, remain firmly embedded in the very conceptual framework that causes the inadequate representation of environmental context systems in the first place.

Some ecological economists point out that much of what is termed 'economic development' has been shaped by the biases of monetisation; that is, creating markets for cutting down, digging up, or selling the natural and human capital that was once outside of the market. Development also implies a preference for moving house-holding, provisioning, and reproductive services from the informal or private sector to the formal and public sphere of the market. That process may indeed generate monetary value or GDP, but the non-measured value of sustaining social and ecological support systems, may be eroded in the process. For instance, a working mother may be less able to attend to her sick child; while daily travel to her city job is GDP positive, but negative in terms of global warming.

A prime example of the misrepresentation of value is the index known as Gross Domestic Product (GDP). Simon Kuznets' invention was meant to create a monetary, and thus commensurable, measure of economic flows that would help policy makers assess the state of the US economy in the aftermath of the great depression. Parts of the economy for which statistical data were not readily available – the household sector, the underground economy, the subsistence economy, natural resource stocks – have remained unaccounted for by GDP. Nevertheless, Kuznets' measure of monetary flow quickly became generalised as a measure of welfare. Not surprisingly, both feminist and ecological economics address measurement questions such as how to value unpaid work, social and community structures, and other previously invisible factors. A more complete economic model would, after all, include expanded measures of efficiency, of the use-value and even intrinsic value of natural capital, or of inter-generational and intra-generational equity. A more outward looking context aware view of the economic process would result in multiple scales for measuring value, respect for social and natural diversity, a concern with justice, with methodological pluralism, and an evolutionary understanding of economic change.

Even so, the question of how invisible social and ecological sustaining functions can be made visible has no easy answer. One approach offered by Herman Daly and John Cobb is the Indicator of Sustainable Economic Welfare (ISEW). A similar approach, put forward by Clifford Cobb, Ted Halstead, and Jonathan Rowe is the Genuine Progress Indicator (GPI).[9] Both ISEW and GPI take personal consumption as the starting point and adjust for (1) defensive expenditures necessary to repair social and environmental destruction, (2) non-renewable energy resources borrowed from future generations, and (3) shifts in the functions provided in households and civil society. These aggregate measures of welfare thus start with basic US-style economic needs and adjust for changes in social and environmental quality or non-economic and non-material needs. Like the GDP, they also create a single numerical indicator that can be easily tracked by policy makers and analysts. The downside of this aggregation is a significant loss of information. As I have argued elsewhere, it also leads to the selective exclusion of non-credentialled experts from the valuation process, and to a reliance on expert assumptions made most explicit in such expert methodologies as cost-benefit analysis.[10]

Multi-criteria measures like the UN Sustainable Development Indicators disaggregate social, economic and environmental dimensions, and provide more transparent information about the social and environmental dimensions of welfare. Both ecological economists like Giuseppe Munda, and feminist economists like Hazel Henderson, have been active in identifying such multi-indicator methods of valuation and their specific criteria.[11] However, multi-dimensional, non-commensurate measures are generally more difficult to interpret meaningfully. The selection of indicator categories and the evaluation of trade-offs between them cannot be easily generalised, but must be flexible to allow for context specific conditions and variations. This is not only an unfamiliar but an uncomfortable task for many economists, since very few have sociological training. The challenges of evaluating trade-offs are generally deemed the prerogative of credentialled experts such as development specialists and planners, and they are often hidden in elaborate assumptions about relative value. Rarely are people holding context specific, local knowledge or those whose knowledge systems have been marginalised, consulted by professionals in the valuation process.[12] Yet it is precisely the context-knowledge of non-credentialled experts that may best capture specific social and ecological characteristics.

No matter how carefully one selects measures of material, social, and cultural wellbeing, generalised 'objective' measures can all too easily ignore the specific needs, options, and perceptions of an individual or social group. As economist Amartya Sen has pointed out, objective measures may in fact reinforce existing cultural, class, and gender biases.[13] This extends not only to the valuation biases of economic abstraction such as 'rational choice', but to the entrenched and gendered methodological bias toward what is readily observable, measurable, quantifiable, and generalisable. As feminist economist Julie Nelson has argued, women whose lives are embedded in material complexity have no difficulty making sense of the qualitatively unobservable, non-measurable, and context specific aspects of economics.[14]

Methods reflect power structures

In the dominant economic model, the market (public) is deemed more valuable than the household (private); universalisable concepts and measures are preferred to local context specific ones; unified theories are preferred to experiential variation. This is not simply a matter of selecting indicators, even multiple ones, which capture complexities. It is also a matter of 'Who' selects the indicators and 'Who' evaluates the trade-offs between different economic scenarios.[15] In other words, feminist economists want to know: whose needs and values are determinative in selecting a set of indicators and in evaluating their relative importance? Should economists listen to Gary Becker's benevolent head of the household – or to the women and children he supposedly represents? Should economists listen to the needs of those who are unaware of, yet materially dependent on invisible ecosystem services? Should economists listen to people for whom an ecosystem is merely an abstract concept, or perhaps, a recreational opportunity? My position as a feminist ecological economist is to prioritise the judgement of people who perceive human wellbeing as inseparably linked to the health and functioning of non-human systems.[16] And I would most certainly disagree with those who reduce ecosystem services to human use-value.

Many scholars of gender and its role in the social construction of knowledge, most notably Sandra Harding, have long critiqued the idea of 'objectivity' in the positivist scientific sense. Similarly, feminist ecological economists including myself have argued for pluralism in theory, and analysis of the way in which hierarchical and dualistic thought patterns constrain people's understanding of complex economic processes.[17] When professionals rely on expert systems without examining their epistemological assumptions, they miss the fact that each discipline brings distinct biases to the selection and valuation process.

It is important for economists and ecological economists to understand how epistemological assumptions, indicators, measures, and assessment methods often reflect existing power structures. If these power relations are not transparent, then economic constructs will simply perpetuate the powerlessness of those who have been excluded from the knowledge-making process. Most commonly this is people – usually women – who are burdened with providing essential social sustaining functions. The inevitable result is that economists leave nourishment, care, stress recovery, waste assimilation, reproduction and restoration uncounted. In turn, this means that modelling is oversimplified and abstract. Models must be inclusive, and based on politically transparent assumptions, be flexible, fairly sophisticated, and allow for cross-influences and context changes.[18] Feminist economist Irene van Staveren, for example, uses modelling techniques derived from chaos theory to capture contextual and relationship-sensitive dimensions of the economic process.[19] Such models can complement narrative approaches that introduce the messy interaction of real people and real communities, located in real spatial, climatic, ecological and cultural life-contexts.

The ability to take the complexities of real-life-contexts into account will rest on what people say about their live-worlds.[20]

Economists, including some ecological economists, have been rather sceptical of the subjective perception and opinion of human actors. And as economists caution, an individual's stated preferences and revealed preferences are two different things.[21] Comparison theory that relies on interview based individual assessments of wellbeing is a case in point. Since people make judgements about their satisfaction level by looking at others' income or social status, comparison studies reveal only a weak connection between 'objective' measures of wellbeing and 'subjective' satisfaction levels. However, the answer to this measurement dilemma cannot lie in hidden assumptions, generalisations, and simplifications. Rather, it must be sought in participatory research and assessment methods that can capture more complexity and context information rather than less.

It is no small task to admit marginalised perspectives and unfamiliar measures like cooperation, variability, or provisioning, into the valuation and decision process. It requires new approaches and new economic sensibilities. At the same time, context specificity should not imply total relativism. Instead, the acceptance of context is a vote for detailed empirical observation, historical awareness, and for generalisable guidelines about functions and services deemed indispensable.[22] This implies collaboration and communication between credentialled experts and the often invisible expertise of locals who challenge and expand standard methods and models. Without the effective representation of situated agents, economic measures and models will continue to ignore the social and environmental dimensions of long-term sustainability in favour of short-term unsustainable 'quick-fixes'. Feminist economists have played a key role in advancing this methodological dialogue and in the process have advanced both theory and practice.

Feminist ecological economics

Feminist ecological economists offer an even deeper methodological critique of economics than feminist economists do. They consider the interrelatedness of economic actors, the importance of family and community in social reproduction, and the centrality of unmeasured non-monetised work in maintaining homes. However, feminist ecological economists integrate these things with the sustaining significance of ecosystems in relation to productivity and wellbeing. This moves context from the periphery of economics to the centre, and what typically has been considered an 'externality', now becomes the focus of analysis. This radical shift in perspective is marked by several practical innovations:

- methodologies rely on data collection rather than existing statistics,
- research design is participatory rather than distanced,
- the interest is citizen deliberation rather than ranking of individual preferences,[23]
- transparency is sought between stakeholder groups and experts,
- new theoretical models redefine the core economic activities of production, consumption, and welfare creation.[24]

Feminist ecological economists move ecological and social indicators that better reflect sustaining functions and processes to the fore as well. This means that complexity rather than reducibility, variability rather than specialisation, diversity rather than homogeneity, provisioning rather than non-satiation, and the ability to cooperate rather than compete, all become indispensable dimensions of a resilient and sustainable economy.[25] Like all measures, these newly admitted dimensions describe the perspectives of individual or collective actors. In the global South the actor might be the bureaucrat who privatises the water supply; the Somali woman who must walk two additional hours to the well due to desertification; the child who never knew a spring clean enough to drink from; or the researcher bringing new water purification technologies to a remote village. In the global North the actor might be the mother who would rather spend time with her children than work a 60-hour week or the father who would rather stay home than drive an hour to get reliable day care for his child. Such agents are rarely one-dimensional. The actors described by feminist ecological economics both make and are shaped by the complexities of their life-worlds. In fact, despite the short-hand assumptions of conventional economic modelling, such agents are quite capable of sorting through the daily chaos of their life-world contexts; they can assess complex information and can articulate their own standpoint.

The work of feminist scholars from the global South has been particularly relevant in articulating multidimensional perspectives and in calling attention to the inadequacies of standard economic valuation methods and models. Prominent among these women are Vandana Shiva, Bina Agarwal, and Asoka Bandarage.[26] By assessing the effects of economic development, industrialisation, structural adjustment, population policies, and imported agricultural methods on women's lives, they not only articulate the specific social and ecological dimensions of economic policies and development strategies, they also point to underlying systemic problems. Recurring themes in this body of work are global–local connections, economic autonomy, and the relationship between gender and the environment. They deconstruct the systemic effects of development policies biased toward the monetary economy and its particular definitions of efficiency, growth, and wealth creation.

Many scholars from the global South bring a further critical dimension to the fore, namely community activism, local participation, and engagement in the social change process. This is not surprising given their exposures to the ecological reality of ecosystem constraints and the feminist reality of relationships associated with the demands of households and communities. When women's lives become the starting point of research, new explanations, theories, measures and methodologies are called for; and so are new solutions, activities, strategies, and stories. When economists work face to face with women in communities, this invariably leads to insights about the importance of social processes and power relations, as well as respect for diverse ways of knowing and valuing. In short: feminist ecological economics has a commitment to methodological pluralism and an openness to 'learning with' those who have grassroots expertise rather than 'learning about' them.

This observation holds for the work of feminist ecological economists in the global South and in the global North. Both groupings seek solutions for local communities and regions while revising accepted disciplinary models, methodologies and explanations.[27] As J.K. Gibson-Graham has demonstrated, this kind of research may include grassroots work in economic and ecological literacy, local economic initiatives and alternative development strategies, the active searching out of relevant empirical data for new models and policies, green community planning and design, and other similarly participatory approaches.[28] To meet the demands of complex, non-hierarchical, and nuanced models that do not aspire to being universal, feminist ecological economists often have to start from scratch. They invariably collect their own data, build their own models, and design their own policies. They often cultivate community-based 'volunteer' work as a way of advancing their chosen field of scholarship while remaining connected to people and places in their own life-worlds.

To summarise: the management of the human household – the economy – has often ignored the workings or *logos* of the natural household. The consequence of this neglect has been the destruction of valuable context systems that provide essential ecological and social services to the economy. Feminist ecological economists seek to change this by focusing attention on what traditional economic constructs have deemed 'externalities'. This radical shift in perspective is accompanied by theoretical and methodological innovations, such as methodologies that rely on data collection rather than existing statistics, research design that is participatory rather than distanced, interest in citizen deliberation rather than ranking of individual preferences, transparency and collaboration between stakeholder groups and experts, new theoretical models that redefine the core economic activities of production, consumption and welfare creation. In bringing such innovations to the field of economics, feminist ecological economists also highlight the gender bias that stands behind the neglect of ecological and social-cultural context systems. This work of 'uncovering' and 'reconnecting' has implications for theory and practice, and it has real-life consequences as well.

Notes

1. Ecological economics emerged as a new field in the late 1980s. The journal *Ecological Economics* began publication in 1989; the International Society for Ecological Economics, founded in 1986, now has chapters in Europe, Russia, India, Australia and New Zealand, Latin America, Brazil, Canada and the US. There are newsletters, listserves, electronic discussion groups, and a substantial literature.

2. Herman Daly, *Ecological Economics and the Ecology of Economics*, Cheltenham: Elgar, 1999; Robert Costanza (ed.), *Ecological Economics: The Science and Management of Sustainability*, Columbia University Press, 1991; Robert Costanza, Olan Segura, and Juan Martinez-Alier, *Getting Down to Earth: Practical Applications of Ecological Economics*, Washington DC: Island Press, 1996; Robert Costanza, John Cumberland, Herman Daly, Robert Goodland, and Richard Norgaard, *An Introduction to Ecological Economics*, Boca Raton, FL: St Lucie Press, 1997; Rajaram Krishnan, Jonathan Harris, and Neva Goodwin (eds), *A Survey of Ecological Economics*, Washington, DC: Island Press, 1995; Sabine O'Hara, 'Discursive Ethics in Ecosystems Valuation and Environmental Policy', *Ecological Economics*, 1996, Vol. 16, No. 2, 95–107; Sabine O'Hara, 'Sustaining Production: Material and Institutional Considerations', *International Journal of Environment and Pollution*, 1998, Vol. 9, No. 2/3: 287–304; Sabine O'Hara, 'The Challenges of Valuation: Ecological Economics between Matter and Meaning' in Cutler Cleveland, Robert Costanza, and David Stern (eds), *The Nature of Economics and the Economics of Nature*, Northampton, MA: Elgar, 2001.

3. Feminist economics has existed as a well-defined field since the early 1990s. The journal *Feminist Economics* began publication in 1995. The International Association for Feminist Economics was formed in 1992 and meets annually in addition to publishing a newsletter, listserve, and discussion group. In German speaking countries, a more loosely knit network *Vorsorgendes Wirtschaften* brings together women economists for conferences, working groups, and publication projects.

4. Marianne Ferber and Julie Nelson (eds), *Beyond Economic Man: Feminist Theory and Economics*, University of Chicago Press, 1993; Heidi Bernhard Filli, Andrea Günter, Maren Jochimsen, Ulrike Knobloch, Ina Praetorius, Lisa Schmuckli, and Ursula Vock, *Weiberwirtschaft: Frauen-Ökonomie-Ethik*, Luzern: Edition Exodus, 1994; Edith Kuiper and Jolande Sap (eds), *Out of the Margin: Feminist*

Perspectives on Economics, New York: Routledge, 1995; Gillian Hewitson, *Feminist Economics: Interrogating the Masculinity of Rational Economic Man*, Northampton, MA: Elgar, 1999.

5. Hazel Henderson, *The Politics of the Solar Age: Alternatives to Economics*, New York: Doubleday, 1981; Hazel Henderson, *Paradigms in Progress: Life Beyond Economics*, Indianapolis: Knowledge Systems, 1991; Sue Himmelweit, 'The Discovery of "Unpaid Work": The Social Consequences of the Expansion of "Work"', *Feminist Economics*, 1995, Vol. 1, No. 1, 1–19; Adelheid Biesecker, 'Shareholders, Stakeholders and Beyond – *Auf dem Weg zu einer Vorsorgenden Wirtschaftsweise*', Bremen: Diskussions-papiere zur Sozialökonomik, 1998, No. 26.

6. Sabine O'Hara, 'Toward a Sustaining Production Theory', *Ecological Economics*, 1997, Vol. 20, No. 2, 141–54.

7. John Gowdy and Sabine O'Hara, *Economic Theory for Environmentalists*, Delray, FL: St Lucie Press, 1995.

8. An exception is the special issue of the journal *Ecological Economics*, edited by Patricia E. Perkins, *Ecological Economics*, 1997, Vol. 20, No. 2; also a volume from the Group of Green Economists, *Ecological Economics: A Programme for Global Reform*, Ottawa, 1992. This included an appendix citing contributions of women, especially from the global South.

9. Herman Daly and John Cobb, *For the Common Good*, Boston: Beacon, 1989; Clifford Cobb, Ted Halstead, and Jonathan Rowe, 'If the GDP is Up, why is America Down?', *Atlantic Monthly*, October 1995, 59–79.

10. O'Hara, 'Discursive Ethics in Ecosystems Valuation and Environmental Policy'; O'Hara, 'The Challenges of Valuation'.

11. Hazel Henderson, *Paradigms in Progress*; Guiseppe Munda, Peter Nijkamp, and Piet Rietveld, 'Qualitative Multi-criteria Evaluation for Environmental Management', *Ecological Economics*, 1994, Vol. 10, No. 2, 97–112.

12. For a critique see for example Clement Tisdell, 'Issues in Biodiversity Conservation Including the Role of Local Communities', *Environmental Conservation*, 1995, Vol. 22, No. 3, 216–22.

13. The term 'option' rather than 'choice' connotes the path dependent nature of what Sen terms 'agency-freedom' and 'wellbeing freedom', see: Amartya Sen, *Inequality Re-examined*, Oxford: Clarendon, 1992; Amartya Sen, 'Capability and Wellbeing' in Martha Nussbaum and Amartya Sen (eds), *The Quality of Life*, Oxford: Clarendon, 1993.

14. Julie Nelson, 'The Study of Choice or the Study of Provisioning? Gender and the Definition of Economics' in Marianne Ferber and

Julie Nelson (eds), *Beyond Economic Man: Feminist Theory and Economics*, University of Chicago Press, 1993.

15. Sabine O'Hara, 'Economics, Ecology and Quality of Life: Who Evaluates?' *Feminist Economics*, 1999, Vol. 5, No. 2, 83–9; also O'Hara, 'The Challenges of Valuation'.

16. J.K. Gibson-Graham, *The End of Capitalism (As We Knew It): A Feminist Critique of Political Economy*, Oxford: Blackwell, 1996.

17. Sandra Harding, *The Science Question in Feminism*, Cornell University Press, 1986; Marianne Ferber and Julie Nelson, *Beyond Economic Man*; Sabine O'Hara, 'Valuing Socio-Diversity', *International Journal of Social Economics*, 1995, Vol. 22, No. 5, 31–49. Also O'Hara, 'Discursive Ethics in Ecosystems Valuation and Environmental Policy', and O'Hara, 'Economics, Ecology and Quality of Life'.

18. For example Esther Redmount, 'Towards a Feminist Theory of Econometrics' in Kuiper and Sap, *Out of the Margin*.

19. Irene van Stavaren, 'Chaos Theory and Institutional Economics: Metaphor or Model?', *Journal of Economic Issues*, 1999, Vol. XXXIII, No 1, 11–24.

20. The term *Lebenswelt* or 'life world' as used by German sociologist Habermas connotes people's lives as well as life contexts. Jürgen Habermas, 'Diskursethik-Notizen zu einem Begruendungsprogram' in Jürgen Habermas (ed.), *Moralbewusstsein un Kommunikatives Handeln*, Frankfurt: Surkamp Verlag, 1983.

21. See for example Richard Easterlin, 'Does Economic Growth Improve the Human Lot? Some Empirical Evidence' in Paul David and Melvin Redner (eds), *Nations and Households in Economic Growth: Essays in Honor of Moses Abramovitz*, New York: Academic Press, 1974; Angus Campbell, Philip Converse, and Willard Rodgers (eds), *The Quality of American Life: Perceptions, Evaluations, and Satisfactions*, New York: Sage, 1976.

22. Much of this methodological alternative was lost after the nineteenth century *Methodenstreit* between the Marginalist versus Historical Schools. See Birger Priddat, 'Die Andere Ökonomie. Eine neue Einschätzung von Gustav Schmollers Versuch einer ethisch-historischen', *Nationalökonomie im 19. Jahrhundert*, Marburg: Metropolis Verlag, 1995. Compare too, Charlene Siegfried, *Reweaving the Social Fabric: Pragmatism and Feminism*, University of Chicago Press, 1996.

23. Mark Sagoff, 'Aggregation and Deliberation in Valuing Environmental Public Goods: A Look Beyond Contingent Pricing', *Ecological Economics*, 1989, Vol. 24, No. 2/3.

24. Examples can be found in the work of Marlene Kim, 'Poor Women Survey Poor Women: Feminist Perspectives in Survey Research', *Feminist Economics*, 1997, Vol. 3, No. 2, 99–117; Michele Pujol, 'A Special Exploration on Field Work and Methodology', *Feminist Economics*, 1998, Vol. 3, No. 2, 119–51; Perkins, *Ecological Economics*, 1997, Vol. 20, No. 2; Adelheid Biesecker, 'Power and Discourse: Some Theoretical Remarks and Empirical Observations', Bremen: Diskussionspapiere zur Sozialökonomie, 1996, No. 14; Ulrike Knobloch, *Theorie und Ethik des Konsums. Reflexion auf die normativen Grundlagen sozialökonomischer Konsumtheorien*, Bern: Paul Haupt, 1994. See also Kuiper and Sap, *Out of the Margin*; Sabine O'Hara, 'Urban Development Between Isolation and Connection: A Study of the Potential for Job Creation in Urban Neighborhoods', *Review of Social Economy*, 2001, Vol. LIX, No 1: 23–43; Sabine O'Hara and Carie McDonald, *Development as if Local Residents Mattered – Results of a Household Survey Conducted in the Town of Poultney, Vermont*, Poultney, VT: Green Mountain College Research Report, 2002; Sabine O'Hara and Jose Vazquez, *The Five Pillars of Economic Development: A Study of Best Practices for the Roanoke Valley*, Salem, VA: Roanoke College Research Report, 2006.

25. See for example John Dryzek, *Rational Ecology: Environment and Political Economy*, Oxford: Blackwell, 1987.

26. Bina Agarwal, 'The Gender and Environment Debate: Lessons from India', *Feminist Studies*, 1992, Vol. 18, No. 1, 119–58; Asoka Bandarage, *Women, Population and Global Crisis: A Political-Economic Analysis*, New York: St Martin's, 1997; Vandana Shiva, *Staying Alive: Women, Ecology and Development*, London: Zed Books, 1989; Jael Silliman and Ynestra King, *Dangerous Intersections: Perspectives on Population Environment, and Development*, Boston: South End, 1999.

27. See Nancy Naples 'Contested Needs: Shifting the Standpoint on Rural Economic Development', *Feminist Economics*, 1997, Vol. 3, No. 2, 63–98; Patricia E. Perkins, 'Public Participation and Ecological Valuation: Inclusive = Radical', paper presented at the Capitalism, Nature, Socialism Conference, York University, Toronto, 2005.

28. Gibson-Graham, *The End of Capitalism*.

Part IV

Energy

The more things are brought together from out of their habitat and locale, the more networks bringing them to the place of consumption are needed. The more they are brought together, the more they are cut out of their habitat and locale. The more they are cut out, the less they can reproduce. The less they reproduce, the less they become. The less they become, the more substitutes for them need to be found. The more substitutes need to be found, the greater the globalization needed to find and transport them ...

In other words spatial centralization creates energy demands and an energy field which can only sustain itself by extracting surplus-value from nature.

Teresa Brennan, *Exhausting Modernity*,
London: Routledge, 2000, p. 129.

11

WHO PAYS FOR THE KYOTO PROTOCOL?

Selling Oxygen and Selling Sex in Costa Rica

Ana Isla

The global system of capitalist patriarchal economics understands the conservation of biodiversity and climate change in terms of enclosures, and more recently, marketable commodities. However, environmental conservation led by neoliberal governments and large NGOs in the global North has become yet another instrument for the colonisation of Third World resources – in particular, women's work, and nature.[1] This chapter describes two interconnected socio-economic aspects of this process: the first is the enclosure of rainforests as 'carbon sinks' or oxygen generators, and the second is the enclosure and commodification of women's labour which results from that move. As forest ecosystems and women's non-wage labour together comprise a complex support system for the survival of local communities, the international conservationist agenda of enclosing rainforests has become a war on subsistence and a cause of rural poverty and displacement. Women are now forced to find a means of subsistence on the margins of the global economy.

Since the Industrial Revolution began, humans have been increasing the quantity of carbon dioxide (CO_2) in the Earth's atmosphere and oceans. These gases are emitted by industrial processes such as fossil fuel combustion, and by modification of land use such as deforestation. If emissions continue at the present rate, current projections suggest that there will be a global increase in temperature of between 1°C and 5°C by 2100, leading to global warming and unstable climatic conditions across the planet.[2] Governments first agreed to tackle climate change at the UN Earth Summit in Rio de Janeiro in 1992. The UN Framework Convention on Climate Change (UNFCCC) evolved into the Kyoto Protocol and set countries an initial non-binding goal of stabilising their emissions. This objective was not met overall. Likewise, targets negotiated at subsequent meetings of the Inter-governmental Panel on Climate Change (IPCC), are unlikely to be met across the board.

In regions of the global South without industrial degradation, intact forest vegetation can store CO_2 that otherwise might trap heat in the atmosphere, driving up temperatures and speeding up climate change. At Rio, the use of tropical rainforests to act as carbon sinks became a central part of the 'sustainable development' agenda and, as noted, this was subsequently incorporated into the Kyoto Protocol. The World Bank has defined sustainable development as management of the entire cycle of life (humankind and nature) with the intention of expanding 'wealth'. This definition allows for management of a nation's portfolio of assets including – built infrastructure; natural resources like minerals, energy, agricultural land, forests; human capital and social capital. The World Bank has noted that many critically important ecological life-support functions provided by natural systems are not measured yet as part of the wealth of nations.[3] Among the services not yet captured by the dominant economic discourse are those provided by forest ecosystems. Yet, rather than see economics as dependent on ecology, capitalist patriarchal reasoning embeds the forest in the economic system as 'natural capital', a resource for sustainable development. This upside down logic is especially problematic for rainforest dwellers living beyond the market economy.

The sexual division of labour and women's oppression by means of it, is affected in powerful ways when forests are commodified for selling oxygen. Rural women and men need economic resources for subsistence and they need intact communities for emotional support. But after conservation enclosure, peasant families evicted from the forest break up as they are forced to migrate into cities looking for employment. Here, those who do not succeed in the market are seen as 'defective', less human and therefore more exploitable. In this context, capitalist patriarchal gender relations convert peripheral women into various kinds of cheap labour. As cheap sex, they provide an opportunity for men to purchase the satisfaction of ego needs as well. Genevieve Vaughan names the process by which men enjoy social dominance through the control of women's bodies 'masculation'.[4] Some men confirm their constructed-gender superiority through sexual violence – degrading anyone in the position of a social 'other'. It seems that just as nature is enclosed in the global South to give back 'life' to the global North, so prostitution is the enclosure of women's and children's bodies to give back 'life' to damaged individuals.

Enclosing the forest to sell oxygen

Mainstream environmentalists articulate the multiple advantages of selling carbon sink capacities. But those from the industrial world have adopted a political stance that sets them and their movement above and beyond class and gender oppression, imperialism, and neocolonialism. Their politics simply reinforces the dominant relations of power under neoliberalism, as they bypass questions of exploitation and poverty, and contribute to displacement of communities on a global level through ill-conceived conservation strategies.[5] To the environmental establishment, rainforest dwellers are 'spectators' only, not political agents.[6] The international sustainable development agenda defines the forest as 'natural capital', while rural women are constituted as 'human capital'. Since capitalist patriarchal economics has converted the sensuous world into an abstraction for the purpose of profit and masculine aggrandisement, forests and women are diminished as ways of being. The double enclosures of the forest and women's labour have become another war on the autonomy and subsistence capacity of peoples in the global South.

Ecologists have provided ample evidence of the natural limits of the planet for industrial growth and consumerism and they reject the myth of unlimited economic growth.[7] These natural limits are already demonstrated by the destruction of resources, the failure of absorptive capacities for wastes, and the irrefutable rise of global warming.[8] While economic growth continues to be promoted as central to sustainable development, Earth Summits in Rio and in Johannesburg have deliberated on the need to reduce the emission of greenhouse gases, air pollution in the form of carbon dioxide, dust particles, and carbon monoxide. But these meetings have failed in their objectives. And it is equally clear that the conventional environmental movement is inadequate to the crisis it faces.

As distinct from the big environmental NGOs, the radical ecology movement argues for a reorientation of economics, replacing competitive free trade and export led development with self-sufficiency and minimal energy and material throughput. Materialist ecofeminists like Maria Mies, Veronika Bennholdt-Thomsen, or Vandana Shiva, advocate alternative consumption norms based on 'enoughness'; 'sufficiency', 'subsistence economies', and 'gift economies'.[9] Ecofeminists recognise that over many centuries, patriarchal societies have fabricated an economy based on *private* property (in Latin *privare* = to rob). Some have suggested that private property and artificial scarcity were created in order to erase the gift economy, practised by women across cultures, generation after generation. Today, most labour in the world remains hidden in the gift economy. The gifts can be identified in women's non-waged household work and in peasant and indigenous people's labour. But even urban industrial workers make forced gifts in the form of 'surplus value' as the unpaid portion of their labour.[10] Other gifts include voluntary work; sex slavery; child labour; and of course, the 'free services' of nature.

The official economy of Costa Rica is an export-oriented economy. However, due to its foreign debt, it plainly demonstrates the problems of export pressure on human and natural resources.[11] For example, in terms of land ownership, United Fruits, a US multinational corporation, has enclosed the southern part of the country with banana plantations; the local business community has enclosed the central valley for coffee plantations; and foreigners and local businesses have enclosed the northwest for cattle ranching. These land grabs by foreign and local businesses have deeply divided Costa Rica in terms of land control and power. To be specific, government statistics reveal that in 1996: 0.71 per cent of individuals with more than 100 hectares own 70 per cent of the country's territory; while 83 per cent of landowners with less than 100 hectares control 1 per cent of the national territory.[12]

The international sustainable development agenda has aggravated this unequal access to resources by intensifying enclosures of land through the Conservation Area System created in 1989 by the then Ministry of Natural Resources, Energy, and Mines (MIRENEM, now MINAE). The Sistema Nacional de Areas de Conservacion (SINAC) implemented the conservation area model to manage the country's wildlife and biodiversity. It divided the country into eleven Conservation Areas, which incorporate wildlife, privately owned lands, and human settlements, and placed them under supervision of the current Ministry of Environment and Energy. In enclosing 25 per cent of national territory, SINAC expanded the enclosure model. As happened in North America, the expropriated land has been organised along the lines of national parks, where indigenous people are excluded and denied any role in sustaining the ecosystems.[13] These expropriated lands are linked by transnational political networks of local and global 'stakeholders' through management categories such as human patrimony, national parks, wet land, biological reserves, protected zones, forest reserves, and wildlife refuges. At the same time, internal boundaries are built, to separate off local people who have traditionally shared the benefits of volcanoes, waterfalls, rivers, hot springs, congo-monkeys, and turtle-spawning havens. The separated lands now become access sites for mining, research, eco-tourism, and selling oxygen.[14]

Natural capital or super-organism?

In the sustainable development framework, forests are simply 'natural capital'. But among other things, rainforest trees are an essential mechanism for flood control. The trees are connected directly to each other through the multitude of creatures that relate to them as food or as shelter or nesting places; through their shared access to water, air, and sunlight; and through an underground system of fungi that links all the trees as a super-organism. Rainforest people are also members of this super-organism.

In the meeting of parties to the Climate Change Convention in Kyoto in 1997, industrial countries agreed to create mechanisms to reduce gases responsible for global warming. The Kyoto Protocol committed industrialised nations to reducing emissions of greenhouse gases, principally carbon dioxide, by around 5.2 per cent of their 1990 levels. Carbon dioxide is primarily discharged by the global North. However, reducing gas emissions implies capital costs for industries in the industrial world. Thus, it was easier for the major emitting corporations, with the backing of their governments, to propose a more self-interested 'solution'; that is, to set up 'a global market' in carbon dioxide and oxygen, making use of the clean forests of poor indebted countries in the global South. According to the Climate Change Convention, countries or industries that manage to reduce emissions to levels below their designated limit are able to sell their 'pollution credit' to other countries or industries that exceed their own emission levels. Following the Convention, the Clean Development Fund evolved into the Clean Development Mechanism (CDM), an arrangement under the Kyoto Protocol that allows industrialised countries with a greenhouse gas reduction commitment to 'invest' in emission reducing projects in indebted countries, as an alternative to more costly emission reduction in their own countries.[15]

Under the Kyoto Protocol, the rainforest is valued economically through its CO_2 securing strategies. The use of forest absorption to compensate for developed countries' emissions was readily adopted by indebted Costa Rica. This country now organises conservation, management of forests, and reforestation, by means of international covenants and sells environmental services to Norway, Germany, Holland, Mexico, Canada, and Japan.[16] During José Figueres' administration (1994–98), the Forestry Law (7575) and the decree DAJ-D-039-98 were signed to regulate payments for environmental services. Certification for forest conservation is legislated by the Forestry Law (Article 22) in the jurisdiction of the Ministry of Environment and Energy (MINAE). Through its Forestry Incentive programme, MINAE receives, evaluates, and approves the terms of conservation programmes and promotes and compensates the owners of forestry plantations. The decree recognises the forest and forest plantation owners, small farmers (*finca*), and Conservation Areas as providers of environmental services eligible to receive payments for services provided.

Globally speaking, emissions produced by coal and oil burned in the industrial world are the leading cause of climate change, but proceed unimpeded. The global North is not held responsible for mitigating its high level of emissions, but simply continues polluting the planet by purchasing carbon credits from indebted countries in the global South. Selling CO_2, to mitigate carbon emissions, is a neocolonial, class- and gender-biased practice that impacts on the ecology of poor countries, on their subsistence economies, and particularly on women.

Selling oxygen is transforming the rainforest, especially where forest farms have been established. Reforestation is promoted among large-scale agricultural entrepreneurs in association with international capital – which class benefits, in addition, from tax relief under Fiscal Forestry Incentives (FFI). FFI reforestation uses foreign forest species of high yield and great market acceptance, such as *melina* (used by the US corporation Stone Forestall), and *teak* (used by Bosques Puerto Carrillo and Maderas). Big projects related to the planting of agroforests are also connected to the interests of big mining corporations. For instance, in Arenal-Huetar Norte conservation area, Industries Infinito (a subsidiary of the Canadian company Vanessa Ventures) obtained permits to operate Mining Crucitas over an area of 1,000 hectares. The company also has a reforestation project of 32 hectares in the area where it planted 20,000 trees to profit from the Forestry Incentive plan. The corporations are allowed to cut the trees after ten years and transform them into wood for floors or paper.

Between 1996 and 2001, it is estimated that some 121,000 to 147,000 hectares of foreign trees were planted; 50 per cent of the species are melina and teak, and the rest, eucalyptus.[17] The government of Costa Rica enthusiastically converted the forest ecosystem into sterile monocultures by planting homogeneous forests, despite the fact that melina, teak, and eucalyptus are not indigenous to its ecosystem. This increases water run off, extraction of soil nutrients, and devastates the productive capacity of soil. Thus, chemical fertilisers are used massively, spread across the area targeted for the plantation. The government's choice to move into monoculture was clearly dictated by pressure from industry for floor wood and paper manufacturing opportunities. All this has had very negative effects on soil fertility, water retention, and biological diversity.

The crisis of gatherers and small farmers

Sonia Torres is a forestry engineer who has researched the consequences of planting teak. She explains how foreign trees produce erosion even on flat land. In the rainforest, biodiversity means that a great number of *leguminosae* with different sized leaves, lessen the impact of rainfall and prevent erosion. She uses the example of teak to illustrate the problem.

> Since the planting of these foreign species, I have observed that teak has a root system that grows deep into the soil, but in the rain forest the systems of nutrient and water absorption are at the surface. In general, nutrients and water are concentrated between 70 and 100 centimetres deep. As a result, teak trees are encircled by flaked soil. In addition, when it rains, the size of the leaf accumulates great amounts of water that then pours violently on to the soil. A drop of water, at a microscopic level, forms a crater; when water falls from 15 metres or more it forms holes. Water descending on soft soil destroys the soil. The far-reaching spread of the roots and the shade produced by the leaves obstruct the vegetative growth on the lower forest layer, which could prevent the soil damage from the violent cascades.[18]

Torres advocates the planting and protection of indigenous tree species that can also feed indigenous populations – from humans to animals to soil bacteria.

This state project of selling oxygen has transformed local communities in Costa Rica. And the expropriation of land from small and medium-sized landholders without compensation has been exposed by Elizabeth Odio:

A symbol of pride to Costa Ricans, the national parks constitute a unique model in the world, which offer innumerable benefits to society in particular and the planet in general, but they are in a critical situation due to the lack of resources to give them sustainability and cancel the debt to the former property owners whose lands were expropriated or frozen for the sake of protection.[19]

By August 1999, the government of Costa Rica owed US$100 million to the evicted *campesinos* and *campesinas*. Around that time, it offered to pay US$6,703 per hectare to the removed families.[20] However, by 2001, 14,917 hectares of land were still not paid for, affecting approximately 745 families made landless and impoverished by the conservation areas system.

In Costa Rica, large projects related to the planting of forests are often connected to international mining interests, to large environmental NGOs, and to government institutions. For instance, in the Arenal Conservation Area, organised by the World Wildlife Fund-Canada, parks such as Arenal Volcano and Tenorio Volcano National Park, and forestry reserves such as Cerro Chato, sell oxygen. But in order to put this oxygen on the market, the Arenal Volcano was declared Arenal Volcano National Park in 1994. From five hectares, the park was extended to 12,010 hectares. As a result, entire communities were forcibly evicted. While most of the land around the volcano was not arable or adequate for cattle ranching, small farmers had long existed in the area. *Campesinos* and *campesinas* who had organised their lives by clearing land for crops and pasture around the Arenal Basin were expelled by the Ministry of Environment and Energy. An injunction brought to the Costa Rica Supreme Court (Division IV of the judicial system), reported heavy losses by *campesinos* living in the Basin area of the Arenal Conservation Area. They lost land, pasture, houses, dairies, and roads. Former property owners are now hut renters (*ranchos*) or slum inhabitants (*tugurios*). Their personal effects such as cars and small electrical appliances were taken by the commercial banks when they could not afford to repay their loans acquired for economic development.[21] When, in desperation, some of them returned to their land to plant yucca, beans, maize and other subsistence foods, they were declared to have broken the law and many were thrown in jail.[22]

In 1996, La Cuenca de Aguas Claras was also declared a forestry reserve. In 2001, more than 200 farmers, men and women, came to be interviewed about their plight at a Town Hall meeting in La Cuenca de Aguas Claras. Since there were too many for face-to-face conversation, they chose Abel Fuentes and Luis Guimo to speak on their behalf, and they declared themselves witnesses to the following account. MINAE had told the community that it was their own

> ... survival way of life [that] is producing deforestation and pollution, and reducing the water level of La Cuenca de Aguas Claras. MINAE exaggerated the level of deforestation to oust almost all the inhabitants because it is reforesting our land in order to sell the oxygen to other countries and get 'donations'.[23]

MINAE's argument for expropriating their land was based on the claim of water reduction in the area. The message of 'water scarcity' is a strategy to convince *campesinos* to let MINAE take over reforestation while the owners of the land are evicted. Abel Fuentes gave evidence of the forced eviction of rainforest dwellers.

> Until 1996, in La Cuenca de Aguas Calientes, 200 families lived and the land was organised as follows: 70 per cent was pastureland, holding around 2,000 cows; 10 per cent primary forest; and 20 per cent combined secondary forest, which was used for beans and pig production. By 2001, we were only three families; the majority were forced into exile. And the land has been re-organised as follows: 90 per cent is primary and secondary forest; 10 per cent is pastureland with less than 200 cows; and land to produce beans extinguished.[24]

Fuentes believes that his rights and his community's rights have been violated with the 1995 law of expropriation. As soon as the law was passed, some of the *campesinos* went to MINAE's office to get more information about it, but were purposely misled by the government. Fuentes declared that:

> ... the government denied our right to know the law. When we requested a copy of it, a representative of MINAE showed us a giant book, saying that he couldn't give us a copy, because of the volume of the decree. However, later, one of our members found the legislation on the internet and printed it on just one page.[25]

Luis Guimo, also a smallholder who still lives within the expropriated land, added:

> When we ask MINAE officials for information, they decide when and where we can get it. When we propose a meeting, they decide when and where we can meet, then they change the hour, the date, or they cancel the meeting without telling us. Many of us live far from the meeting place and sometimes we have to ride a horse for three hours to go to a meeting and it is disappointing to arrive and learn that the meeting has been cancelled.[26]

The theft of forest from local communities who use it to sustain themselves has become a death sentence for small and medium-size landholders; their needs are dismissed by government and they are declared enemies of the rainforest.

Under global neoliberalism, the eviction of rainforest dwellers is justified by the ideology of 'progress' and the assumption that they will become 'developed' through employment in the cities. Conversely, rural people know that it is only industrial labour, professional and business classes, who find well-paid jobs and upward mobility in urban centres. *Campesinos* and indigenous forest dwellers know that there is a surplus of 'unskilled' – or more correctly 'autonomous' – workers in cities. They are like the *sans papier* immigrants of Europe, whose basic needs cannot be met by global capitalist patriarchal societies and whose human rights are routinely violated.[27] The ecofeminist Maria Mies argues that community members in the Third World dispossessed from their livelihood cannot expect to become dependent on wages. Peripheral humans, landless women and men, will not have the good fortune of their peers from the global North in finding a job and sharing the wealth extracted from colonies.[28] For the truth of the matter is that they themselves are the colonies.

The crisis of women and children

The power of the industrial world to redesign rainforest areas as 'oxygen generating machines' seriously exacerbates global social inequalities. As a new structure of international capitalist accumulation emerges, the disintegration of the ecosystem that supported local subsistence communities has powerful effects on the sexual division of labour and on women's oppression in the global South. In Costa Rica, when rural families are violently displaced and impoverished, their women are encouraged to migrate to San José and to tourist areas in the hope of earning an income for themselves and dispossessed families through the cash economy. In the first instance – and often the last – these impoverished women earn all or part of their living as prostitutes. Prostitutes in Costa Rica are women at work supporting children and other loved ones. They are 'in the market' not by choice but out of necessity. According to Casa Alianza, a US non-profit organisation for homeless children and kids at risk, along with these women, an astonishing number of children are bought, sold, and generally abused.[29] By complying with the desires of men from the so-called developed world, they all contribute to the global tourism industry, to the wealth of businessmen, and to state coffers.

Indebted Costa Rica, under pressure from the World Bank and International Monetary Fund (IMF), has become a primary eco-tourism and sex-tourism destination since the early 1990s.[30] Eco-tourism links conservation areas with tourist spectacles, and promises a world of leisure, freedom, taste, and safe risk. At the same time, sex-tourism portrays an image of women's and children's bodies as simple, pure, exotic, and erotic. This image of Costa Rica entangles two aspects of contemporary capitalist patriarchal economics: the domination of creditors (industrial centres) over debtors (rural periphery) and the parallel domination of 'masculation' over compliant women's bodies.[31] As Costa Rica is impoverished by foreign debt, the mark of international power relations is stamped on the bodies of its women and children.[32] White men of all classes cross borders for racialised sex tourism. Sex tourists, usually men in their 40s and 50s, come mainly from creditor countries, such as Europe, the US, and Canada. Likewise, most of the pimps who profit from the organisation of sex-tourism are men from the global North. They bring with them an alien political economy and culture, material relations and perceptions of how the world works.[33] On the internet, there are more than 70 websites selling Costa Rican women. They are commercially constructed as a 'body-for-others', objects of desire, bodies for men's use.

Between 1992 and 1996, 313,525 Canadians visited Costa Rica. In 1997 alone, 36,032 Canadians visited, while by 2002 this number had increased to 50,000. A CBC report made it quite clear the extent to which Canadian men engage in sex-tourism. These men can be found at the El Rey hotel in San José, where secret videos for sex and teenagers are waiting to be bought and women are sold for $10–20.[34] In San José alone 2,000 girls are working in the sex trade, and trafficking is a growing problem.[35] Many teenagers sold into the sex industry in Costa Rica are victims of traffickers from Nicaragua, Guatemala, and Honduras. These criminal traffickers threaten to kill the girl's parents and siblings if they are identified. The 'wealth' generated by these women goes to the IMF and the World Bank as interest payment on Costa Rica's outstanding foreign debt.

As Costa Rica slides into a subordinate position internationally, the entire country is humiliated. It becomes a paradise for paedophilia. Men interested in young girls, gay male tourists (and so-called straight tourists wanting experiences with boys) come to engage in sex with or take pornographic pictures of children. Child pornography is an established industry in Costa Rica.

In San José alone there are more than 300 brothels with an average of 10 women and children working in each. This would suggest that some 3000 women and girls are formally employed as prostitutes in a city of 278,373 people. 1.1 per cent of the city's entire population is prostituted ...[36]

Women and children involved in sex work commonly contract sexually transmitted diseases or die of AIDS-related illness.[37]

By 2001, Casa Alianza and other international groups put the Costa Rican government under intense scrutiny for lack of action against the sexual abusers of children, most of them tourists. In an economy increasingly based on enclosure and resourcing of the natural and human commons, governments do not want to stop the sex trade because they know that this is the only way for women and children to earn a living. The official attitude is one of general indifference to reports of this criminal activity. In 2001, ex-president of Costa Rica, Miguel Angel Rodriguez said on CBC's *20/20 Report* that there were 'only 20 or 30' children being sexually exploited in Costa Rica, even though the US Department of State estimated 3,000 children as victims of commercial sexual exploitation in Costa Rica.[38] The government also protects the sex industry because, as noted above, it generates hundreds of millions of dollars per year to help pay off its foreign debt.

Although prostitution is prohibited in Costa Rica by law, there is no enforcement of the law to stop abuse and disposal of the bodies of poor and marginalised members of society. To dull the misery of sexual activity with five or six men daily, many enslaved women and children turn to drugs and alcohol. In 2001, three young street girls went missing and were eventually found cut into pieces and strewn around San José.[39] No one was charged with the crime. By 2001, there were only four US citizens and one Costa Rican in jail awaiting trial for the sexual exploitation of children, despite 230 criminal complaints to Casa Alianza.[40] The police are part of the problem. On 10 August 1999, the Costa Rican Special Prosecutor Against Sex Crimes received a judge's order to raid The Green Door, a private club operated by a US citizen offering female escorts and minors for sex to visiting businessmen and foreign residents. With assistance from the Minister of Public Security, Rogelio Ramos, the US criminal escaped.[41] Further, as the CBC programme reported, when young girls are arrested, the victims are personally punished by police demands for oral sex.

In Costa Rica, women are also sex tourists. Some lonely US, Canadian, and European women likewise take advantage of their class and race status to lure needy locals into intimacy. Young boys and men engage in 'romance tourism' with these women, usually well-off, single, professionals who travel to resort areas and may provide a willing man with drinks, dinners, shopping sprees, jewellery, and other luxury goods in exchange for sex and companionship. In this criminal environment, women can be as exploitative as men are, but women can also be endangered by these 'romantic companions'.[42]

Resisting narrow environmentalism

The definition of rainforests as oxygen generators destroys sustainable ways of living and creates poverty by expropriating or diminishing the capacities of the forest to sustain its dwellers. In Costa Rica, *campesinos* know that their human rights have been violated by MINAE and organisations that call themselves environmentalist. As Luis Guimo said:

> They used to come to us for information, and we provided it. I personally boarded people and allowed them to use my horses to move about comfortably. Things are changing, we cannot collaborate anymore. MINAE told me that I have to sell my *finca* to the state and at the price the state decides. We are not leaving. They have to kill us if they want our land.[43]

The enclosure of Costa Rican rainforest for global capital accumulation, has condemned rural families, especially vulnerable women and children to destitution. Ironically, Costa Rica as a country stands in much the same situation as its prostitutes – kept in financial debt by pimps, in this case, the World Bank and IMF, mining firms and environmental NGOs. But neither the nation nor its women can earn enough to pay off debts and regain autonomy.

In spite of all this, Costa Rican women and men are fighting back and defending their rights to a secure livelihood. They are exposing the fallacy of a 'sustainable development' that does not acknowledge its class, gender, imperialist, and neocolonial roots. They are bringing pressure to bear on governments, investors, academics, and environmentalists. International women activists, in particular, are joining their Costa Rican sisters in this struggle for a just and healthy world – for as they say: 'No blank cheque to the Kyoto Protocol!' The ecology, women's, workers, and indigenous, movements should support the Kyoto Protocol only if it is committed to imposing limits on carbon emissions produced by the lifestyle of the global North. The Framework Convention or other strategies for the reduction of global warming cannot be endorsed if they depend on expropriating the subsistence economies of others.

Notes

1. The discourse of neoliberal environmentalism gained currency at the Rio Earth Summit in 1992. For a manifesto see: Stephan Scmidheiny (ed.), *Changing Course: A Global Business Perspective on Development and the Environment.* Cambridge, MA: MIT Press, 1992.
2. For fundamentals of physical geography see, Online Available HTTP: <www.physicalgeography.net/fundamentals/9r.html> (accessed 15 June 2006). For fundamentals of climate change see the Pew Center Report, Online Available HTTP: <www.pewclimate.org/global-warming-basics> (accessed 15 June 2006).
3. World Bank, 'Measuring the Wealth of Nations' in *Expanding the Measure of Wealth: Indicators of Environmentally Sustainable Development*, Washington, DC: World Bank ESD Studies Monographs Series, 1997, No. 17, 19–39.
4. Genevieve Vaughan (ed.), *The Gift: Il Dono: A Feminist Analysis*, Rome: Meltemi Press, 2004, p. 17.
5. John Bellamy Foster, 'The Ecological Crisis and Ecological Conditions before the Industrial Revolution' in *The Vulnerable Planet: A Short Economic History of the Environment*, New York: Monthly Review Press, 1994. Foster does not integrate the gender aspect of these processes: see Ariel Salleh, 'Sustaining Nature or Sustaining Marx? An Ecofeminist Response to Foster and Burkett', *Organization & Environment*, 2001, Vol. 14, No. 4, 443–50.

6. Susana Hecht and Alexander Cockburn, *The Fate of the Forest: Developers, Destroyers and Defenders of the Amazon*, New York: Penguin, 1990.

7. Herman Daly, *Beyond Growth: The Economics of Sustainable Development*, Boston: Beacon, 1996; Mathis Wackernagel and William Rees, *Our Ecological Footprint: Reducing Human Impact on the Earth*, Philadelphia: New Society, 1996.

8. Elmar Alvater, 'Ecological and Economic Modalities of Time and Space' in M. O'Connor (ed.), *Is Capitalism Sustainable? Political Economy and the Politics of Ecology*, New York: Guilford, 1994.

9. Wolfgang Sachs, *The Development Dictionary: A Guide to Knowledge as Power*, London: Zed Books, 1992; Vandana Shiva, *Staying Alive: Women, Ecology and Development*, London: Zed Books, 1989; Veronika Bennholdt-Thomsen and Maria Mies, *The Subsistence Perspective*, London: Zed Books, 1999; Vaughan, *The Gift: Il Dono*.

10. Vaughan, *The Gift: Il Dono*; see also discussion of the Marxian concept of 'surplus value' in Maria Mies, Veronika Bennholdt-Thomsen, and Claudia von Werlhof, *Women: The Last Colony*, London: Zed Books, 1988.

11. Ramachandra Guha and Joan Martinez-Alier, 'Poverty and the Environment: A Critique of Conventional Wisdom' in *Varieties of Environmentalism: Essays North and South*, Oxford University Press, 1998.

12. Government of Cosa Rica, *El Estado de la Nacion en Desarrollo Humano Sostenible*, San José: Imprenta Editorama, 1997.

13. Hecht and Cockburn, *The Fate of the Forest*.

14. Ana Isla, 'A Struggle for Clean Water and Livelihood: Canadian Mining in Costa Rica in the Era of Globalization', *Canadian Women's Studies*, 2002, Vol. 21/22, No. 4, 148–54; Ana Isla, 'Conservation as Enclosure: An Eco-feminist Perspective on Sustainable Development and Biopiracy in Costa Rica', *Capitalism Nature Socialism*, 2005, Vol. 16, No. 3, 49–61; Ana Isla, 'The Tragedy of Enclosure: An Ecofeminist Perspective on Eco-Tourism in Costa Rica', Women's Studies Paper Series, Brock University, St Catharines, Ontario, 2005.

15. For the Clean Development Fund (CDM), Online Available HTTP: <www.unfccc.int/kyoto_protocol/mechanisms/clean_development_ mechanism/items/2718.php> (accessed 14 February 2007).

16. Govt. of Cosa Rica, *El Estado de la Nacion*, p. 129.

17. Ministry of Environment and Energy (MINAE), *Plan Nacional de Desarrollo Forestal 2001–2010*, San José: Government Printer; Ronnie De Camino, O. Segura, L. Arias, and I. Pérez, 'Forest Policy

and the Evolution of Land Use: An Evaluation of Costa Rica's Forest Development and World Bank Assistance', 1999, Online Available HTTP: <www.wrm.org.uy/english/tropical_forest/WorldBank.html> (accessed 14 February 2007).

18. Sonia Torres, Coordinadora Frente Nacional de Oposicion a la Mineria, interview with the author, July 2001.

19. Elizabeth Odio, 'Modelo Unico en el Mundo', *Al Dia*, 24 August 2001, p. 2.

20. Irene Vizcaino, 'Deuda Millonaria por Las Expropiaciones', *La Nación*, 29 August 1999, p. 6a.

21. Yehudi Monestel Arce, 'Campesinos Precaristas en su Propia Tierra', *Eco Catolico*, 17 January 1999, p. 11.

22. *Siete Dias de Teletica*, Newscast, 19 January 1999.

23. Luis Guimo, interview with the author, July 2001.

24. Abel Fuentes, interview with the author, July 2001.

25. Ibid.

26. Guimo, interview.

27. William Robinson, *Transnational Conflicts: Central America, Social Change, and Globalization*, London: Verso, 2003; Bennholdt-Thomsen and Mies, *The Subsistence Perspective*.

28. Maria Mies, *Patriarchy and Accumulation on a World Scale*, London: Zed Books, 1986.

29. Casa Alianza, Media Release: 'Man Charged in Costa Rica for "Dishonest Abuse" of Children', 9 January 2001, Online Available HTTP: <www.casa-alianza.org.uk> (accessed 15 June 2006).

30. Isla, 'The Tragedy of Enclosure'; see also 'Dream Getaway: Fantasy Resort Adult Vacations', 2005, Online Available HTTP: <www.1dreamgetaway.com/packages.htm> (accessed 15 June 2005).

31. Vaughan, *The Gift: Il Dono*.

32. Jackie Roddick, *The Dance of the Millions: Latin America and the Debt Crisis*, London: Latin America Bureau, 1988.

33. Jan Pettman, 'Body Politics: International Sex Tourism', *Third World Quarterly*, 1997, Vol. 18, No. 1, 93–108, p. 96.

34. Victor Malarek, 'Prostitution in Costa Rica', *20/20 Report*, Canadian Broadcasting Corporation, 17 February 2004.

35. Casa Alianza, 'Man Charged in Costa Rica'.

36. Global March Against Child Labor – Information on Costa Rica, 2006, Online Available HTTP: <www.globalmarch.org/resource-centre/world/costa%20rica.pdf> (accessed 1 June 2007).

37. Casa Alianza, Media Release: 'Third Street Girl Goes Missing in Costa Rica', 14 March 2001, Online Available HTTP: <www.casa-alianza.org.uk> (accessed 15 June 2006.

38. Malarek, 'Prostitution in Costa Rica'.
39. Casa Alianza, 'Third Street Girl Goes Missing in Costa Rica'.
40. Casa Alianza, 'Man Charged in Costa Rica'.
41. Casa Alianza, Media Release: 'Costa Rica Policeman Convicted for Helping Child Pimp Escape', 31 January 2001, Online Available HTTP: <www.casa-alianza.org.uk> (accessed 15 June 2006).
42. Jacqueline Sanchez Taylor, 'Tourism and "Embodied" Commodities: Sex Tourism in the Caribbean' in Stephen Clift and Simon Carter (eds), *Tourism and Sex: Culture, Commerce and Coercion*, London: Pinter, 2000.
43. Guimo, interview.

12

HOW GLOBAL WARMING IS GENDERED
A View From the EU

Meike Spitzner

The situation regarding CO_2 emissions in industrialised countries is well known: CO_2 emissions are far too high and must be reduced dramatically. The level of 21 t/a (tons per annum) of CO_2 emissions emitted per capita in the US is undoubtedly too much, but so is the 10 t/a per capita in Germany.[1] While there is a rapid increase of energy consumption in regions of the global South, such as China and India, the actual *production* of climate problems today is overwhelmingly an effect of decisions and actions taken in the global North. The EU categorises its emission sources as:

- Power generation 35 per cent
- Energy branch 5 per cent
- Industry 13 per cent
- Tertiary sector 7 per cent
- Transport 27 per cent
- Residential energy consumption 13 per cent.[2]

As these figures suggest, global warming is not only predominantly brought about by the global North, it is overwhelmingly an effect of decisions and actions, made by men occupying positions in institutions set up and staffed by men.

Common but differentiated responsibilities?

Now surveys show that women and men perceive social and environmental risks differently. Women's higher sensitivity to risk, to social and environmental qualities, and their competencies in caring labour, lead them to view market-based international climate policies less positively than men. Fewer women than men believe that technology can solve environmental problems as long as a resource heavy consumerist economy is maintained. More women than men reject the use of nuclear power.[3] In addition to renewable energy sources and energy saving, women in Europe are also demanding sustainable public transport and decentralised social infrastructures.[4]

Despite a relative lack of technological knowledge among most women, research shows that women in general are more able than most men to recognise the urgency of global warming and to adjust their personal energy consumption, for instance by changing shopping habits.[5] On the other hand, sociological data from Europe suggests that many men appear to identify culturally with high-powered technologies.[6] Trips taken by men are overwhelmingly by car; tend to be single purpose and longer distance journeys; a lower awareness of the environmental costs of transport can be assumed here. But there is also a gender specific difference in free time due to social pressures on women to serve the daily demands of dependants. In Europe, many more women than men travel by public transport, or even travel on foot. Car use by women generally involves multiple short drives and meets several purposes on the one trip. Women's mobility as measured by motorised kilometres per capita is far less than men's but women's daily movement activity in multi-tasking is significantly greater.[7]

However, neoliberal policy changes have the effect of forcing more women to use private vehicles. The withdrawal of expenditure on public transport infrastructure affects the availability of trams for children and the elderly, and provision of adequate footpaths for baby prams. There is a decline in government support for schools, hospitals, and other care facilities, such that these become 'thinner on the ground' requiring care givers to travel further to access them. The contraction of social welfare benefits to widows and divorced wives, single mothers, and disability carers means more women must look for work. This in turn satisfies the neoliberal trend to an informal, flexibilised, part time labour force. Women's daily routines are characterised by multi-tasking and 'spatio-temporal scatter' across fewer and fewer social resources, so testing their capacity for integration and time management. Women's traditional unpaid labour in the reproductive sector, is now matched by new commitments in the productive sector. Their unpaid time spent moving between one labour activity to another, adds to their exploitation by the patriarchal economy. This invisible extraction of unpaid time from women is a form of surplus value, which further benefits capital accumulation.

Women in the global South have been quick to point out how *impacts* of climate change will be gender specific; but attention to gender and the *production* of climate change came late to the debate. Now it is women in the North, who are taking initiatives and focusing on the 'malestream' obsession with end-of-pipe solutions. Women's socially learned multi-tasking means they can be highly effective organisers and citizen activists on questions of transport, environment, energy, peace, and health. For two decades, European women have been linking gender justice and environmental sustainability, through research into transport science, economics, policy planning, and development studies.[8] At the same time, networks for social change have emerged, such as the Women's Working Group in the Forum on Environment and Development, ENERGIA, GENANET, LIFE, and WECF. Meeting in Milan in 2004, some of these NGOs formed a Gender and Climate Change Network.[9]

Clearly, international climate policy should rest on gender sensitive measures, but at this stage, the agreements that constitute the emerging international management regime – the United Nations Climate Change Convention and the Kyoto Protocol – make no reference to international agreements on social justice and the empowerment of women. Decisions adopted at annual Conferences of the Parties (COP) reveal activities and regulations in this policy arena to be designed in a totally 'man-made' way.[10] This androcentrism is no surprise, for women are under-represented in all relevant political and economic decision-making bodies – local, national, and international. The same kind of political exclusion affects the UN Framework Convention on Climate Change. At the first Conference of the Parties – COP1 in Berlin, 1995 – a large women's conference, 'Solidarity in the Greenhouse', was organised as a side event. Two hundred and fifty women came from all over the world, calling for effective climate protection. But the following COPs had no participating women's organisations. Worse than this, five years later, at COP6 in Den Haag, a side event on women and climate change was marginalised.[11]

From procedural to substantive change

Over 15 years of international climate negotiations, only one resolution has dealt with gender asymmetry, and that focuses on participation procedures and not on the substantive socio-economics of gender and climate change. Adopted at COP7 in Marrakesh 2001, on the initiative of the then Moroccan President of COP, this resolution invited 'Parties to give active consideration to the nomination of women for elective posts in any body under the Convention or the Kyoto Protocol' and it requested 'the Secretariat to maintain information on the gender composition of each body ... and to bring this information to the attention of the Parties whenever ... a vacancy occurs'.[12] The Secretariat now runs this resolution on each COP agenda. And in addition, a spreadsheet showing the gender composition of UNFCCC bodies goes to the COP President and negotiators in advance of elections. A reminder leaflet in negotiators' mailboxes appears to be the main initiative towards the engendering of climate policy.

This is not the kind of policy action envisioned in the 1992 Rio Declaration of the World Summit on Environment and Development. Nor does it reflect the vision of the Beijing Declaration and Platform of Action (BPA) at the Fourth World Conference on Women in 1995. The latter calls explicitly for a paradigm change in designing policies and measures to control global warming. It calls for action on the 'international consensus' that sustainable development cannot be realised in the absence of gender justice. The BPA also advises governments and agencies to implement the following instruments:

- gender analysis of all programmes, measures, and actions;
- gender budgeting in all respective areas;
- generation of knowledge on the structural linkage of gender and environmental sustainability;
- full participation of women in decision-making processes;
- securing women's access to power and resources (empowerment).[13]

The principle of 'common but differentiated responsibilities', incorporated into the 1987 Montreal Protocol, is one of the three key principles (along with the precautionary principle and the principle of sustainable development) in the Climate Change Convention (Article 3). However, this principle of 'difference' applies only to nation states.[14] A dual standard of responsibility for so called developed and developing countries is established by the Convention, but there is no parallel application of the principle of difference in relation to gender inequality: that is, to gender and the production of global warming or to gender and the response to global warming. Thus while it is argued that 'industrialised countries' have been the leading cause of climate change, have greater financial and technological resources for responding to the problem, and consequently, must shoulder most of the burden, there is no analogous reasoning in relation to the asymmetry of gender power and responsibilities.

It is not only politicians who ignore gender issues in climate policy, but academics, and NGOs do as well. For this reason, there are few resources available for research and knowledge generation; few facilities for gender competent debate; and few established lobbying networks globally speaking. The result is man-focused or androcentric data, androcentric concepts, androcentric policy, and androcentric regulatory instruments.

A first step in transforming this state of affairs is to ensure that policy data in all fields is gender disaggregated, generated by gender sensitive methods and categories, and analysed along gender lines. For example, systematic data on the gender ascribed caring economy would demonstrate its lower climate change impact. Conversely, it would show clearly the high impact of the market driven economy, and the high impact of specific leisure activities that are preferred by men. Gender competent studies would demonstrate how global warming is likely to entrench, if not exacerbate, existing gender and class inequalities.[15] In developing countries, environmental degradation caused by climate change will affect poor women disproportionately, since as a gendered reproductive labour force, they are primary, hands-on, natural resource users. In nearly all non-industrial societies, where development and urbanisation have occurred, women carry responsibility for managing the natural resource base of the subsistence economy. Women worldwide have almost exclusive responsibility for the care of other humans. As climate change sets in train harsh conditions and new scarcities threaten vulnerable groups, women's unfairly large (unpaid economic) workload will increase. As things stand, 70 per cent of the world's poor are women, mostly unsupported mothers and elderly, lacking any social and economic capacity to adapt to unanticipated environmental impacts.

The failure of the UN Framework Convention on Climate Change to assess gendered impacts of climate change is one thing; the lack of gender analysis of the production of climate change, is another. Government planning for transport infrastructure, for instance, remains oriented to the private car and, as such, prioritises men's interests, values, and economic capacities. What pass for 'scientific' mobility methodologies, infrastructure, and transport policies, actually end up justifying rather than mitigating, climate-damaging transport volume. This gender skewed policy results in costs to public space and higher expenditures for households. Again, the poor – disproportionately women, children, youth, and the elderly – are inconvenienced, even endangered by inadequate public transport provision. Yet, it is their public transport usage that is less environmentally problematic.[16]

A gender lens is essential in steering sound political responses to global warming and in negotiating mitigation practices that do not simply displace the burdens of social change on to already vulnerable groupings. For instance, instruments like the Clean Development Mechanism (CDM) of the Kyoto Protocol could be used proactively to promote gender equality and empowerment by facilitating women's access to renewable energy technologies.[17] Usually however, technological innovation does not enact distributive justice, but follows the established social hierarchy of gender and class by directing profits towards middle-class men and leaving women with traditional 'clean up' roles. In short: the dominant debate on so-called 'common' climate policy is nonsensical. Rational dialogue is undercut by the dominant social norms of competitive masculinity, with its attendant over-valuation of technologies, markets, and large-scale projects. Most European researchers and policy makers avoid the simple question of: Who emits and why? Rather the focus is on developing countries, self-servingly understood as 'under-technologised' and needing further capital investment. The economic North is not given to reflection on the direct relation between global warming and its own complicity in globalising industrial productivism. If the Third World or women are appraised at all, it is as victims, not as 'alternative consumers' or 'non-polluting producers'.

A chance for gender post 2012?

Despite this negative assessment, there has been a modest reorientation of the climate regime in the direction of gender justice and sustainability. At COP8 in Delhi 2002, the ENERGIA group, in cooperation with UNDP, organised a big public event on gender and energy. At COP9 in Milan 2003, ENERGIA and LIFE/ GENANET, called an informal meeting drawing in 30 people. Also in Milan, the Swedish Environment Minister Lena Sommestad, on behalf of the Women Environmental Ministers Network, introduced a focus on gender and energy in the global South. These activities marked a new starting point for networking and closer cooperation. A website was set up to prepare for the COP10 in Buenos Aires 2004, the themes were: adaptation and mitigation from a gender perspective.[18] At COP11 / COP-MOP1 in Montreal 2005, a Research Workshop was organised by GENANET with the aim of elaborating a research agenda, to be part of the Four Assessment Reports of the Intergovernmental Panel on Climate

Change (IPCC).[19] A first strategy workshop series was set up to discuss how the Post Kyoto Regime beyond 2012 could be engendered; climate talks with ministers took place; and a gender statement went to the COP11 plenum.

The 2005 negotiations entered a new phase, concerned with developing the Kyoto Protocol beyond the commitment period of 2008–12. It opened up an opportunity for women to influence agenda-setting negotiations at an early stage, with a view to modifying the Protocol's conceptual framework and instruments. The Gender and Climate Network published a position paper, emphasising the most relevant actions to be undertaken.[20] A special publication of GENANET, the German Federal Government's Focal Point on Gender Justice and Sustainability, outlined the basics of a gender competent climate policy. To paraphrase:

- All climate-protection measures, programmes, and instruments must be submitted to a *gender analysis*.
- *Women* must be involved at all levels of negotiation; not through representation based on numbers, but by *ensuring the participation of gender experts* in energy, transport, agriculture etc.
- The gender perspective must be *universally* integrated by *mainstreaming* in negotiations and in the formulation of climate-protection policy at *national and international* levels, in *the South and in the North*.
- Policies and programmes must recognise gender as a structural hierarchy and take into account the differing *situations* of women and men – their different needs, opportunities, priorities and goals.
- All problems must be analysed for *gender-problematic dimensions* and in a *gender-differentiated way*. New guidelines should elicit gender-sensitive national reporting schemes for the Climate Change Convention. It is precisely in the North that this data is lacking.
- Gaps in the knowledge of links between gender and climate protection must be closed by *designing and financing relevant research* projects.

- A monitoring system is needed at national and international levels to *ensure universal integration of the gender perspective* and where necessary, to call for its implementation.[21]

At COP12/COP-MOP2 in Nairobi, 2006, women ran a continuous caucus to focus their lobbying.[22] Statistics were calculated on the gender composition of delegations. LIFE organised a side event on gender and climate protection, as well as providing information desks, and again a gender statement went to the plenum. At COP12 the integration of women was 33 per cent of the UN Secretariat Units and Bodies; 27 per cent of the Non-governmental Organisations (all observers); 25 per cent of Intergovernmental Organisations; 15 per cent of the Parties; and 0 per cent of observer nations (three men).[23] The number of substantive adjustments of climate policy towards gender balance or even references to gender within COP12 decisions was zero.

Meanwhile the corporate sector, directed largely by be-suited men in the global North and their followers in the global South, spends billions in public moneys on 'cooperation' and on public relations, mystifying politicians and communities alike as to the science of climate change. Profit-making 'win/win' solutions to global warming are promoted – carbon trading, sequestration, nuclear power – at once confusing the UN Framework negotiations and undermining serious national efforts at mitigation.[24] Moreover, such proposals leave intact the highly problematic productivist economy and consumer lifestyle of the global North, increasingly emulated by the global South. These so called win/win alternatives generate new unknown risks to be carried by the public at large, they are regulation intensive, transport heavy, and environmentally destructive. Most importantly, they take no account of the priorities of women as managers of everyday life. The struggle continues[25] ... although to achieve a truly 'multilateral' climate policy, women citizens need funds for participation in climate change negotiations, funds to prepare for meetings, funds to elaborate and document opinions. Here it seems they are entrapped in the circularity of androcentric reasoning. For if governments and agencies do not *gender disaggregate statistics* on climate change, how can they be convinced that global warming is gendered in both causes and effects?

Notes

1. See Ulrike Roehr and Meike Spitzner, 'Global Environmental Change and Gender', paper presented to the UNEP Global Women's Assembly on Environment: Women as the Voice for the Environment – WAVE, Nairobi, 2004. Roehr has pioneered this field.

2. Leonidas Mantzos and Pantelis Capros, *European Energy and Transport: Trends to 2030 – update 2005*, Institute of Communication and Computer Systems, National Technical University of Athens, commissioned by EC, Brussels, 2006, Online Available HTTP: <www.ec.europa.eu/dgs/energy_transport/ figures/trends_2030_update_2005/index_en.htm> (accessed 31 May 2007).

3. Ulrike Roehr and LIFE e.V *FrauenUmweltNetz*, 'Gender and Energy in the North', Expert Workshop on Gender Perspectives for Earth Summit 2002, hosted by the German Federal Ministry for Environment and Heinrich Boell Foundation, 2001, Online Available HTTP: <www.earthsummit2002.org/workshop/Genderper cent20&per cent20Energyper cent20Nper cent20UR.pdf> (accessed 10 May 2007).

4. Meike Spitzner, 'Women at the Crossroads with Transportation, the Environment and the Economy: Experiences and Challenges in Germany', *Women & Environments International Magazine*, No. 70/71, 31–4.

5. Roehr and LIFE, 'Gender and Energy in the North'.

6. Meike Spitzner, *Transformation and Privatisation of Netbound Infrastructures and Gender*, Berlin: Deutsches Institut für Urbanistik, Networks Paper, 2004, No. 13, Online Available HTTP: <www. networks-group.de/veroeffentlichungen/DF9369.pdf> (accessed 10 May 2007).

7. European Parliament, *Women and Transport in Europe*, Brussels, 2006, prepared by Jeff Turner, Kerry Hamilton (UEL), and Meike Spitzner (Wuppertal), with Leo Seserko (OKAR/Slovenia) and Alena Krizkova (Czech Republic), Online Available HTTP: <www.europarl. europa.eu/EST/download.do?file=9558> (accessed 10 May 2007).

8. For an early overview: Meike Spitzner and Ute Beik, 'Reproduktionsarbeits-Mobilitat' in Meike Spitzner et al. (eds), *Entwicklung der Arbeits und Freizeitmobilitat*, Wuppertal Institute, 1995, Vol. 5, 40–140. See also: Christa Wichterich, 'Die Erde Bemuttern: Frauen und Okologie nach dem Gipfel in Rio', Koln: Schriftensreihe der Heinrich Boll Stiftung, 1992, Vol. 16.

9. The NGOs include: Women's Working Group in the Forum on Environment and Development, Online Available HTTP: <www.forum-ue.de/47.0.html>; Global Network on Gender and Sustainable Energy (ENERGIA), Online Available HTTP: <www.energia.org/>; Focal Point on Gender Justice and Sustainability (GENANET), Online Available HTTP: <www.genanet.de/leitstelle.html?&L=1>; Women's Environment Network (LIFE), Online Available HTTP: <www.life-online.de/index.html>; Women in Europe for a Common Future (WECF), Online Available HTTP: <www.wecf.org/>. For the new Gender and Climate Change Network (GENDERCC), Online Available HTTP: <www.gendercc.net> (all sites accessed 8 March 2008).

10. Minu Hemmati, 'Gender and Climate Change in the North: Issues, Entry Points and Strategies for the Post-2012 Process', commissioned by GENANET, Frankfurt, 2005.

11. Ulrike Roehr, 'Gender Relations in International Climate Change Negotiations', Updated 2006, Online Available HTTP: <www.genanet.de/klimaschutz.html?&L=1> (accessed 8 March 2008).

12. For COP7 Marrakesh Decisions – FCCC/CP/2001/13/add.4 and FCCC/CP/2001/L.22, see *Earth Negotiations Bulletin*, 2001, Vol. 12, No. 189, Online Available HTTP: <www.iisd.ca/vol12/enb12189e.html> (accessed 10 May 2007).

13. UN, *The Official Report of the United Nations Fourth World Conference on Women, Beijing Declaration and Platform of Action*, 1995, Online Available HTTP: <www.un.org/womenwatch/daw/beijing/index.html> (accessed 10 May 2007).

14. The principle of 'common but differentiated responsibilities' is supported by developing countries and recognised by the UN General Assembly, the UNCED Preparatory Committee, Second World Climate Conference, Toronto Conference Statement, Hague Declaration, and Noordwijk Declaration. It is reflected in Principle 7 of the 1992 Rio Declaration and became part of Article 3 of the UN Framework Convention on Climate Change in 1994, Online Available HTTP: <www.unfccc.int/resource/docs/convkp/conveng.pdf> (accessed 10 May 2007).

15. See Elizabeth Cecelski and Joy Clancy, 'Why Women and Energy?', ENERGIA, Gender Perspectives on Energy for CSD-9, 2001, Online Available HTTP: <www.energia.org/pubs/papers/csd9pospaper.pdf> (accessed 10 May 2007). On the negative gender impacts of emissions trading, see: Ulrike Roehr, Irmgard Schultz, Gudrun Seltmann, and Immanuel Stiess, 'Klimapolitik und Gender – Eine Sondierung möglicher Gender Impacts des Europäischen Emissionshandelssystems', JET-SET Arbeitspapier, 2005, No. II/05, Online

Available HTTP: <www.wupperinst.org/uploads/tx_wibeitrag/gender.pdf> (accessed 10 May 2007).

16. The European Parliament transport study in 2006 (see note 7 above) set out to rectify this.

17. Margaret Skutsch, 'CDM and LULUCF: What's in It for Women?', Gender and Climate Change Network, Netherlands, 2004, Online Available HTTP: <www.gencc.interconnection.org/skutsch2004.pdf> (accessed 9 June 2007).

18. Roehr, 'Gender Relations in International Climate Change Negotiations'.

19. GENANET, 'Global Gender and Climate Change Research Workshop: What do we know? What do we need to find out?', 2005, Online Available HTTP: <www.genanet.de> (accessed 10 May 2007).

20. GENANET and WECF, 'Gender and Climate Change. Input from Women to Governments, preparing their Submissions Regarding Article 3.9 – Consideration of Commitments for Subsequent Periods for Annex I Parties of the Kyoto Protocol', 2005, Online Available HTTP: <www.genanet.de/fileadmin/downloads/themen/g_cc_article3.9.pdf> (accessed 3 June 2007).

21. GENANET, 'A Healthy Climate? Gender Justice and Climate Protection', 2005, Online Available HTTP: <www.genanet.de/fileadmin/downloads/themen/Healthy_climate_english.pdf> (accessed 20 June 2006).

22. GENANET, 'Women's Caucus at COP12 / COP-MOP2', 2005, Online Available HTTP: <www.genanet.de/fileadmin/downloads/themen/Themen_en/Womens_caucus__lobbying__points_14Nov.doc> (accessed 10 May 2007).

23. Updates on women in the UNFCCC process, Online Available HTTP: <www.genanet.de/unfccc.html?&L=1> (accessed 1 June 2007).

24. Intergovernmental Panel on Climate Change Report on Carbon Sequestration, Online Available HTTP: <www.arch.rivm.nl/env/int/ipcc/pages_media/SRCCS-final/IPCCSpecialReportonCarbondioxideCaptureandStorage.htm> (accessed 20 May 2007). For a critical perspective: Rie Watanabe et al., 'The Impacts of Carbon Capture and Storage (CCS) as Clean Development Project Activities on Long Term Targets', forthcoming. The proposal for parallel tracks in climate policy is the subject of ongoing research at the Wuppertal Institute.

25. See Minu Hemmati and Ulrike Roehr, 'A Huge Challenge and a Narrow Discourse: Ain't No Space for Gender in Climate Change Policy?', *Women & Environments International Magazine*, 2007, No. 74/75, 5–9.

13

WOMEN AND THE ABUJA DECLARATION FOR ENERGY SOVEREIGNTY

Leigh Brownhill and Terisa E. Turner

I repeat that we all stand before history. My colleagues and I are not the only ones on trial. Shell's day will surely come for there is no doubt in my mind that the ecological war that the Company has waged in the Delta will be called to question and the crimes of that war be duly punished.

Ken Saro-Wiwa, on being sentenced to hang,
Port Harcourt, Nigeria, 1995

Climate change and global warming are gaining unprecedented public attention, with accelerating frequencies of extreme weather events and new findings on dangerous emissions of carbon dioxide, and other gases that trap the sun's heat, increasing the temperature of the earth's atmosphere. The climate change deniers, paid by major oil companies, are in retreat.[1] In their wake, come advocates of various solutions to global warming: neoliberals who recommend 'free' markets and 'advanced' technologies as solutions; and Leftists who recommend shifting to an entirely new political economy; both address gender, but in different ways. In this chapter, we extend a Left perspective on energy use and global warming, one that is both gendered and rooted in the global South. Our position draws on 'the subsistence perspective' as practised by Nigerian women and their communities and as articulated by many ecofeminists worldwide.[2] This vision of ecological sustainability beyond economic globalisation is encapsulated in the Abuja Declaration for Energy Sovereignty enacted by international activists in 2006. What follows is an account of community resistance to Big Oil in Nigeria, in the years leading up to this critical gathering at Abuja. We will then present and comment on the Declaration.

In past decades, oil wealth was seen as the means of eradicating poverty, underdevelopment, debt, and neocolonial usurpation. But in the new millennium, even the IMF speaks of the 'curse of oil'. Big Oil has caused absolute immiseration, war and dictatorship, pollution and civil conflict, debt and militarisation, environmental disaster, and climate chaos. As we speak, oil revenues turn states into battlegrounds where cities are bombed and thousands of innocent people die. But none of this is inevitable. Beginning in the early 1980s as the Reagan–Thatcher dogma of 'There is No Alternative' was used to enforce corporate rule through privatisation and 'structural adjustment', a new popular resistance to oil emerged and women in the global South were at the forefront of it.[3] This followed the terrible costs of oil exploitation borne by women who depend on farmland for their livelihoods. A loud 'No!' came in 1984 from ten thousand Nigerian women who confronted the US oil company Pan Ocean. These women damned the curse of oil with their curse of nakedness. In the two decades to 2007, this refusal by women, indigenous peoples, small farmers, traders, urban poor, environmentalists, some waged workers and their allies throughout the world, has become more sophisticated.[4] Lessons have been learned and new political links have been established. The Abuja Declaration reflects this maturity.

Neoliberal approaches to women and climate change

When it talks about women and global warming, the ruling class seems to fall into two camps. The first camp constructs women as perpetrators of climate change; it blames and demonises women, especially those with high birth rates. It adopts the logic of Garret Hardin's discredited 'tragedy of the commons' and the assumption that poor people in the global South mismanage resources and overuse wood fuels. The neoliberal approach to their 'carelessness' is more 'development and growth' through the imposition of private property rights across indigenous and communal land. Meanwhile, the UK government's Stern Review in 2006 claims that privatisation and growth of a market in carbon emissions offers the solution to global warming.[5] But those who work closely with such communities, as we do in Nigeria, know that privatisation simply means more enclosures, more dispossession and more desperation for women and the poor.[6] And, as will be revealed in our Nigerian case study, a further aspect of privatisation is the expansion of militarism, to enforce the end of common property rights.

The second camp frames women not as perpetrators but as victims of climate change. Since almost nothing is known about the gender specific implications of climate change, this perspective adopts a disaster management approach. It is true that women and the poor, especially in the global South, are at the bottom of the social order and hurt most by floods, droughts, resource wars, pestilence, and extreme weather events. But the solution offered is a paltry policy of 'gender sensitive adaptation, coping and mitigation'.[7] Women, at least in the global South, are constructed as 'social capital', albeit leaning on 'aid' to muddle through. The 'add gender and stir' policy ubiquitous in the field of international development, is a poor response to understanding women's actual relation to the construction of a progressive energy policy. Moreover, while 'women and development' analysts proffer their consultancy services to rectify the absence of gender disaggregated studies on impacts of climate change, they overlook women's ongoing resistance, North and South, to the powers that simultaneously create poverty and environmental problems.

The Left alternative to climate change and social justice spelled out in this chapter recognises and defends social and communal entitlements to built and natural environments against corporate 'growth' and its uncosted 'externalities'. The Nigerian communities described here, represent the standpoint of exploited and dispossessed peoples everywhere, who struggle against the perpetrators of global injustices and climate change. The women who are prominent at the forefront of these ecological life and death struggles are there precisely because they are life-givers who draw their daily subsistence from the environment that corporate profit-taking destroys.[8] These resisters are grounded in, and elaborate, a politics of subsistence social relations. It is a 'commoner' perspective, which sees the hierarchical and exploitative social relations of capitalism at the root of climate change. The first premise of subsistence politics is that there can be no just reversal of planetary ecological decline as long as the market mind-set and its political economy remains in place. Major social changes will be required to realise social justice and ecological sustainability.

Corporate monopolies over resources must be replaced by the communal socialisation of energy production and distribution. Corporate sovereignty and neoliberal marketisation leads to environmental degradation in manifold ways. It facilitates the worst business practices, encouraging pollution and rapid depletion of natural fertility through uncontrolled extraction of soil, timber, diamonds, and oil. In the global South, these economic processes have led to the displacement of millions of people from commonly owned lands, forcing them on to ecologically fragile terrain that is inadequate to their subsistence. The neoliberal scenario is the reason why the poor unwittingly engage in deforestation of marginal lands and become vulnerable to soil erosion, drought, flood, attendant disease, and inevitable conflicts. Their politically sanctioned insecurity also contributes to high fertility rates as people seek to improve chances for survival by adding to the family labour force. We contend that it is this inequality in control of resources that is driving up the earth's temperature. Only the elimination of corporate power over resources can reduce the level of carbon emissions necessary to stabilise human interactions with nature. But few governments, agency, or even NGO experts, appear to understand the links between the political economy of capitalism and existing levels of carbon emissions.

Gendered, ethnicised, class struggle

It is imperative to examine alternatives to capitalist productivism, exploitation and excess. The social relations of subsistence, for example, are characterised by political autonomy, collectivity, and commoning. Here, meeting the life needs of all is the first priority of economic activity. Within this life-centred alternative, social harmony, reciprocity and the movement towards egalitarian social relations both require and facilitate symbiotic interactions with nature. This perspective has been well elaborated by ecofeminists including Maria Mies, Hilkka Pietila, Mary Mellor, Claudia von Werlhof, Silvia Federici, Veronika Bennholdt-Thomsen, Ellie Perkins, Ariel Salleh, and Vandana Shiva.[9]

The subsistence political economy is 'actually existing'. It is the very foundation of capital accumulation. When we say 'the very foundation', we mean that commodification is parasitical upon the existing subsistence political economy mainly managed by women. Capital is dependent upon and cannot survive without the life-centred work of women, peasants, indigenous peoples, youth, the informal sector and all waged and unwaged workers – plus nature. But the converse is not true. Subsistence is autonomous from capital and must become more so if human communities are to survive. People defending subsistence are those engaged in environmental defence and restoration in the face of ever more intense financial and military attack.

We offer the following case study to illustrate this dynamic. But before we go to our account of women's direct action for climate justice, a methodological note is in order. We give great weight to what is happening, that is, to empirical and historical accounts of what actual people have done and are doing in real situations. We theorise these actions in that we try to understand them within the framework offered by the subsistence perspective. We theorise gendered, ethnicised, class struggle, as pursued by social forces for and against capital accumulation and social forces for and against subsistence commoning. Two points are important here. First, the exploited class is global and includes both waged and unwaged people. Second, most women – North and South – are unwaged and are fighting both corporate agents and men from their own class who are assimilated into the capitalist economic project. It is these women who, in refusing corporate enclosure, stand for nature and against men who choose to collaborate with capital. These unwaged women are not negotiating for a reformist deal. In fighting for the essentials of their livelihoods, they are defending an ecosystem, a political economy of subsistence, and a conception of humanity that does not admit of class domination. Note here that class, ethnicity, and gender are not separate categories.

In theorising the actions of insurgents against corporate rule, we problematise, in particular, the organisational forms from which they draw their power and their potential to prevail. Therefore an important element of this gendered, ethnicised class analysis – what we call revolutionary ecofeminism – is that those who confront capital do so through a double-sided organisation that is simultaneously local and global, deriving as it does from a mix of indigenous subsistence social relations on the one hand, and responding to exogenous corporate social relations, on the other.[10] So far we have pointed to the social relations that characterise the political economies of capital and subsistence. The following case study inquires into the energy relations that characterise climate change. It asks what energy relations are subsistence actors trying to protect and extend?

Women's 'gift' to humanity

In 1999 Nigerian women led a remarkable global initiative to halt Shell Oil's irresponsible and dangerous burning of natural gas. This coordinated international action and its aftermath suggest tactics that if more widely adopted might help stop climate change. The coordination was taken a step further in 2006 when member groups of Friends of the Earth International from 51 countries met in Nigeria's capital and issued the Abuja Declaration on Energy Sovereignty. More of this later.

In Europe and elsewhere, Shell uses valuable natural gas for electricity, for petrochemicals, and for pressure maintenance in oil wells. But in Nigeria, to save money, Shell and other oil companies flare or burn off a great deal of gas associated with oil production. In June 2005, the Port Harcourt organisation Environmental Rights Action claimed that:

> More gas is flared in Nigeria than anywhere else in the world. Estimates are notoriously unreliable, but roughly 2.5 billion cubic feet of gas associated

with crude oil is wasted in this way everyday. This is equal to 40% of all Africa's natural gas consumption in 2001, while the annual financial loss to Nigeria is about US $2.5 billion. The flares have contributed more greenhouse gases than all of sub-Saharan Africa combined. And the flares contain a cocktail of toxins that affect the health and livelihood of local communities, exposing Niger Delta residents to an increased risk of premature deaths, child respiratory illnesses, asthma and cancer.[11]

Environmentalists in Nigeria, notably from among the Ogoni, Ijaw and other ethnic groups in the oil-rich Niger Delta, have persistently tried to douse these fires. Since 1993, Ogoni Day has been celebrated to mark the anniversary of the day that Ogoni people launched their struggle against Shell and forced the oil company off their lands. On 10 November 1995, Ken Saro-Wiwa and eight other activists were hanged by Nigeria's military dictatorship in what was described by one UK Queen's Counsel as 'an act of state-sponsored murder'. Those executed were part of an indigenous movement known as MOSOP or Movement for the Survival of the Ogoni People. In this movement, Ogoni women were prominent and their objective was to shut down the polluting operations of Shell.[12] On 1 January 1999, activists in the Niger Delta launched 'Operation Climate Change'. To protest Shell's gas flaring and complicity in the murder of Saro-Wiwa, Niger Delta women and their allies staged simultaneous actions in Nigeria and the UK. These actions featured shutdowns of Shell, on an international basis, on and after Ogoni Day, 4 January 1999.

While business-suited environmentalists occupied Shell's London headquarters, women and men in the Niger Delta closed down gas flares. Thirteen activists from three human rights and environmental groups occupied Shell headquarters. They barricaded themselves in the Managing Directors' offices and broadcast the event to the outside world via digital cameras, laptop computers and mobile phones. Six hours later, police cut off electricity, smashed down the wall and arrested the activists. Shell declined to press charges. One participant pointed out that the London occupation aimed

... to show real solidarity with people in the Niger Delta rebelling against Big Oil and its private security force (the Nigerian army). It was becoming increasingly easy for multi-national corporations to isolate struggles and resistance. The strength of linking together undermines their ability to do this ... Oil companies, with their hideous environmental and social record, combine a series of struggles not only in the developing world but in the UK too.[13]

Converging with and reinforcing these movement efforts was an earlier Kaiama Declaration issued on 11 December 1998, by the newly formed Ijaw Youth Council. This group was part of the multi-ethnic, pan-Delta Chikoko movement. In the Declaration they resolved that all land and natural resources belonged to local communities and demanded that

> ... all oil companies stop all exploration and exploitation activities in the Ijaw area. We are tired of gas flaring, oil spillages, blowouts and being labelled saboteurs and terrorists. We advise all oil companies staff and contractors to withdraw from Ijaw territories by the 30th December 1998 pending the resolution of the issue of resource ownership and control in the Ijaw area of the Niger Delta.[14]

Operation Climate Change was initially planned as a ten-day programme of non-violent civil disobedience. In the end, it lasted for several weeks. Actions targeted five oil companies operating in the Delta. Two hundred organisations endorsed a January 1999 letter to Shell, Chevron-Texaco, Mobil, Elf, and Agip. The letter warned the companies that the 'World is watching' and they should suspend operations in Nigeria immediately.[15]

The Shell-backed military Nigerian administration responded with a state of emergency. Two warships and up to 15,000 troops were deployed and women were raped by soldiers. Several crude oil flow stations were occupied, and villagers also attempted to shut down the gas flares. On 4 January 1999, soldiers using a helicopter and boats owned by Chevron, attacked environmentalists who were occupying a drilling rig, killing over fifty people and destroying dozens of homes.[16] Enraged by the rapes and murders, dozens of women's groups from across the Delta, mobilised in a multi-ethnic umbrella organisation called Niger Delta Women for Justice, and took to the streets in Port Harcourt. On 11 January 1999 hundreds of women from Niger Delta Women for Justice, in conjunction with the Ijaw Youth Council, marched to deliver a protest letter to the military administrator of Rivers State, decrying the rape of women and land. The protesters dressed in black and carried placards, some of which read 'Justice for Ijaws and their Neighbours'; 'The Women are Aggrieved, Stop the Killing'; 'Ijaws are United in their Declaration; Let us Dialogue'; and condemned the oil companies that have 'Love for Oil, Hatred for the Owners'.[17]

Big Oil and state violence

A witness told Reuters press that demonstrators 'were confronted by three lorry loads of policemen who fired into the air and tear gassed the crowd of surging women'.[18] The protesters demanded that the government open dialogue on the Kaiama Declaration and that the police release all political prisoners. The soldiers arrested at least 34 of the women, one of whom claimed that soldiers had stripped her naked and flogged her with *koboko* or cow hide whip. Others sustained injuries whilst fleeing from the rampaging soldiers. In 1999, Annie Brisibe, of Niger Delta Women for Justice and Friends of the Earth Nigeria's Climate Change project, stated that

> I've been involved in organizing political awareness workshops for women through the Niger Delta Women for Justice movement ... We focus on creating awareness about what a polluted environment can do to people. We point out the activities of transnational corporations – the gas flares caused by the oil industry, the improper waste management, the carbon dioxide and sulphur emissions – and make the connections between all of this and the frequent environmental problems in the Niger Delta.[19]

The operations of Agip, Chevron-Texaco, Mobil, and Shell were seriously impacted by Operation Climate Change. Shell production of some 400,000 barrels of oil per day (bdp) – fully half of the super-major's total Nigerian output – was interrupted by the initiative to stop gas flaring and expel the company from Nigeria. Another 40,000 bpd of oil flow was interrupted from five of Shell's flow stations in June 1999. Isoko youth occupied the flow stations located in five communities, in Otomoro, Egini, Oweh, Uzere, and Oroni. Some 100,000 bpd were interrupted in November 1999 by Ijaw communities demanding compensation for other oil spills. Seven of Shell's oil flow stations were allowed to reopen only upon agreement with the Ijaw in August 1999, ten months after community members occupied Shell's oil facilities.[20] Shell suffered a 95 per cent drop in profits in the fourth as compared to the third quarter of 1998, or a loss of US$350 million. The *Financial Times* reported in London that 'up to a third of output was halted at one point last year by piracy and sabotage by activists demanding a fairer share of revenues for the region's impoverished inhabitants'.[21] Output interruptions and financial losses were even greater in 1999, and Shell was forced to make a public concession and promise to stop all gas flaring in Nigeria by 2007.

Environmentalists in Nigeria and the UK described the operation to shutdown Shell gas flares as 'a gift to humanity' because it sought to cut carbon emissions that threaten human life as a whole. The aftermath for those engaged in this campaign unfolded over the subsequent eight years along three axes:

- first, deepening militancy within the Niger Delta around the demand for democratic 'resource control';
- second, achievement of significant success in expelling oil companies from the Niger Delta; and
- third, the experience of violent counter-insurgency at the behest of the Nigerian state and foreign oil companies.

This third dimension of the aftermath exposed the power relations between women who try to interdict perpetrators of ecocide and those men who profit from expanded oil production with its escalating deadly emissions.[22]

In 2005, the Nigerian women's groups, including Niger Delta Women for Justice, who had helped achieve a moratorium on gas flaring, were labelled 'terrorist' by the government which was being drawn ever more deeply into the US global 'war on terror'. This demonisation of women reveals the link between the imperial ambitions of President Bush's 'War without End' and Big Oil's manufacture of 'enemies' out of women fighting for a life-centred economy on their community lands. This corporate–government link constructs environmentalists, and especially women who reach for global consciousness and practical solidarity, as immediate targets for repression. The Nigerian women's 'gift to humanity' is, in consequence, a double gift. First, it provoked a leap in global consciousness about the common fate of all humans if specific polluters amongst the world's tiny clique of 400 plus billionaires run rampant beyond any democratic control. Second, the African women's gift of direct action to stop gas flaring accelerated an international groundswell of coordinated mobilisations over Big Oil. These started with the 4 January 1999 occupation of Shell's London headquarters and continued in subsequent actions including an International Day of Protest, Action and Carnival of the Oppressed in financial centres around the world on 18 June 1999. Further international actions were directed against the World Trade Organization in November and December 1999. And after the people's victory against governments and international financial institutions at Seattle, hundreds of manifestations against corporate rule occurred around the world.

Moving forward to 8 July 2002, 600 Nigerian women occupied Chevron-Texaco's Escravos oil export terminal and tank farm for eleven days. This production shutdown coincided with oil consumption boycotts against the impending US attack on Iraq.[23] A year later on 15 February 2003, anti-war mobilisations culminated in an historic global peace march involving as many as 50 million people across all continents. The Iraq war has brought citizens in the global North to a new awareness of links between Big Oil, US militarism, carbon emissions, and extreme weather events. Between 21 and 28 September 2006, US and international activists gathered in Washington using civil disobedience to promote a 'Declaration of Peace' in Iraq and Iran. In January 2006, Nigerian courts ordered Shell to stop the flaring of natural gas from specified oil wells in the western Warri zone of the Niger Delta. The oil giant refuses to comply – but is facing more legal challenges under a concerted, international campaign to prosecute Big Oil for damages resulting in climate change. A second precedent of global import was announced on 19 September 2006, in the Nigerian newspaper *Punch*, where it was reported that the government intended to cancel Shell's licence in the eastern Niger Delta block covering Ogoniland, because Shell's operations there had lapsed for more than ten years, due to the campaign of the Movement for the Survival of the Ogoni People.[24]

In a 23 September 2006 interview, Dr Owens Wiwa said:

> It was Ogoni women who were most instrumental in preventing Shell from operating in Ogoniland over the past decade. This is a major success because not only have we driven Shell out non-violently, but we have set a precedent for all Nigeria and indeed the whole world: without local people's agreement, no oil company can go in. A tremendous price has been paid in loss of life. But government's revocation of Shell's operating licence is a tremendous victory and it is due largely to the commitment of ordinary village women, mostly organized through the Federation of Ogoni Women's Associations.[25]

The shutdown of all Shell operations in Ogoniland meant less gas flaring, less carbon emissions, and less global warming. And it was not limited to Ogoniland. Across the Delta, some 600,000 barrels per day, or about a quarter of Nigeria's total production, was stopped throughout 2006.[26] This entails a massive cut in greenhouse gases.

So how did Nigerian women and their allies accomplish this major political achievement? Can their tactics be generalised? The activists mirrored Shell's global corporate reach by organising simultaneous shutdowns of Big Oil across national boundaries. The coordinated direct actions that followed Operation Climate Change show these civil disobedience tactics generalised in global movements against the depredations of Big Oil, and indeed against war. As the urgency of the global warming crisis is realised by people worldwide, there is every reason to believe that peaceful direct action for popular control over petroleum will expand. And similarly, we can expect that women's – local and international – initiatives and coordinations will continue to be key features of this agenda to reverse climate change.

But the success of Nigerian communities does not end here. From 28 to 29 September 2006, member groups of Friends of the Earth International (FoEI) from 51 countries including Nigeria's Environmental Rights Action (ERA) and other national and international civil society groups, representatives of Niger Delta Communities, and journalists gathered in Abuja for the International Conference on Climate Change. This conference, with the theme 'Minimizing Climate Change Impact and Curbing Global Energy Chaos', was one of the activities of the Biennial General Meeting of FoEI. It concluded by putting forward a model for the democratic control of natural resources – the concept of Energy Sovereignty.

The Abuja Declaration

Observations

Following presentations and robust discussions at the conference, participants observed that:

1. All struggles, whether social, economic or environmental are interlinked with political struggles. Therefore, there is the need to link the different messages from around the world and adopt broad strategies that clearly address the issues of Climate Change and Energy Sovereignty, since it is the flawed and exploitative international economic system that drives the climate change phenomenon.
2. There is the need to synchronize the various energy struggles around the world by adopting a global strategy for resisting environmental degradation, destruction of local livelihoods, and rights abuses associated with corporate controlled energy sourcing and consumption globally.
3. There exist attempts by corporations to promote other sources of energy primarily nuclear as an alternative. Nuclear expansion must be resisted it has inherent and irreversible negative impacts.

4. Alternative energy production must not lead to further impoverishment of peoples.
5. The extraction of crude oil has led to unprecedented human rights abuse, environmental problems, fostering political and social conflicts in the Niger Delta and in other communities globally, which have been responded to by the militarization of community lands and sovereign states. In this militarized condition, women in particular have been victims.

Resolutions

Arising from the observations, participants resolved that:

Another energy future is necessary based upon:

- Abandoning the belief in export led growth in favour of servicing local (basic) needs;
- Restructuring the price and production of energy;
- A new approach to restructuring ownership of the energy regimes; and
- Abandoning the mistaken dichotomy between 'development and environment'.

We therefore:
1. Endeavor to work with and support community struggles towards energy sovereignty and democratic control of natural resources that will be the basis for alternative fair and just trade regimes that link producers with consumers eliminating corporate led control of our energy systems. It is essential that women are fully involved in all negotiations over energy production and allocation of natural resources.
2. Call for fair trade and just direct deals between producers and consumers, built upon energy sovereignty and the transition to alternative energy that cut out the oil middlemen, oil companies and oil speculators. These direct deals in oil can involve barter (as in Venezuela with Cuba, Argentina, and Uruguay) thereby avoiding the use of the US Dollar.
3. Call on Governments across the world to declare a global moratorium on new oil and gas exploration and development

until full eco-restoration and reparations is implemented in communities already impacted by extractive industries.

4. Call on Governments in both South and North to focus more on responsible energy consumption and the development of decentralized democratically controlled technology for easy utilization of clean energy like wind and solar energy.

5. Call on Governments of the South to develop gender responsive and clear policies toward attaining 'Energy Sovereignty'. Such policy should promote sustainable energy, local community control of energy along with the protection of the environment and local livelihoods from corporate and state abuse.

6. Recognize the alliance between the Nigerian and other governments and the oil multinationals in the form of Joint Venture Agreements that negate communities' interests. The terms of these JVA must be made public and repudiated. These JVA must be replaced with democratically controlled government and local community agreements.

7. The Niger Delta crisis should be resolved through dialogue and democratic/political interventions. Such interventions must include communal control of communal resources, protection of local political interests and strict enforcement of environmental standards and codes.

8. Neoliberal trade agreements and economic policies that have the effect of stripping people of their entitlements to basic resources for a just and human existence and increase the impoverishment of peoples' must be terminated; finally

9. The super profits of the oil multinationals must be redirected towards clean-up reparations, and the transition to safe energy alternatives under democratic control.

Meena Rahman
Chair, Friends of the Earth, International

Nnimmo Bassey
Executive Director, Environmental Rights Action/
Friends of the Earth, Nigeria.[27]

The Abuja Declaration demonstrates the fact that 'There is An Alternative' to corporations and the wider system of accumulation for which they are linch pins – the weapon-dollar petrodollar alliance.[28] It breaks from the 'bait and switch' strategies that discredit so many UN, World Bank and IMF initiatives. The bait is crocodile tears about poverty, HIV-AIDS, climate change, and the switch is the call for remedies through more 'growth' and private sector subsidies. In short, the switch offers more influence to the very perpetrators of the global crisis. Shocking in this regard is Big Oil's demand that the World Trade Organization force oil-rich societies to 'open' their economies to transnational control of trade and investment in all 'services' related to oil and gas. The Abuja Declaration rejects neoliberalism in favour of local economic sovereignty. It spells out how to put this into effect. It is not only about disempowering transnational corporations, but replacing them with direct transactions between sovereign communal groups. The example of Venezuela's Bolivarian revolution with its direct deals of oil for doctors is cited as a model. But the Declaration goes one step further and calls for reparations. The profits Big Oil is reaping from war-related energy price hikes must be taken back and used to clean up Big Oil's ecological mess that threatens life itself. Finally, the Abuja Declaration makes the crucial, and in a sense obvious, point that only a democratically organised people is capable of containing climate chaos. No solution to the impending ecocide brought to you by Big Oil is available without a popular move to shut down the oil companies. In advocating popular sovereignty and international coordinated democratic action against Big Oil, the Abuja Declaration goes beyond the narrow lie contained in Bush's 'You're Either With Us or Against Us', to embody and launch what Maude Barlow of the Council of Canadians calls 'a third global force'.[29]

Notes

1. According to a January 2007 report by the US organisation Union of Concerned Scientists, Exxon paid US$16 million to a network of 43 PR groups in the years between 1998 and 2005, in order to pacify

public concern over scientific findings on climate change; Online Available HTTP: <www.ucsusa.org> (accessed 5 March 2007).

2. Maria Mies and Veronika Bennholdt-Thomsen, *The Subsistence Perspective*, London: Zed Books, 1999.

3. Sokari Ekine, *Blood Sorrow and Oil: Testimonies of Violence from Women of the Niger Delta*, Oxford: Centre for Democracy and Development, 2001; Terisa E. Turner, 'The Land is Dead, Women's Rights as Human Rights: The Case of the Ogbodo Shell Petroleum Spill in Rivers State, Nigeria, June–July 2001', see Niger Delta Women for Justice, Online Available HTTP: <www.ndwj.kabissa. org/PressRelease/News2/news2.html#LandisDead> (accessed 4 June 2006).

4. Anon., 'Climate Justice Now! The Durban Declaration on Carbon Trading', 10 October 2004, Online Available HTTP: <www. sinkswatch.org> (accessed 12 November 2006).

5. *Stern Review on the Economics of Climate Change*, September 2006, Online Available HTTP: <www.hm-treasury.gov.uk/ independent_reviews/stern_review_economics_climate_change/ stern_review_report.cfm> (accessed 15 October 2006).

6. Ana Isla, 'The Tragedy of the Enclosures: An Eco-feminist Perspective on the Kyoto Protocol', Canadian Society for Ecological Economics Conference, York University, Toronto, 2005.

7. See Focal Point Gender Justice and Sustainability – GENANET, Online Available HTTP: <www.genanet.de> (accessed 12 November 2006).

8. Terisa E. Turner and Leigh Brownhill (eds), Special Issue on Gender, Feminism, and the Civil Commons, *Canadian Journal of Development Studies*, 2001, No. XXII.

9. A valuable compilation of ecofeminist analyses is presented in Ellie Perkins (ed.), *Women & Environments International*, 2002, No. 54/55.

10. Terisa E. Turner and Leigh Brownhill, 'We Want Our Land Back: Gendered Class Analysis, the Second Contradiction of Capital and Social Movement Theory', *Capitalism Nature Socialism*, 2004, Vol. 15, No. 4, 21–40. See also Terisa E. Turner and Leigh Brownhill, 'Ecofeminism as Gendered, Ethnicized Class Struggle: A Rejoinder to Stuart Rosewarne', *Capitalism Nature Socialism*, 2006, Vol. 17, No. 4, 88–96.

11. Environmental Rights Action and Friends of the Earth, *Gas Flaring in Nigeria: A Human Rights, Environmental and Economic Monstrosity*, report by the Climate Justice Programme, ERA, and FOE Nigeria, 2006, Online Available HTTP: <www.climatelaw.

org/gas.flaring/report/exec.summary.htm> (accessed 14 September 2006).

12. Timothy Hunt, *The Politics of Bones: Dr. Owens Wiwa and the Struggle for Nigeria's Oil*, Toronto: McClelland and Stewart, 2005; Ike Okonta and Oronto Douglas, *Where Vultures Feast: Shell, Human Rights, and Oil*, New York: Verso, 2003.

13. Anon., 'Sabbing Shell', *Do or Die*, 1999, No. 8, Online Available HTTP: <www.eco-action.org/dod/no8/shell.html> (accessed 15 October 2006).

14. Anon., 'Office Politics', *Weekly Schnews*, 1999, No. 197.

15. Anon., 'Vital Statistics: A Sampling of Shell's Activity in Nigeria over the Last Four Years', *Drillbits & Tailings*, 1999, Vol. 4, No. 18, Online Available HTTP: <www.moles.org/ProjectUnderground/drillbits/4_18/vs.html> (accessed 22 September 2006).

16. Anon., 'Big Trouble for Big Oil', *Do or Die*, 1999, No. 8, Online Available HTTP: <www.eco-action.org/dod/no8/shell.html> (accessed 15 October 2006).

17. Collins Obibi, 'Ijaw Women Protest Troop Deployment to Bayelsa', *The Guardian* (Amsterdam), 12 January 1999.

18. Anon., 'Nigerian police disperse protest by Ijaw women', *Reuters Inter Press Service*, Port Harcourt, Nigeria, 11 January 2000; Anon., 'Protesting *Ijaw* Women Dispersed, Beaten: At least 34 Women Arrested: Victims Stripped Naked', *OGELE Bulletin of the Ijaw Youth Council*, 11 January 1999, Online Available HTTP: <www.lists.essential.org> (accessed 15 October 2006).

19. Ann Doherty, 'Operation Climate Change: An Interview with Annie Brisibe of Friends of the Earth Nigeria', *Link Magazine*, 1999, No. 91, Online Available HTTP: <www.foei.org/publications/link/91/e91climatechange.html> (accessed 14 June 2006).

20. Anon., 'Vital Statistics'.

21. William Wallis, 'Ethnic Riots Lead to Fears for Oil Output', *Financial Times*, 9 June 1999, p. 6.

22. Turner and Brownhill, 'We Want Our Land Back'.

23. Terisa E. Turner and Leigh Brownhill, *The New Twenty-First Century Land and Oil Wars: African Women Confront Corporate Rule*, New York: International Oil Working Group, 2005. This is also available through First Woman: East and Southern African Women's Oral History and Indigenous Knowledge Network, Online Available HTTP: <www.iowg.org>.

24. Anon., 'Editorial', *Punch* (Lagos), 19 September 2006, Online Available HTTP: <www.nigerian-newspaper.com/punch-newspaper.htm> (accessed 28 October 2006).

25. Owens Wiwa, interview with Terisa Turner, September 2006, Toronto.
26. Anon., 'African Continent to Remain a Key Spot for Investors, African Oil and Gas', Platts.com News Feature, 20 July 2006, Online Available HTTP: <www.platts.com/Oil/Resources/News%20Features/africanenergy/index.xml> (accessed 14 September 2006).
27. The Abuja Declaration is Online Available HTTP: <www.eraction.org/index.php?option=com_content&task=view&id=14&Itemid=12> (accessed 15 October 2006).
28. Bichler and Nitzan Archives, Online Available HTTP: <www.bnarchives.yorku.ca/> (accessed 12 November 2006).
29. Council of Canadians, Online Available HTTP: <www.canadians.org/> (accessed 15 October 2006).

Part V

Movement

All species, peoples, and cultures have intrinsic worth
All beings are subjects who have integrity, intelligence, and identity not objects of ownership, manipulation, exploitation, or disposability ...

The earth community is a democracy of all life
We all have a duty to live in a manner that protects the earth's ecological processes, and the rights and welfare of all species and all people. No humans have the right to encroach on the ecological space of other species and other people ...

All beings have a natural right to sustenance
Resources vital to sustenance must stay in the commons. The right to sustenance is a natural right because it is the right to life. These rights are not given by states or corporations ...

Earth Democracy globalizes peace, care, and compassion
Earth Democracy connects people in circles of care, cooperation, and compassion instead of dividing them through competition and conflict, fear and hatred.

Vandana Shiva, *Earth Democracy*,
London: Zed Books, 2006, pp. 9–11.

14

ECOFEMINIST POLITICAL ECONOMY AND THE POLITICS OF MONEY

Mary Mellor

Ecofeminism, as its name implies, brings together the insights of feminism and ecology.[1] Feminism is concerned with the way in which women in general have been subordinated to men in general. Ecologists are concerned that human activity is destroying the viability of ecosystems. Ecofeminist political economy argues that the two are linked. This linkage is not seen as stemming from some essentialist female identification with nature, for which some early ecofeminists were criticised, but from women's position in society, particularly in relation to masculine-dominated economic systems.[2] What ecofeminist political economy explores is the gendering of economic systems. It sees a material link between the externalisation and exploitation of women and the externalisation and exploitation of nature.[3] For ecofeminist political economy, 'the economy' is a boundaried system that excludes or marginalises many aspects of human existence and of nonhuman nature. This problem of externalisation is one explored by many green and feminist economists, but finding a solution is more problematic.

One solution is to incorporate 'externalised' aspects of human existence within the market form, but this is not a solution if the market itself is seen as the source of the problem. A more radical approach seeks to expand the notion of the economy from the narrow neoclassical focus on market determination and rational choice or the productivist focus of left economists, to a much wider conception of human activities in meeting needs. More expansive concepts have been adopted by feminist economists such as 'provisioning' which cover all aspects of human needs including nurturing and emotional support – much of which still remains in the home and the community.[4] Another approach is to try to withdraw from the market or make it more locally responsive.[5] For some this means dropping out of the money-based market economy entirely and moving towards subsistence as a means of production.[6] Another approach is to look for transformative spaces within current economic structures.[7] This is reflected in the considerable enthusiasm for alternative economic forms such as LETS, time banks, or other mutual or cooperative structures.[8]

However, as well as exploring radical and innovative alternatives, it is also necessary to challenge the capitalist market as a structure. Through violence, patriarchy, nepotism, colonialism, and market manipulation, the capitalist economy has gained control of the sources of sustenance for many of the world's people as well as other species.[9] As Michael Perelman argues, 'virtually no land ownership in the world has either honest or honourable origins'.[10] This chapter will argue that control of banking and finance has also been central to capitalist accumulation and growth. What has made the situation much more complex is that through the market, the capitalist economy has intertwined the servicing of human needs (where profitable) with the creation and meeting of wants.

So how can the capitalist market be challenged in a way that provides a feasible alternative at a systemic level? As the exploration of externalities shows, the market system places a boundary around certain limited activities and functions that are defined by their value in money terms. Ecofeminist political economy points to the dualist construction of the modern market economy and the way in which economic valuing and the social dominance of men are directly connected. This chapter will explore first the basis of that dualism and then explore the critical question of money issue and circulation that has largely been ignored by both radical and conventional economists.

Dualist economics

Orthodox economics is a theory written by men about men, one that pushes women to the economic margins by ignoring women's work and women's issues.[11] This leads to a dualism in economic thought in which 'the economy' is carved out of the complexity of the whole of human and non-human existence.

The Economy and its Other

Accorded High Value	Accorded Low/No Value
Economic 'Man'	Women's work
Market value	Subsistence
Personal wealth	Social reciprocity
Labour/Intellect	Body, emotions
Skills/Tradeable Knowledge	Feelings, wisdom
Able-bodied workers	Sick, needy, old, young
Exploitable resources	Eco-systems, wild nature
Unlimited consumption	Sufficiency

The money-valued economy takes only what it needs from nature and human life to fuel its activities and only provides products and services that are profitable. This has led Susan Donath to argue that instead of mainstream economics with its 'single story' of competitive production and market exchange, there needs to be a 'distinctively feminist economics' based on the 'other economy' representing care, reciprocity, the direct production and maintenance of human beings.[12] As the pioneering work of Hilkka Pietila and Marilyn Waring has demonstrated, what is unvalued or undervalued by the economy is the resilience of the ecosystem, the unpaid and unrecognised domestic work of women and social reciprocity, particularly as represented in non-market economies.[13]

Ecofeminists see the capitalist market as a small part of a much greater sustaining whole. Maria Mies sees it as the tip of an iceberg with, below the water line, the invisible economy that includes the world of unpaid work and subsistence and natural resources.[14] For Hazel Henderson, the market sector is the icing on a multi-layered cake.[15] Beneath the icing lies the public sector, the non-market sector and 'Mother Nature' so called. The filling of the cake is the informal 'cash' economy', which, in practice, forms a large part of the world's money-based economies.

Women's position in relation to the money-valued economy is complex. Women can be present in the economy in large numbers as consumers and employees. There are women who do well economically, and some women exploit and oppress other women and the environment. What ecofeminist political economy focuses upon is not women per se, but 'women's work', the range of human activities that have historically been associated with women both inside and outside of the market place. Women's work is the basic work around the human body that makes other forms of activity possible. It secures the body and the community. If a woman enters the valued sphere of economic life she must leave her woman-work behind; childcare, domestic work, responsibility for elderly relatives, subsistence work, community activities. The valued economy is therefore limited and partial in relation to the whole of women's lives.[16]

From the perspective of ecofeminist political economy, the market economy and its public sector support system, represents a public world as defined by dominant men, a masculine-experience economy, a ME economy that has cut itself free from the ecological and social framework of human *being* in its widest sense. Its ideal is 'economic man', who may also be female. Economic man is fit, mobile, able-bodied, unencumbered by domestic or other responsibilities. The goods he consumes appear to him as finished products or services and disappear from his view on disposal or dismissal. He has no responsibility for the life-cycle of those goods or services any more than he questions the source of the air he breathes or the disposal of his excreta. The ME economy is disembodied because the life-cycle and daily cycle of the body cannot be accommodated in the fractured world of the money-valued economy. The ME economy is also disembedded from its ecosystem; it is not limited by local growing seasons and where possible dumps its waste on poor, marginalised communities.[17] 'Economic man' is the product of an ahistoric, atomised approach to the understanding of human existence.[18]

Ecofeminist political economy expands on earlier criticisms of the disembedding of the economy from society, emphasising in particular the dimensions of space and time. Women's work is spatially embedded because it is, of necessity, local and communal, centred on the home. Those doing domestic duties, reflecting bodily needs, cannot move far from those responsibilities. In subsistence economies women's work, and subsistence work generally, is embedded in the local ecosystem. In contrast to its spatial limitations, women's work is unlimited in terms of time characterised by repetition and presence: watching, waiting, nursing, cooking, cleaning, fetching and carrying, weeding. Much of women's work involves being available, always on call, so much so, that many women take paid work as a break from the demands of domestic life.[19] For many, this is a labour of love, but it can also be seen as an imposed altruism.[20] While women's work may be carried out as an expression of love and/or duty, for many there is fear of violence and/or lack of any other economic options. In their historical association with the life and needs of the human body, women have been seen as weak, emotional, irrational, even dangerous and subjected to domestic violence.[21]

The core argument of ecofeminist political economy is that the marginalisation of women's work is ecologically dangerous because women's lives as reflected in domestic and caring work represent the embodiedness of humanity, the link of humanity with its natural being. Women's work represents the fundamental reality of human existence, the body's life in *biological time* the time it takes to rest, recover, grow up and grow old. Equally there is a time-scale for the environmental framing of human activities. *Ecological time* is the time it takes to restore the effects of human activity, the time-cycle of renewal and replenishment within the ecosystem. As formal economic systems have been constructed, women's work has become the repository of the inconvenience of human existence. Moreover, the pattern of exclusion that affects women's work is, in turn, related to other exploitations, exclusions, and marginalisations. The valued economy has gained its power and ascendancy through the marginalisation and exploitation of women, colonised peoples, waged labour and the natural world increasingly on a global scale.[22]

The precarity of global capitalism

The ME economy as a growth-oriented capitalist market system, has claimed hegemony over all other economic systems, including the public sector, and over economic thought.[23] The beneficiaries of the ME economy take no moral responsibility, since all negative outcomes are attributed to anonymous market forces. Despite this power, it is a system in which people do not feel economically secure or happy, even in the richest countries.[24] What advocates of the market do not acknowledge is the precariousness of its seemingly transcendent position. What is ignored is its immanence in and dependency on the sustaining systems that underpin it.[25]

One of the main mechanisms that separates the formal economy from unacknowledged and unpaid body work is the creation and allocation of money within society. This is compounded by one of the main features of late twentieth century globalisation, the fact that it is largely a financial phenomenon. More than 90 per cent of trade in money terms is just that, trade in money, money products and money services. This has been accompanied by a massive expansion of global currency and credit, particularly dollars, that have given the US virtually unlimited resources to supply it with goods and services and conduct its military adventures. The dominance of the dollar as one of the 'hard' currencies compares with the vulnerability of countries with soft currencies. This has been a particular problem where countries with soft currencies have been encouraged or forced to borrow money in hard currencies. Taking advantage of this situation, transnational corporations source and manufacture in low wage economies (a combination of absolute low wages and unequal currency values). They borrow money where it is cheapest and sell where the price is highest. The capacity of governments to tax international corporations, or companies generally, has become increasingly difficult, particularly where there are no physical assets.

One of the most notable aspects of the dominance of finance in contemporary capitalism is that investment has moved from what Marx saw as the traditional capitalist model of money invested in commodity production to produce increased money value at the point of sale. Money is now invested in money itself as a commodity. A recent, and illustrative example is the hedge fund. Hedge funds do not invest in companies as such; they only gamble on small changes of currencies, shares or goods values. This is a more extreme version of general stock market trading where only around 5 per cent of trade relates to direct investment in companies (i.e. initial purchase of shares). So much so, that in the absence of any other investments, even insurance companies and similar repositories of pensions and other personal savings in the UK are becoming involved in hedge funds, which might be better described as gambling syndicates. While the vulnerabilities of the rich in the investment of money would not be of concern to ecofeminists or radical economists, their operation can reveal a great deal about the operation of finance capital.

Hedge funds reveal a particular aspect of capitalist accumulation, the role of credit finance in speculation. Because the profit on these small scale gambles is so miniscule they cannot generate sufficient income to make a profit for investors. The investor's money is therefore 'leveraged' up many times to create enough volume of profit to provide a return to the original investors. Leverage is a nice word for credit. Long Term Capital Management when it had to be rescued by the US Federal Reserve in 1998, is said to have had $5 billion in assets and 'exposure' of nearly a trillion. ENRON failed with $2 billion in assets and debts of $20 billion. What these examples show is the importance of credit access to investment. What is most remarkable is that this money can disappear as investments fail without any noticeable impact on the global economy as if they are dipping into a magic well. The trick is also used by companies involved in mergers, acquisitions, privatisations, or management buy outs. The tool that is being used is the social phenomenon of money creation. In capitalised money systems, money/credit issue is a means by which those who have control over, or access to, the money/credit-creation process can establish ownership and control over the means and direction of production. This credit fuelled grab of assets is effectively a form of primitive accumulation. For example in Britain, private companies are undertaking highly leveraged investments in the public sector through private finance initiatives. By borrowing money they are effectively acquiring state assets. These would have remained entirely in the public sector, but for the present ideological commercially oriented rejection of state investment. Private equity firms are also engaged in highly leveraged takeovers of publicly quoted companies taking them back into private unregulated ownership. In a commodified market system, money and credit are the means by which property and value are accumulated.

A number of thinkers, particularly linked to the green movement, have seen the issue of money and credit as an important question and a possible mechanism for socio-economic change.[26] The particular feature they point to is the fact that commercial banks can issue money they do not have. One of the innovations of commercial banking that enabled capitalism to establish itself was the issue of credit well beyond the assets that the bank or lender holds. This is known as reserve banking. Given that in the UK, 97 per cent of new money is entering the economy as debt, this additional 'nothing' money is also a major factor in driving economic growth and needless employment and consumption. Historically, new money entered the economy mainly through state action as notes and coin. In many countries this is still the case, but the pressure towards more commercial money issue will be intense in all countries that are 'modernising'. As Herman Daly points out, an understanding of how banks create money is comparatively recent and Steve Keen argues that neoclassical economics still theorises banking as barter between savers and borrowers.[27] Even where banking theory acknowledges this is not the case, it maintains that there is a control on bank issue through the demand that banks hold specific levels of reserve funds. But as Keen has argued in the case of the UK, in practice such a reserve does not exist, but is represented by another layer of credit in the central bank.

Given the prevalence of debt-based money issue and the virtual non-existence of fractional reserve banking, the money currently issued into our society is effectively created out of nothing. In Kenneth Galbraith's oft repeated words, 'the process by which banks create money is so simple that the mind is repelled. Where something so important is involved, a deeper mystery seems only decent.'[28] As James Tobin has pointed out, 'a long line of financial heretics have been right in speaking of "fountain pen money" – money created by the stroke of the bank president's pen when he approves a loan and credits the proceeds to the borrower's checking account'.[29] Victoria Chick defines bank deposits as 'privately issued forms of money' and Daly argues that 'money creation has become a source of private income'.[30] In Britain and the US, increasingly money is being issued as personal debt, in addition to the long established lending for mortgages. In September 2006, UK personal debt (excluding mortgages) was £3,560 per person.[31] This is a source of profound instability as the dynamics of the economy depends on people's willingness to take on credit. A fundamental problem of debt-based money is that it creates a growth imperative within the economy. People must find work of any sort, not only to meet current expenses but also to service their debts.

Why growth is made 'an imperative'

While conventional economic theory would see money as 'a medium' of economic activity, it can be seen as an institutional form in its own right, with its own independent dynamic.[32] It is increasingly being recognised that money issue and circulation is crucial to economic development. This has given rise to widespread interest in micro-credit for local level market development. While credit is essential for those who are financially excluded in contemporary economies, it is questionable whether such a neo-market solution is the way forward for economically marginalised communities.

Under finance capital, money/credit issue is a means by which those who have control over, or access to, the money-creation process can establish ownership and control over the means and direction of production. Money is the means by which property and value are accumulated. The core feature of 'total' money economies, where the bulk of the population have no direct access to the means of sustenance, is that most people have no choice but to engage with them. People have to work for wages if they want to eat. Money is not just a medium of exchange or a store of value, it enables the basic circuits of life in the ME economy. Within a capitalised economy, therefore, access to money becomes a crucial question, together with the allocation of money-based value. Economic investors who build up their assets on debt may describe themselves as wealth-creators, whereas in fact they are more correctly described as, quite literally, money-makers. In the process they may produce valuable, useful and sustainable products; on the other hand, they may not. The most important point is that money issue is an independent dynamic within an economy. It does not just represent economic activity; it creates it. If the power of the capitalist market economy is to be broken and alternative economic forms established, the unchallenged access of the capitalist market to new money issue cannot remain. Money issue and access is a vital question for ecofeminist political economy not only because of its impact on women's marginalisation and on the environment, but because of its impact on the right to livelihood and on economic democracy.

Given that money is central to the functioning of capitalism and is the main mechanism dividing the dualist economy, money access and circulation is a vital issue for ecofeminist analysis.[33] In a system where priorities are driven by 'effective demand' access to money is a core political issue. The importance of seeing money as a social institution is that its issue and circulation cannot be seen as 'natural'. In an early statement, Culbertson argued,

> ... the progressiveness, efficiency, and stability of an economy ... depends largely upon the quality of judgement applied by the suppliers of funds. This fact is not sufficiently appreciated. The reason for this is that people tend to accept whatever pattern of economic events emerges as inexorably

ordained by fate, rather than seeing it as determined by institutions and habits of behaviour that could have been quite different.[34]

This understanding is vital because of 'the central role of financial decisions *in allocating the resources of the economy*'.[35] Chick also points out that 'money confers on those with authority to issue new money the power to pre-empt resources'.[36]

The importance of revealing the operation of the money system is that it is arguably one of the institutions of capitalism that is most vulnerable to critical analysis. Money is one of the most intangible and social aspects of the economy. It is, and has been, a source of instability and insecurity. It demonstrably has no basis for its value, particularly given its inflationary history, and currently virtually uncontrolled credit issue in some countries. Also, the money system, unlike private property is already acknowledged to be within the public sphere of influence, and therefore could be subject, if politically desired, to democratic control. For Chick, the money system is essentially social, where 'social organisation influences monetary circulation'; she also sees 'a mutuality of state and social support of money in the modern western economy'.[37]

Even though the mechanism of money creation is now largely understood, Daly argues that its impact has not been addressed, 'although today the fact that commercial banks create much more money than the government is now explained in every introductory economics text, its full significance and effects on the economy have still not been sufficiently considered'.[38] Chick adds that the key issue is whether money is 'a creation of the state or of private consensus', but the more important question is whether it is subject to democratic control.[39] The irony of the current situation is that money creation is effectively in private hands through commercial decisions in the banking system, but the state still retains responsibility for managing and supporting the system, albeit at arm's length through central banks. It is therefore politically important to make public the fact that society collectively bears ultimate responsibility for the failures of the commercial money creation system, but has no influence on the overall direction of how finance is invested or used. In the process, government issue of money through borrowing is frowned upon while companies like Long Term Capital Management and ENRON appear to have virtually unlimited lines of credit and are 'bailed out' when they collapse. Perelman points to the further irony that while 'the financial system can bail out a Long Term Capital Management for a few billion dollars ... nobody knows how to recover depleted energy sources or to rescue devastated environments on a global scale'.[40]

As new money in the economy is effectively produced out of thin air, there is a strong case for putting that money into the hands of the people as a whole, rather than into the market. This is particularly important in global terms where the huge issue of state and commercial borrowing is being used to finance military adventures and asset acquisition under capital de-regulation. The ability to use money issue for the process of capital accumulation depends also on the global dominance of particular currencies. Credit money is therefore also an issue of global exploitation. However, economic gain from the exploitation of credit money is not just a feature of commercial companies, it has long been used by governments on an international level. Understanding and challenging money issue within the dominant currency economies is therefore vital. The desire of many green thinkers to build sustainable local economies will be continually frustrated if the generation and circulation of credit continues apace, particularly on the global level.

Challenging the money system

There are two major concerns about the current way of issuing money. First this money is a national resource and should be subject to democratic control and used for social purposes. The second is that such expenditures determine the priorities of the economy. Both are vital for the creation of a complex but ecologically sustainable and just economy. Ways of changing the economic system through the money system are currently being debated.[41]

One of the first changes that would take place is that the use of newly issued money would be democratically determined, together with the decision as to whether it should be subject to interest or issued debt free. It may be that the choice would be to allow new money to be used commercially, but it is highly unlikely that people would vote for a purely speculative use. It may be that a green and socialist society would still retain a commercial market sector, but this would need to be funded by real investment, that is already circulated money, and be subject to strict environmental and employment regulations. Most importantly, people could have a say in the priority for commercial investment, rather than always being at the end-of-pipe as a consumer. At present, given that money is issued largely into the private sector, it has to be taxed back out again (with difficulty) into public use. Socially issued money could go the other way round with social use expenditure carried out first with the commercial sector having to earn the money through socially relevant and ecologically sustainable activities.

One possibility is to issue new money as a Citizen's Income.[42] This could be a universal income or it could be used to influence the economy through being issued or enhanced selectively, for example, by region. A basic income could be paid to people who live or settle in underpopulated regions or to support regional populations with particular difficulties. New money issue could also be allocated to a local development bank to help establish local production, local food provisioning, and local power generation. Equally, new money could be channelled towards supporting women's work and lives and away from the profit-based producer–consumer economy. A case can be made of course, that any money system, no matter how democratically run or administered, will be destructive as it treats the material world and personal services as measurable by money. I would argue this is not the case. Under capitalism money is the mechanism of commodification. But under a different system, social money, free of the demands of profit, could be used as a mechanism of social integration and solidarity.

Ecofeminist political economy argues that the capitalist market is disembodied and disembedded, carved out of the totality of human existence within the natural world. An analysis of women's work shows how the dualist 'economy' fails to acknowledge its true resource base and how it is parasitical upon sustaining systems, including the environment. As a result, these are exploited and damaged. This chapter has described how ecofeminist political economy challenges the false boundaries of the dualised economy to begin the process of creating a provisioning system that will meet human needs and enhance human potential without destroying the life of the planet.

A provisioning economy would start from the embodiment and embeddedness of human lives, from the life of the body and the ecosystem, from women's work and the vitality of the natural world. Prioritising the life-world of women's work would mean that patterns of work and consumption would be sensitive to the human life-cycle. Necessary production and exchange would be fully integrated with the dynamics of the body and the environment. Provisioning of necessary goods and services would be the main focus of the economy in which all work would be fulfilling and shared. The idea of sufficiency would come before the dynamics of the market or the profit-motive. Priorities would be determined by the most vulnerable members of the community, not its 'natural' leaders as defined by economic dominance. To achieve this, the market economy must be challenged and pathways to a sustainable economy identified. The money system is not the only determinant of the functioning of the dualist economy, but it does influence economic directions and priorities. Making the issue of new money subject to democratic control, is essential to begin the process of building a non-gendered, egalitarian and ecologically sustainable provisioning economy.

Notes

1. See Mary Mellor, *Feminism and Ecology*, Cambridge: Polity, 1997; Ariel Salleh, *Ecofeminism as Politics: Nature, Marx, and the Postmodern*, London: Zed Books, 1997.
2. For a preoccupation with 'essentialism' see: Noel Sturgeon, *Ecofeminist Natures*, New York: Routlege, 1997; Catriona Sandilands, *The Good-Natured Feminist*, University of Minnesota

Press, 1999. For (non-essentialist) materialist ecofeminist writing: Maria Mies, *Patriarchy and Accumulation on a World Scale*, London: Zed Books, 1986; Ariel Salleh, 'Nature, Woman, Labor, Capital: Living the Deepest Contradiction' in Martin O'Connor (ed.), *Is Capitalism Sustainable?*, New York: Guilford, 1994; Mary Mellor, 'Women, Nature and the Social Construction of "Economic Man"', *Ecological Economics*, 1997, Vol. 20, No. 2, 129–40.

3. Ellie Perkins (ed.), 'Special Issue: Women, Ecology and Economics', *Ecological Economics*, 1997, Vol. 20, No. 2; Ellie Perkins and Edith Kuiper (eds), 'Explorations: Feminist Ecological Economics', *Feminist Economics*, 2005, Vol. 11, No. 3, 107–48.

4. Julie Nelson, 'The Study of Choice or the Study of Provisioning: Gender and the Definition of Economics' in Marianne Ferber and Julie Nelson (eds), *Beyond Economic Man*, University of Chicago Press, 1993; Marilyn Power, 'Social Provisioning as a Starting Point for Feminist Economics', *Feminist Economics*, 2004, Vol. 10, No. 3, 3–19; Nancy Folbre and Michael Bittman, *Family Time: The Social Organisation of Care*, London: Routledge, 2004.

5. Colin Hines, *Localisation: A Global Manifesto*, London: Earthscan, 2000.

6. Veronika Bennholdt-Thomsen and Maria Mies, *The Subsistence Perspective*, London: Zed Books, 1999; Veronika Bennholdt-Thomsen, Nicholas Faraclas, and Claudia von Werlhof (eds), *There is an Alternative: Subsistence and Worldwide Resistance to Corporate Globalization*, London: Zed Books, 2001.

7. J.K. Gibson-Graham, *The End of Capitalism (As We Knew It)*, Oxford: Blackwell 1996; Paul Langley and Mary Mellor, '"Economy" Sustainability and Sites of Transformative Space', *New Political Economy*, 2002, Vol. 7, No. 1, 49–65.

8. Richard Douthwaite, *Short Circuit: Strengthening Local Economies for Security in an Unstable World*, Totnes: Green Books, 1996; Richard Douthwaite, *The Ecology of Money*, Totnes: Green Books, 1999; Richard Douthwaite and Daniel Wagman, *Barataria: A Community Exchange Network for the Third System*, Utrecht: Strohal, 1999; Mary-Beth Raddon, *Community and Money*, Montreal: Black Rose, 2003.

9. Joel Kovel, *The Enemy of Nature: The End of Capitalism or the End of the World*, London: Zed Books, 2002.

10. Michael Perelman, *The Perverse Economy*, Basingstoke: Palgrave Macmillan, 2003, p. 147.

11. Edith Kuiper and Yolande Sap, *Out of the Margin*, London: Routledge, 1995; Ferber and Nelson, *Beyond Economic Man*; Julie

Nelson, *Feminism, Objectivity, and Economics*, London: Routledge, 1996.

12. Susan Donath, 'The Other Economy: A Suggestion for a Distinctly Feminist Economics', *Feminist Economics*, 2000, Vol. 6, No. 1, 115–23, p. 115.

13. Hilkka Pietila, *Tomorrow Begins Today*, ICDA/ISIS Workshop at Forum '85, Niarobi, 1985; Marilyn Waring, *Counting for Nothing*, Sydney: Allen and Unwin, 1988.

14. Bennholdt-Thomsen and Mies, *The Subsistence Perspective*.

15. Hazel Henderson, *Creating Alternative Futures: The End of Economics*, West Hartford: Kumerian Press, 1996.

16. Nancy Folbre, *Who Pays for the Kids?*, London: Routledge, 1993; Susan Himmelweit (ed.), *Inside the Household: From Labour to Care*, London: Macmillan, 2000; Agneta Stark, 'Warm Hand in Cold Age: On the Need for a New World Order of Care', *Feminist Economics*, 2005, Vol. 11, No. 2, 7–36.

17. Robert Bullard, *Dumping in Dixie: Race, Class and Environmental Quality*, Boulder: Westview, 1994.

18. Susan Feiner, 'Portrait of Homo Economicus as a Young Man' in Martha Woodmansee and Mark Osteen (eds), *The New Economic Criticism*, London: Routledge, 1999; Ferber and Nelson, *Beyond Economic Man*.

19. Martha MacDonald, Shelley Phipps, and Lynn Lethbridge, 'Taking its Toll: The Influence of Paid and Unpaid Work on Women's Well-being', *Feminist Economics*, 2005, Vol. 11, 63–94.

20. Mary Mellor, *Breaking the Boundaries*, London: Virago, 1992, p. 251.

21. Anna Agathangelou, *The Global Political Economy of Sex*, Basingstoke: Palgrave Macmillan, 2004.

22. Mies, *Patriarchy and Accumulation on a World Scale*; Rosi Braidotti, Ewa Charkiewicz, Sabine Hausler, and Saskia Wieringa, *Women, the Environment and Sustainable Development*, London: Zed Books, 1994; Wendy Harcourt (ed.), *Feminist Perspectives on Sustainable Development*, London: Zed Books, 1994; Christa Wichterich, *The Globalised Woman*, London: Zed Books, 2000.

23. Frances Hutchinson, Mary Mellor, and Wendy Olsen, *The Politics of Money: Towards Sustainability and Economic Democracy*, London: Pluto, 2002.

24. Robert Lane, *The Loss of Happiness in Market Democracies*, New Haven, CT: Yale University Press, 2000; Richard Layard, *Happiness: Lessons from a New Science*, London: Penguin, 2005.

25. Mellor, *Feminism and Ecology*.

26. James Robertson, *Transforming Economic Life*, London: Schumacher Society and New Economics Foundation, 1998; James Robertson and John Bunzl, *Monetary Reform: Making it Happen!*, London: International Simultaneous Policy Organisation, 2003.

27. Herman Daly, *Ecological Economics and the Ecology of Economics*, Cheltenham: Elgar, 1999, p. 142; Steve Keen, *Debunking Economics: The Naked Emperor of the Social Sciences*, London: Pluto, 2001, p. 289. See also Peter Soderbaum, *Ecological Economics*, London: Earthscan, 2000.

28. John Kenneth Galbraith, *Money: Whence it Came and Where it Went*, London: Penguin, 1975, p. 29.

29. J. Tobin, 'Commercial Banks and Creators of Money' in D. Carson (ed.), *Banking and Monetary Studies*, Homewood, IL: Unwin, 1963, p. 408.

30. Victoria Chick, *On Money, Method and Keynes*, Basingstoke: Palgrave Macmillan, 1992, p. 141; Daly, *Ecological Economics*, p. 141.

31. *BBC News*, 27 September 2006.

32. Randall Wray, *Credit and State Theories of Money: The Contribution of A. Mitchell Innes*, Cheltenham: Elgar, 2004; Geoffrey Ingham, *The Nature of Money*, Cambridge: Polity, 2004.

33. Hutchinson, Mellor, and Olsen, *The Politics of Money*; Mary Mellor, 'The Politics of Money and Credit as a Route to Ecological Sustainability and Economic Democracy', *Capitalism Nature Socialism*, 2005, Vol. 16, No. 2, 45–60.

34. J. Culbertson, 'Government Financial Policy in the Effective Market Economy' in Carson, *Banking and Monetary Studies*, p. 152.

35. Ibid., p. 151.

36. Chick, *On Money, Method and Keynes*, p. 141.

37. Ibid., p. 164, p. 142.

38. Daly, *Ecological Economics*, p. 142.

39. Chick, *On Money, Method and Keynes*, p. 141.

40. Perelman, *The Perverse Economy*, p. 93.

41. Mercy Harmer, 'A Green Look at Money' in Nancy Scott Cato and Miriam Kennet (eds), *Green Economics*, Aberystwyth: Green Audit, 1999; Daly, *Ecological Economics*; Douthwaite, *The Ecology of Money*; Robertson, *Transforming Economic Life*; Bernard Lietaer, *The Future of Money*, London: Century, 2001; Robertson and Bunzl, *Monetary Reform*; Mellor, 'The Politics of Money and Credit'.

42. Clive Lord, 'An Introduction to Citizen's Income' in Scott Cato and Kennet, *Green Economics*.

15

SAVING WOMEN: SAVING THE COMMONS

Leo Podlashuc

The practice of Savings among autonomous communities in the global South is a material antithesis to the logic of neoliberalism. Contra individual consumerism and the false consciousness of aspirational society, savings collectives founded upon the social ecology of daily livelihood subtly deconstruct the oppressions of industrial-modernity. Through a reassertion of the commons as shared conservation and production of resources, Shack/slum Dwellers International (SDI) is developing a transnational social movement mainly of dispossessed women resisting the neo-apartheid of market practices, while shifting the site of historical agency from elite agendas to people's agendas. The grassroots exchange programmes that led to this proliferating social movement were formally initiated by Argentine Jesuit Father Jorge Anzorena in Asia during the 1970s.[1] Unlike earlier worker organisations based on socialist or anarchist agendas, this people's programme was directed at an 'unconscious class', the 'poorest of the poor' in the global South, a constituency that Marx called the *lumpenproletariat*. Today, in 2007, SDI groups are active in Angola, Argentina, Bolivia, Brazil, Cambodia, Colombia, East Timor, Ghana, India, Indonesia, Kenya, Laos, Malawi, Mozambique, Namibia, Nepal, Pakistan, Philippines, Sierra Leone, South Africa, Sri Lanka, Swaziland, Tanzania, Thailand, Uganda, Vietnam, Zambia, Zimbabwe.[2]

Savings is the first principle of SDI and guides all of its rituals. SDI savings groups are face-to-face communities based upon the daily collection of money for self-help or crisis needs. These small local groups link hundreds of poor families together across cities in the global South, forming what SDI call 'Federations'. These are linked to regional affiliations, which in turn are attached to the transnational confederation of shack/slumdwellers that make up SDI. What appears on the ground as a small self-help or crisis collection group is thus attached to a vast network of similar autonomous groups across the global South, capable of pooling considerable resources and rallying masses of members in concerted action. As this chapter will show, savings is a pragmatic, collective response to poverty; it is a social exercise; it is an instrument for pedagogy; it is a vehicle for advocacy; it is a heuristic device; and it is an internationally active grassroots political movement.

The semantics of savings

Savings is a survival strategy that follows the contours of poverty yet whose formulation and material location acts as a 'ritual' for social cohesion, uplift and agency.[3] Succinctly, each day groups of women from slums go from home to home and gather savings from each other in order to collectively address the livelihood struggles they share. It is important to note that savings is not simply a financial issue like micro-credit, rather it is a social exercise. As SDI folk say, it is a method for collecting people, of creating social solidarity within the atomised milieu of poverty. According to slumdweller Jockin Arputham, 'savings activity is the glue that holds together the community groups, and underlies their other activities'.[4]

Savings exemplifies the way in which SDI appropriates and reconfigures as *praxis*, a clichéd and functionary verb of capitalist practice. Saving, to 'save' is a word with a useful ambiguity, it can mean both to set aside for later, to conserve, as well as to rescue and redeem. Saving can be understood in both material and ideological ways. Its use as praxis resonates closely to Paulo Freire's project of a 'true word'.[5] In material terms, the idea of saving is of course not limited to the capitalist modality. As a conscious activity, anticipating and preparing for the future is a central element of what it means to be human. Theoretical constructions of the future imply the capacity to overcome temporal limitations, to survive beyond the moment and of being able to hold over for later. It is a significant existential indicator of the ability to endure, of having material surplus. It is central to a notion of hope, both materially and psychically, as it enables envisioning, of being able to imagine alternative outcomes from those dictated by circumstances, leading to transformation of existential conditions. The concrete implications of saving stand in marked contrast to the survival struggles of the urban poor. For the poorest of the poor the immediacy of need and urgency of poverty often prohibits any consideration of the future. As praxis, savings directly engages in challenging this limitation, constructing through collective practice from the many minute occasional surpluses of the individually poor, a common fund that represents material possibility beyond survival. In this way savings seeks to transcend the material and initiates the production of hope, critical to transformative imaginaries.

The creation of an imagined future brings the word's second level of meaning into play: redemption, linking the parallel religious meaning of saving (as in saving souls) to the material one. As will be explained in greater detail below, the social aspects of collective saving provide an answer to the anomie and mutual hostility of the slums. Members engage with each other in new sociable ways, imbuing them with a sense of deliverance from pervasive alienation and aloneness. Academic Arjun Appadurai captures this semantic duality:

> Creating informal savings groups among the poor (now canonized by the donor world as 'micro-credit') is a major world-wide technique for improving financial citizenship for the urban and rural poor throughout the world, often building on older ideas of revolving credit and loan facilities managed informally and locally, outside the purview of the state and the banking sector. But in the life of the Alliance (SDI), 'savings' has a profound ideological, even salvational status.[6]

Saving as word and action seems to offer the appropriate content and semantic complexity for an effective neo-Freireian praxis. It fuses material and ideological elements, combining pragmatism with salvational qualities. In both cases the important premise is the implicit recognition of a trans-temporal possibility, of a future. To 'save' is to recognise the possibility of a tomorrow, reflecting and offering the possibility of surviving the immediate. The material and social aspects of these savings schemes feed back into the social character of the groups, breaking down hostility and building a sense of community.

Saving and savings groups are not new. One might say that they go back historically to the early moments in anthropological time when humans first began to collectively hoard a surplus to carry them through lean times. They are critical to future survival. Whether it be grain-seed, herds of sheep or flakes of hard flint and obsidian for implements, saving has been a perennial shadow activity of the human social process, occurring spontaneously and repeatedly all over the world around diverse material needs. It can be argued that collective conservation practice is a direct corollary of *gattungswesen* or species being, produced logically by the human collective capacity to imagine the future.[7] Conservation and commonwealth are integral to conceptions of the commons. Savings groups de-individualise surplus, that by collectivising, suggests a commons approach to material scarcity. As a group formulation, saving has always provided a solution to scarcity overcoming individual material and temporal limitations. In this sense, savings groups can be seen as an embodiment of hope – and an 'embodied materialism'.[8]

One such savings collective is Mahila Milan, a group of predominantly Muslim street women from the Byculla area of Central Mumbai. This community's history of saving encapsulates the organic spontaneity of the process as well as indicates the increasingly complex social relations that emerge with it. To understand this process it is worth quoting Sheela Patel, Director of the Society for the Promotion of Area Resource Centres (SPARC):

> Savings began with Mahila Milan saying, 'We want to build a house. But no one will give us a free house; we will have to take a loan. How will we take a loan? No one will give us a loan. They will say, "you are bad girls, you don't have anything." So let's save money.' They started to put some money aside. The minute they started putting a certain amount of money aside, there was a demand 'why don't you give each other loans? That we should help each other.' Then Lakshmi's husband was in trouble, so she came back to the group and said, 'I need a loan'. So they started this daily savings thing.[9]

Mahila Milan's idea of savings was in this case a spontaneous grassroots answer to the pavement dwellers' need for a secure home. But in addressing this question it also provided the capacity to deal with the many other immediate crises that were commonplace in their lives. As Patel continues:

> The whole thing of starting a crisis and consumption savings and loans programme emerged from the daily savings. They said, 'OK we will have two savings schemes. We will put on one side the money for housing and we won't touch it, and then in case, we will put aside a little bit for when we desperately need it.' So, they first gained the ability to protect their savings for the long term and then they produced the second one. When they produced the second one they realised that they still were all indebted to moneylenders ... paying very high interest, and all they could afford to pay back each month was only interest. They were really desperate, which again forced the savings scheme to deal with this issue. Making it now a constantly borrowing and savings scheme. So now there are three types of loans and savings. For housing, for income generation, and for crisis and consumption. The same group of people manage all of these.[10]

This ability to respond and overcome problems, indicative of a self-creating, self-reflecting instrument, synthesising action and imagination bears the hallmarks of praxis. In this case it represents an organic praxis located in the ranks of the lumpen-proletariat. Mahila Milan took a commonplace idea and through the practice of daily life fashioned it to satisfy a broad spectrum of poverty needs. As it was practised it responded directly to the concrete needs and demands placed upon it. It developed a life of its own and contrary to orthodox dismissal of the underclass, proved enduring beyond the immediacy of the crisis that created it. Defying the atomised opportunism generally attributed to the lumpenproletariat, savings has in fact become a sustained cultural practice.

Community and autonomy

At the close of the Cold War, when a triumphant neoliberalism became the dominant hegemony, there were a great number of schemes operating all over the globe with a specific focus on saving money for the poorest of the poor. They were in the global South however, generally disconnected and localised, typical of the atomising impact of super power pressures on the Majority World. The opportunities provided by the new era in terms of communication and travel suggested the possibility of overcoming these divisions. The world was ready to accommodate expressions of grassroots banking. Micro-credit and micro-financing moved from the periphery to mainstream practice, allowing institutions like the Grameen Bank to flourish. In a sense, micro-financing has now become paradigmatic within development programmes and key to notions of extending and deepening citizenship.[11] The idea has spread all over the world and it is this common practice that SDI both helped establish and build upon. Savings, in its SDI formulation, is currently practised in around 30 countries, with many hundreds of thousands of savings schemes linked together in Federations that are affiliated to the social movement.

The savings group is seen as the hub of the entire SDI federating process. The exclusivity of formal banks effectively prohibits the lumpenproletariat from using their facilities; requiring identity documentation, legitimate addresses, basic numeracy and literacy, demanding bank charges, minimum balances, refusing to accept deposits in small coinage, and so on. As a result the shack/slumdwellers find it impossible to access banks and other formal institutions. This leaves what little cash they do acquire in jeopardy, always at risk of loss to fire, theft, extortion etc. This insecurity, in turn, encourages the poor to squander the little they have so as not to run the risk of such loss, thereby prohibiting any conservation of assets and reifying the slough of poverty. Savings schemes are essentially informal and autonomous cash banks in the slums. They originate in the perennial collective banking practices of the poor, typified by South African *stokvels*.[12] They are an autonomous grassroots alternative to market created institutions that specifically address the social and material needs of shack/slumdwellers. A crucial element of these savings schemes is the fact that the majority of members – nine cases out of ten – are women. The importance of this is that generally amongst the poor, 'it is the women who are in charge of keeping the hours, running household expenses, deciding where things are kept in the home and so on'.[13] Savings groups create a buffer against the many crises that poor women experience, allowing these women to ride out crisis moments and to survive until alternatives arise. After that, the survivor's savings go to help others.

An additional limitation of formal banking institutions is the fact that should the poor actually manage to save in banks or post offices, their savings never entitle them to loans. As Joel Bolnick points out, 'they save their hard-earned cents so that the banks can lend that money to the wealthy and middle classes'.[14] Savings schemes answer this need, rather like the currently popular micro-finance principle, allowing the savers to benefit directly from their own savings. But in savings groups the savings of the people work for the people themselves. Members of these schemes can take loans for small business ventures or for crises in their families. Flexibility characterises the design of savings groups. There is no exact template, rather a series of practices that the group shapes and colours by their specific needs. Bolnick describes it as 'a survival mechanism, which follows the contours of poverty directly'.[15] This is done generally in two ways. Firstly, as 'daily savings' it follows the temporal rhythm set by poverty. The goal of most savings groups is for savings to be collected daily. Daily saving matches informal earning patterns, and as such works with the rhythms of poverty. Secondly, it sets no limitations on the amount saved, any amount large or small is accepted; it is the act of saving which counts.

A significant social factor is that collective saving works to reduce the stigma of poverty. The shame of lack compounds the anomie of the slums. Savings challenges this directly; poverty is exposed, ritualised, and accommodated. In going from shack to shack, pavement bedroll to bedroll, members of the savings group discover each other intimately. Little can be hidden and in this way poverty is shared, discovered, understood and through this dialogue, defanged. Adding pennies to the collective coffer, as a slumdweller remarked, 'is the sound of poverty laughing at itself'.[16] Savings becomes a social ritual, a time for sharing gossip and news, an all-embracing discipline of social inclusion providing a reassuring regularity in an otherwise chaotic and merciless environment. In this way saving mobilises and builds social cohesion within the ranks of the poor. The system is devised to be as inclusive of the 'poorest of the poor' as possible, practised so that no one member of a settlement is left out. By continually triggering new savings groups, including ever more people meeting every day, the collective saving process steadily increases its scale.

When these savings groups are linked to the wider network of Federations, they amass considerable amounts of money and people. These funds are ploughed back into the communities through slum development projects such as collective sanitation blocks, land acquisitions etc. The projects represent an autonomous approach to development, reflecting grassroots initiative. This challenges orthodox social theory's dismissal of the underclass as not having a capacity for anything beyond immediate self-interest. Drawing funds from their own savings provides slumdwellers with the material autonomy to set their own terms. In this way, saving seems to re-capture the essential spirit of non-aligned development and Steve Biko's self-reliance, and makes it core to the construction of the social movement.[17]

The savings process has thus evolved a logic of aggregation identical to its collection methodology, incrementally building Federation networks into a large social movement, in effect creating webs of solidarity. A favoured metaphor used by the shack/slumdwellers is that they are like many small weak fish that combine in a school. The school acts as one, mimicking a large fish and as such they can then enter the sea of big fish.[18] As Patel puts it:

> ... when people produce these big numbers ... banks come to you and say, 'Will you come and save in our place? Can we help you?' Then we say, 'What are you offering?' These kinds of relations are not done for love but for what suits them. So it serves also your purpose of how to use this money to leverage other money. Another important aspect of savings, also of enumeration or any of the rituals is how your internal action can leverage external resources. It's what we call: Corporate means for revolutionary ends.[19]

By this is meant that SDI's poor 'revolutionise' development, seizing control of the process and dictating the terms of its unfolding. This self-determination of the agenda of their upliftment within a paradigm of scarcity and commodification is both radical and problematic. While their prominence certainly amounts to a seizure of resources from below, it is also true that the dialectics of engagement operate equally in all directions, and the structural implications of this replication of the hegemonic narrative seem contradictory to the ethos of collectivity and commons that rally the initial savings groups in the first place.[20] Be that as it may, savings does provide a means of multiplying the power of the many few into a unified mass-movement of the Majority World poor. This solidarity underpins SDI's quest for autonomy.

Savings as *praxis*

Under globalised capitalism, cities are the inevitable spatial focus of the cash nexus. The contradictions of this subsumption express themselves clearly in urban spatialities. Slums are the spatial nexus of multiple crises of exhaustion, but under universal commodification, the paramount scarcity is felt in financial terms. Slums are concentrated sites of cash exhaustion. SDI savings contest this exhaustion by asserting cash as a new form of 'the commons'. In this radical form, cash ceases to be the instrument of oppression but the tool for liberation. Challenging this exhaustion creates dialogue around cash, savings de-individualises cash and collectivises it. Savings thus identifies a primary obstacle that in a commodified world economy limits shack/slumdwellers' humanity through lack of money. By creating a commons of shared savings SDI groups build the foundation for transforming this limitation and overcoming it. The SDI formulation of savings resonates closely with Freire's praxis of 'cultural action'.[21] Savings, like Freireian dialogical practice, is capable of multiple unfoldings using cash to create social subjectivity.

As with Freire's methodology, the SDI praxis of savings creates dialogue between reflex and theory (as a 'true' practice) as well as across the normative issues of what is and what ought to be. These normative imaginaries, to envision a better future, are key to social transformation, for SDI norms are not imposed but appear to evolve from the logic of social action. Savings collectives emerge from the concrete livelihood struggles of the oppressed themselves, the authenticity of which grounds their hope in reality. When these savings collectives start generating utopian imaginaries, they generally move from oppositional to dialogical intercourse and begin to establish degrees of autonomy from the forces that limit them. Freire observed that history places 'limit situations' upon the poor.[22] Generally these confine and inhibit those within them, but under the right conditions, these can be read positively, and limits become the points of envisioning what could be. SDI's savings groups as dialogical processes provide just such positive visions to transcend the slum as a limit situation. Their construction of a cash commons redefines 'being' as being from more, rather than being from nothing. Savings it seems, as a praxis of dialogue, transcends the zero-sum nature of poverty, by providing options for change and a sense of what the future could be.

In a Freireian fashion, savings redefines the limitations of the cash nexus in a radical way: cash as social relations. Freire made the point of contrasting what he called the 'banking' model of education with a 'problem solving' model.[23] Banking is passive and does not encourage active intervention. For SDI, banks are closed, hermetic institutions that separate people from their money. As commodified service providers they are corporate accumulation devices, whose 'bottom line' is profit. Deconstructing Freire's metaphor of 'banking' in a literal sense, savings collectives move from banking money to dialoguing it. Dialogical saving is directed toward problem solving. It reflects a collective investigation of poverty and finds solutions to it. In this way, savings becomes a collective grassroots research process into the problems facing shack/slumdwellers. Savings, for SDI, is an embedded emancipatory action involving actively 'embodied' participation in a material struggle. This provides dialogue between structure and agency, grounding action in a critical reading of reality. As pointed out, according to Freire this conversation creates a dialogical knowledge that avoids passive fatalism and false hope. It becomes a praxis of conscientisation and mobilisation, creating a bottom up methodology of knowledge specific to poverty alleviation.

International mobilisation

Savings is the first step in SDI's mobilisation strategy. In around 30 countries across the global South where SDI operates, a multitude of shack/slumdwellers practise savings. This is the first node of aggregation in their social movement and the beginning point for all their activities. The day-to-day business of SDI is saving, and all else follows from it. The social movement is propagated by the sharing of the experience of poverty through the dialogue of saving. Through ritualised collective saving, shack/slumdwellers discover the similarities of their livelihood struggles and become conscientised of their shared plight. Contrary to orthodox Marxism and its misgivings about the lumpenproletariat, the praxis of savings reveals the capacity of the atomised poor to empathise with each other's struggles and how savings resonates with the material logic of their situation, revealing its structural limitations and possibilities for change.

The ritual of women going from shack to shack every day and sharing details of their lives in the practice of saving, builds deep-felt social commitment to the collective. This is reflected in the words of a Zambian member:

> Savings – you are building your future through the group. Before collecting, the women (collectors) they ask me about my life; they ask – are you OK? Do you need anything? Is your last-born daughter better? The Savings group looks out for each other. So you are not in your family alone, you are part of a bigger thing. Yes, a community![24]

The quality of social intimacy that savings collectives produce is the key to their capacity to mobilise the marginalised. This seems to override even the material considerations, as Zimbabwe activist Beth Chitekwe-Biti points out:

> Actually saving in Zimbabwe does not make sense! Inflation is too great. If you save money it loses value! So for us in Zimbabwe, savings is a ritualistic effort of coming together. People asking about money is an excuse for more social encounter. Money is just a way to make people come together![25]

Social ritual appears to be paramount, justified by the material linkages. The interplay between the material and the social in a situation of scarcity goes to provide an antidote for the anomie and hostility of urban involution, building trust and a sense of attendant community. The sociality arising from savings collectives challenges the prejudiced vision of the lumpenproletariat as an irremediably criminal and dangerous class.

Savings builds trust amongst members through establishing materially collateral relationships. Members 'take a risk' together and being in it altogether quite clearly goes to forging collective responsibility and a sense of group identity. This collective identity is in turn extended to the broader Federation and ultimately trans-nationally as SDI. Savings as praxis becomes a global mobilisation strategy that appears to break down and overcome the enclave and ghetto formation, which is generated by the apartheid logic of current market forces. It seems to reach deep into a common sense of alienation and exclusion and fosters an overarching social identity, what slumdwellers call being the 'poorest of the poor'. This sociality is located primarily in women, amongst whom the implications of belonging to a mass sorority resonates profoundly, as Patel observes:

> ... just as you pay your membership fees to join a union, so your savings book is your ID card in the Federation. For me over time, apart from the fact that it is an ID card, it produces a new focus on women's collectives within the community. It's always the women who do this, so it's an acknowledgement of the role women already play.[26]

SDI's Federation allies generally operate three levels of savings and loan structures simultaneously. These echo the three categories Patel described earlier of crisis and consumption saving; income generation saving; and saving for houses and larger projects. South Africa's Federation of the United Poor (FEDUP) illustrates these.

- *NsukuZonke* (daily savings): for consumer, production and crisis loans, made amongst savings collective members. Each group is divided into smaller clusters for daily savings. Collectors visit members and collect whatever is available from one cent upward. Members' contributions are recorded in their own savings books as well as savings scheme record books. Savings are banked regularly. Withdrawals are allowed.
- *Inqolobane* (the granary): for larger production and enterprise loans. *Inqolobane* are regional funds to which all groups make monthly contributions.
- *uTshani* (housing savings): deposits for *uTshani* housing loans, as a kind of collective insurance against low repayments.[27] In this way the largest institutional form of savings assumes the collective responsibility for default. As the terms under which *uTshani* makes loans available to Federation members changes, savings towards land and infrastructure and housing will be treated differently. Savings may be used as deposits or collective guarantees. Savings towards housing may be used for deposits towards much smaller incremental loans for house building, or for direct investment in the house in order to construct a bigger house.

These incremental and concentric institutions match the way in which SDI mobilises people. The process seeks to be horizontal, and social hierarchy is actively discouraged. The outcome is what the shack/slumdwellers refer to as 'Federation'. Regional, national and transnational links via the Federation network provide the scale to create a mass-movement, while the focus on the primary unit of the savings scheme ensures that everywhere and everyone is equally important. Nevertheless, there is an inevitable and constant tension between these scales, the mass social movement on one hand, and the local savings scheme on the other. This tension is communicated and mediated by the parallel praxis of international visiting or Exchanges, thus creating deeply interwoven layers of connectedness. The cross-pollinating of people and process across the global South compels consistency and cohesion – an encyclopaedic linkage of knowledge that transcends their particularised experience.

While savings in many ways conforms to the concept of praxis found in the earlier 'Hegelian' writings of Marx, and in particular echoes Freireian methodology, it does challenge orthodox perceptions of the lumpenproletariat as an incompetent political actor. As socially self-created activity in response to external conditions beyond individual control, savings praxis goes some way to restore the dialectical foundation of emancipation as an active reflex to material conditions rather than an artificial creation of Marxist vanguardism. A collective self-interest is generated. Many members claim to feel that their 'salvation' comes through the group. The group becomes the vehicle for their collective uplift and self-determination. Unlike the orthodox vanguard approach, in unifying intellectual and mass action defined by self-creating activity, savings groups come to resemble Antonio Gramsci's chimerical understanding of the Modern Prince as – not a concrete individual, but an organism of collective will.[28] The sentient cadres of SDI combine to form a transnational social movement with the same general characteristics, constructing as it were, an 'intellectual-moral bloc' from below.[29] The global savings movement is made up of five tiers that correspond to the contours of poverty. The first tier is that of individual savings collectives on pavements or streets. The second tier is made up of settlement networks. The third is regional linkages hosting the settlements. The fourth tier is the national Federation of schemes. The fifth and international tier is that of SDI as such.

Urban involution alienates poor people in many different ways, but the overarching outcome is the way in which it atomises and individualises them. This alienation by separation is an amplification, intensification and reified expression of the neoliberal imperative of individualism. The effect is one of ubiquitous xenophobia, isolation and mutual hostility. Social constructions in this Hobbesian milieu tend toward insular, intolerant proto-fascist groupings such as street gangs, mafias, and militant religious sects. Standing against this tendency, SDI's savings collectives appear to act as a catalyst for reconstructing the integration of the individual into a more open idea of community, reconstituting in a way the Hegelian and early Marxist focus upon *gattungswesen*. Savings collectives are based upon daily social contact. By seeing the similarity of each other's plight and participating in each other's lives, savings scheme members overcome aloneness and reconvene as a social group. The savings group's capacity to act as an extended 'family' appears to be the key in this regard. The spontaneous upwelling of this familiarity suggests that it is based upon a pervasive common sentiment, akin to Erich Fromm's and Freire's 'social unconsciousness', an immanent class-consciousness among the ranks of the lumpenproletariat.[30]

Saving women

A key aspect of SDI is the fact that the bulk of its members are women, and that savings schemes deliberately focus upon foregrounding and empowering poor women. Few Marxists have thought about how to specify women as an historically relevant class, though Rosa Luxemburg was an exception. She also observed that capital accumulation presupposes the exploitation of ever more 'non-capitalist' milieux for the appropriation of more labour, more raw materials and more markets.[31] Veronika Bennholdt-Thomsen and Maria Mies continue this argument with specific reference to women and subsistence farmers, whom they recognise as contending with 'ongoing primitive accumulation and colonisation'.[32] According to Mies, the work of women and small peasants is conditioned by a similar logic:

> Their exploitation follows the example of the exploitation of nature as a resource which is allegedly free and inexhaustible. The means for the creation and maintenance of such an exploitative relationship is not the labour contract, as in the case of the wage labourer, but violence, physical and structural violence.[33]

Women, like natural resources, are considered 'free goods' and are exploited and appropriated by the industrial system in the same way as life. In the slums, this oppression is doubled. For just as capitalism requires a hinterland, so cities need the same. Under current conditions of ecological exhaustion, slums become satellite hinterlands attached conveniently within the city. Compounding the problem for women within slums, women become embodied hinterlands within these other hinterlands, unilaterally exploited. In validation of Mies' neo-Luxemburg conjecture, SDI evidence shows that women are the moment of intersection of most of the material and social vectors in the slums. They represent the nexus for social, biological and emotional reproduction of not just the class – but of the species – *gattungswesen*. To borrow Ariel Salleh's term, they are a 'meta-industrial class', seen to be outside of, yet indispensable to the functioning of capitalist economics.[34]

Yet, while observations of the structural relations of the poor show that women are central to the creation, maintenance of productive relations at large, as well as the wellbeing of community, this recognition is denied to them – even within their own terrain. They are unacknowledged and this lack of recognition is fundamental and complicit with the insidious frontier-like machismo that the apartheid form of hegemony takes in the slums. This insular patriarchy is so alienating that women themselves seem unaware of their oppression. Chicago based Indian academic-activist Srilatha Batliwala writes:

> ... so deep seated is the non acknowledgment of this role that women play, that even in the settlement itself, group discussions amongst women do

not consciously articulate this. The stark difference in what is seen and what is told indicates a clear absence of linkage between the two. It is as though women retain their experiences at a very intra-personal level and do not move their 'actually having done the task' to seeking acknowledgment for having done it. It is as though this is arrested at the doing stage itself. The spokespersons ... the individual male leader on the other hand has learnt to opine ... regardless of the accuracy of his generalizations, his ability to make these statements on behalf of all makes him the 'agent' for communication between the outside and the inside.[35]

Thus, women in the ranks of the poorest of the poor find that their *weltanschauung* is entirely filtered and mediated by a reified masculine expression of domestic hegemony. As a result, there is a deep-seated disconnection and social amnesia about the real strategic role of poor women, one that is taken for granted and denied even amongst themselves.

Contrary to those feminisms which disembody women in a neo-Platonic way, savings collectives as a predominantly women's movement reflect an embodied feminism, grounded in an ontology of historical victimisation and material empowerment. This resonates with perceptions of the African American scholar W.E.B. DuBois and with bell hooks' writing, and it is central to ecofeminist thought. The view of SDI is that women are simultaneously at the centre of and yet most exploited element in the slums. Their role as provider and nurturer confers upon women a deep and unrecognised burden of responsibility as the final repository of resources. Inevitably women are the 'holders' as Salleh characterises their protective labour, here applied to the conservation of economic reserves. This material and social centrality also makes women the most significant vector for change. In dialectical terms, if you transform women, then society is transformed.

Savings schemes are, in effect, a recognition that the locus of social possibility lies in the hands of women; that women are the single most important subject for political agency. Yet, the manner in which this is being done through SDI, does not directly threaten the prevalent systemic patriarchy, rather it is a process of pragmatic stealth. A Zambian SDI member makes this strategy clear:

> My husband does not work. I have 8 children and 7 grandchildren. I am renting the shack. I must feed my family. I want to start the business but my husband does not allow me. He gets very jealous. I must beg and scratch. I joined the Saving Group. I wanted to do something. My husband is not encouraging. But He does not object! It's women's business. So Savings is approved! He does not suspect a hidden agenda. The savings group was good advice.[36]

Thus without overtly challenging the masculine status quo, SDI, by institutionalising the centrality of women in savings collectives, has created a counter-power base with a domestic focus. The 'coming out' of slum women as the 'holders' of the commons of cash, contributes to transforming them from being the object of plunder to subjects of power. Women, previously sidelined and abused by the frontier machismo of the slums and shantytowns are through their role in savings collectives, commanding respect as the creators of social and financial stability and possibility. Savings, although not ending deeply entrenched gender bifurcation, does valorise and foreground the role of women.

Savings complies largely with the kind of problem-solving education that characterises Freire's 'pedagogy of the oppressed'. The daily practice of savings reveals to shack/slumdwellers their educational limitations in a positive and unthreatening way. Savings collection involves basic writing and accounting skills, and a needs-based incentive for learning. Celine D'Cruz makes the point:

> The process of savings and credit also builds the capacity of women to prioritize their credit needs, manage their moneys and book-keeping. All these skills come to use when addressing other issues in the community whether it be housing, sanitation or solid waste, so in fact the savings and credit process equips these communities to handle all the other issues that it wants to address.[37]

This praxis of learning happens at the immediate level of everyday slum life amidst the shanties and on the pavements. However, the pedagogy does not stop here, the process of savings is extended across space, networked to other Federation groups. As Bolnick points out:

> Poor settlements have vast stores of knowledge. The people of the communities are the only ones who could have the experiential basis for determining their own hierarchy of needs. They are best equipped to create their own priorities.[38]

Conscientisation and empowerment

Savings praxis initiates a social response to crises that converts the atomised poor from passivity to agency and from dependence to autonomy. The collective agency of the savings group provides many shack/slumdwellers with a focus of loyalty. It can become the house, *khan*, clan or tribe for a disconnected and alienated poor, adding an important secular and apolitical layer of identity superimposed upon their other prior and often restricting identities of religion, language, ethnicity, caste and tribe, that remain vestigial but ineradicable. Resonant with Biko's vision of self-reliance and restoration of the dignity of the oppressed, SDI claims that, 'savings is rooted in an affirmation of the dignity and strength of the homeless'.[39] This empowerment goes beyond the limitations of self-help, it also includes the premise of self-sufficient development. A priority evolved by savings has been to empower the poor to take command of the development agenda within their area. The strategy is to mobilise agency beyond the initiating crisis and turn it into a permanently ongoing process of social and material transformation. In this the methodology seems to aspire to a condition of permanent revolution, of continuously sustained community action. But whatever the underlying motivation, the evidence indicates that this strategy continues to resonate with communities, consolidating and reinforcing the sense of autonomy and collective pride.

The global crises of commodification and ecological exhaustion, as well as natural disasters such as climate change and HIV-Aids, have created a broad-reaching commonality amongst its victims that challenges the enclave formation of an increasingly apartheid-capitalist practice. SDI recognises the implications of global change and uses the rhetoric of engaging the neoliberal system on its own terms. The social movement makes a bold attempt in some arenas to mimic the strategies of corporate resource management to set its own development agenda and lever external resources – economic, political, social, and cultural. Synthesised within the dialectic of the globalised market economy, slumdwellers in SDI savings groups are learning to use corporate means for their collective ends. This is an irony rooted in pragmatism.

Some SDI activists draw cynical parallels between liberal economic discourse and liberal democratic practice, equating democracy with the market, wherein a parallel commodification occurs, only with political parties paid for in votes rather than cash.[40] In keeping with this critique, savings schemes try instead to emulate a progressive social actor, which transcends the 'divisive strategy of political-democratic practice', as one Kenyan activist put it.[41] What emerges from the combined efforts of the many savings groups is a Federation of the poor that seeks a different economic dispensation located in the idea of a redistribution of resources toward the poor by the poor themselves. This agenda resonates closely with earlier socialist and counter-hegemonic projects seeking economic democracy before political democracy. Cleverly, SDI skirts around politics to avoid dissipating its energy in what it perceives as futile and divisive pro-hegemonic exercise. Instead it focuses upon building a broad-reaching local and transnational populism and a radical approach to ownership and production located in a politics of social reproduction and a new commons. In a sense, savings praxis creates collective actors whose primary aim is to create fields of autonomy that in turn have a political impact. Another African SDI activist describes savings groups as

> ... the vanguard of their insurrection against the system which has rendered them abject. These face-to-face associations are in effect economic cadres whose task is to sabotage the normal flow of capital, blocking and inhibiting

its usual flow toward the rich and wealthy, undermining the established patterns of accumulation.[42]

While this view is not shared throughout SDI's rank and file, it does capture something about the way SDI operates. Certainly it confirms their self-conscious choice to refer to themselves as 'Shack/slum Dwellers International', revitalising the traditional counter-hegemonic and socialist appellation of the 'International'.

Despite the lack of a revolutionary consensus, the general principle behind creating savings groups is that they are the precondition for an alternative, communal accumulation strategy located in the ranks of *lumpen* slumdwellers – and the women who constitute the majority of them. Savings schemes are intended to be the repositories for the financial surplus of poor communities. Instead of being absorbed back into the flows of the rich via the invisible hand of the market, money is retained amongst the poor; circulated and made to work within the community and network of savings groups. This siphoning off and retention of their assets suggests a deliberate withholding of their funds, a cash boycott of the formal market. Certainly by resisting participation in the system of production that oppresses them, savings can redirect these resources to defending their social reproduction, 'to saving people'. In this way, the material aggregation provided by saving sets in motion a materially rooted, embodied social process of collective conscientisation – located in social reproduction and carried forward by a broad-based transnational linkage of the global South and its underclass.

Notes

1. Asian Coalition of Housing Rights, *Face to Face: Notes from the Network on Community Exchange*, Bangkok, 2000, p. 4. In conjunction with Savings, the practice of horizontal Exchanges involves poor community groups within SDI building political links by travelling across the global South. In these exchange visits, they bond, share, and learn from each other's lives in poverty. Exchanges are the mechanism for intellectual and social connection within the social movement of SDI. Incidentally, Father Jorge is Ché Guevara's second cousin. See also Leo Podlashuc, 'Class for Itself? Shack/

slum Dwellers International: The Praxis of a Transnational Poor Movement', Unpublished doctoral thesis, University of Technology, Sydney, 2007, p. 251.

2. Shack/slum Dwellers International (SDI), Online Available HTTP: <www.sdinet.org> (accessed 27 November 2007).

3. Anon. slumdweller, interview with the author, June 2004, Zenzeleni, South Africa. Transcript held in the SDI (1996–2006) *Archives*, CORC, Unit 7, Campground Centre, Durban Road, Mowbray, Cape Town, South Africa.

4. Jockin Arputham, interview with the author, August 2003, Durban: SDI *Archives*, p. 407.

5. Paulo Freire, *Cultural Action for Freedom*, Harmondsworth: Penguin, 1970, p. 33.

6. Arjun Appadurai, 'Deep Democracy: Urban Governmentality and the Horizon of Politics', *Environment and Urbanization*, 2001, Vol. 13, No. 2, 23–43.

7. For species being, see: Karl Marx, *Economic and Philosophic Manuscripts of 1844*, Moscow: Progress Publishers, 1956, p. 12.

8. Ariel Salleh, *Ecofeminism as Politics: Nature, Marx, and the Postmodern*, London: Zed Books, 1997, pp. 175–8.

9. Sheela Patel, interview with the author, June 2004, Sydney: SDI *Archives*, p. 324.

10. Ibid., pp. 324–5.

11. For the Grameen project, see, Online Available HTTP: <www.grameen-info.org> (accessed 27 November 2007).

12. *Stokvels* are grassroots collective savings groups used by the poor in South Africa, for burials, weddings, emergencies, school uniforms, presents, etc.

13. Sheela Patel, interview 2004: SDI *Archives*, p. 46.

14. Joel Bolnick, interview with the author, October 2005, Cape Town: SDI *Archives*, p. 389.

15. Ibid., p. 156.

16. Anon. slumdweller, interview with the author, December 2004, Old Fadama, Ghana: SDI *Archives*, p. 730.

17. Steve Biko, *The Testimony of Steve Biko*, London: Temple Smith, 1978.

18. Anon. slumdweller, interview with the author, September 2004, Cape Town: SDI *Archives*, p. 81.

19. Patel, interview 2004: SDI *Archives*, pp. 730–1.

20. However, it can be argued from an ecofeminist perspective that the gendered character of this class is 'a saving grace' against such hegemonic subsumption, as it anchors savings practice in the logic of reproduction, as distinct from productivist political economy.

21. Freire, *Cultural Action for Freedom*, p. 21.

22. Ibid., p. 80.

23. Ibid., p. 54.

24. Anon. slumdweller, interview with the author, September 2004, Cape Town: SDI *Archives*, p. 278.

25. Beth Chitekwe-Biti, interview with the author, August 2005, Durban: SDI *Archives*, p. 280.

26. Patel, interview 2004: SDI *Archives*, p. 731.

27. Ted Baumann, Joel Bolnick, and Diana Mitlin, 'Working Paper on Poverty Reduction in Urban Areas', *Environment and Urbanisation*, London: International Institute for Environment and Development, 2002.

28. Antonio Gramsci, *The Modern Prince and Other Writings*, New York: International Publishers, 1957.

29. Antonio Gramsci, *Selections from Prison Notebooks*, London: Lawrence and Wishart, 1971.

30. Erich Fromm, *Beyond the Chains of Illusion*, New York: Simon and Shuster, 1962.

31. Rosa Luxemburg, *The Accumulation of Capital*, New York: Monthly Review, 1968.

32. Veronika Bennholdt-Thomsen and Maria Mies, *The Subsistence Perspective*, London: Zed Books, 1999, p. 30.

33. Ibid., p. 12.

34. Salleh, *Ecofeminism as Politics*, pp. 164–6.

35. Srilatha Batliwala, 'Reorganisation of Communities to Ensure Women's Central Participation', 2004, Online Available HTTP: <www.justassociates.org> (accessed 27 November 2007).

36. Anon. slumdweller, interview with the author, December 2004, Kampala: SDI *Archives*, p. 270.

37. Celine D'Cruz, interview with the author, August 2004, Durban: SDI *Archives*, p. 16.

38. Joel Bolnick and Sheela Patel, *Regaining Knowledge: An Appeal to Abandon Illusions*, Mumbai: Society for the Promotion of Area Resource Centers, 1994, p. 56.

39. Anon. slumdweller, interview with the author, September 2004, Cape Town: SDI *Archives*, p. 96.

40. Joel Bolnick, interview with author, December 2004, London: SDI *Archives*, p. 17.

41. Anon. slumdweller, interview with the author, November 2004, Nairobi: SDI *Archives*, p. 49.

42. Anon. slumdweller, interview with the author, November 2003, General Santos City, Philippines: SDI *Archives*, p. 370.

16

FROM ECO-SUFFICIENCY TO GLOBAL JUSTICE

Ariel Salleh

How relevant is ecological economics in the current struggle between forces for global integration and forces for local autonomy? Can the hybrid discipline respond to the knowledge base of a new green and culturally diverse labour movement? This chapter broadens the notion of reproductive labour as developed in feminist political economy, in order to analyse the nature of ecological work – provisioning activities, that are at once economic, sustainable, and autonomous. It finds that *eco-sufficiency* is already modelled by the global majority of labour – indigenous, peasant, and care-giving workers. But the question is: can theorists in the global North share intellectual and political agency with these *meta-industrial* workers and can they grasp the idea of *metabolic value* as a domain construct in economics?

The relevance of ecological feminism to ecological economics was acknowledged quite early on by figures as eminent as Martin O'Connor, Ramachandra Guha, Joan Martinez-Alier, Bina Agarwal, and Richard Norgaard.[1] Agarwal supported its relevance in a postcolonial context, pointing to women's skill in traditional agriculture and medicine, and how socially constructed care-giving roles are compromised when peasant and indigenous women lack property. Ecofeminism is indeed an 'environmentalism of the poor', and even in the global North, women, as a result of their regenerative labours, experience kinds of poverty and pain that are unknown to men.[2] This is why Veronika Bennholdt-

Thomsen and Maria Mies recommend a methodology of working with the 'view from below',

> ... to demystify the delusions created by those 'on top' that their life and lifestyle are not only the best possible ones but also the image of the future for everybody on this planet ... [In fact] the so-called good life is possible only for a minority and ... [enjoyed] at the expense of others: of nature, of other peoples, of women and children.[3]

At this stage, mainstream economics, and much ecological economics, by conceptualising what is meaningful to men with eurocentric leanings, works with a 'view from above'. Economics as a sustainability science deals merely with the tip of the productivist iceberg, while the greater part of economic transfers between humans and nature are not even named.

Towards that naming, this chapter will compare an ecological economics guided by abstract market indicators, with models of provisioning that engage with ecological integrity. Too much of what passes for economic expertise today, is so decontextualised as to be inaccurate. Worse, the professional advice itself, is marketed as a commodity. A plethora of policy 'measures' exist to mitigate climate change, biodiversity loss, chemical or nuclear emissions, but taxes and subsidies, green engineering, and bioethical formulae, simply stitch up an incoherent neoliberal system tailored to individual gain. Sociologists have various theories about how capitalist production has disconnected humanity from nature. Peter Dickens identifies the modern 'alienated consciousness' as an inevitable outcome of the industrial division of labour.[4] In related vein, John Bellamy Foster explains diminished human capacity for ecological understanding as a corollary of the 'metabolic rift' between town and country. Corporate globalisation and free trade has now multiplied and magnified this rift across the face of the earth. It is certainly true that the more technologically mediated life tasks are, the more people lose a psychological sense of their own organic interchange with nature. Silvia Federici uses the word 'amnesia' to describe this loss of knowledge – and environmental abuse is an expression of that interior splitting.[5] But this dissociated instrumental rationality has not colonised every part of the globe. People in many locations do understand their material embodiment in nature, and they know how to practise eco-sufficiency.

A major foundational thinker in ecological economics, Nicholas Georgescu-Roegen was seriously committed to seeing humans meet their needs in an ecologically sound way. In sharp contrast to Keynesian convention, he brought an awareness of biological systems and the thermodynamic principles that apply to them into economic reasoning.[6] Stephen Bunker carried this sensitivity forward, observing that:

> The long-term maintenance of human life depends on energy transformation processes of which we are not yet aware ... Extraction and production originally occurred together in social formations bounded by a single regional eco-system. In such conditions, human needs usually distributed extractive activity across a wide range of species and minerals; relatively little matter and energy were extracted from each of a large number of forms, so biotic chains could reproduce themselves stably ... Industrial modes of production ... inevitably undermine the resource bases on which they depend ... The idea that nature can be socially created is thus a peculiar illusion based on a partial vision.[7]

However, to be fully adequate to the task, an ecological economics – just like green political theory or environmental ethics – will draw on the conceptual lenses of psychology, sociology, political, and cultural studies too.[8] The latter especially, can enrich the professional imagination in the search for alternatives to the growth paradigm. Beyond these inputs again, stands the sex/gendered depth analysis or 'bioenergetics' introduced by an embodied materialist analysis.[9] Currently, in ecological economics 'embodied energy' refers to exosomatic facts, for example the quantity of fuel invested in the life-cycle of a product from manufacture, through transport, to consumption. In ecological feminism, embodied energy refers to subjective or endosomatic energy flows, through human labour, sexuality, and generative nature at large. Clearly, such an idea has the potential to make a profound intervention in what Donella Meadows dubbed the 'pre-analytic vision' of ecological economics.[10]

The difference between an externalising or 'scientistic' perception of natural energy and an embodied one is apparent in this extract from *Wikipedia*:

> Natural capital can be considered the planetary endowment of scarce matter and energy, along with the complex and biologically diverse ecosystems that provide goods and services directly to human communities: micro- and macro-climate regulation, water recycling, water purification, storm water regulation, waste absorption, pollination, protection from solar and cosmic radiation, etc.[11]

Here 'scarcity' appears as an ontological constant rather than a man made anomaly; and living systems are projected as effectively 'dead matter' or capital, potentially commodifiable goods and services. There is little sense of active human co-evolution – rather, it is 'the planet' (not women's bodies, for instance) that endows the system with human resources. The extract bypasses the historically gendered, class, or racialised context of economics leaving the objectifying capitalist patriarchal vocabulary of human and natural capital unexamined. Now of course, *Wikipedia* is not academia, but it does reflect the state of play. The psychology of externalisation is assisted by all kinds of quantifying devices, and this in the face of overwhelming evidence of regional, temporal, and other empirical incommensurabilities in the economic field.

Another typical distancing technique is projection of the economy as 'an engine'. For Robert Costanza, this machine runs on four kinds of measurable capital – built, human, social, and natural, all readily substituted one for another in production. The achievement of human satisfaction or Quality of Life (QOL) depends on getting the balance of system components right.[12] Consequently, Costanza and colleagues translate the holistic work of Chilean economist Manfred Max-Neef into a reductive number crunching North American QOL study as follows:

> We split off [sic.] a new category titled 'reproduction' from Max-Neef's subsistence category ... acknowledging the importance of reproduction has significant policy implications particularly regarding women and their role [sic.] in society.[13]

Why should reproductive activities be 'split off' from subsistence? And why should reproductive activities be split off 'as women's role'? Men are quite capable of regenerative forms of labour and the life affirming epistemology learned from doing them. For example, the meta-industrial provisioning of peasants or gatherers, demonstrates an economic model that synergises the satisfaction of human needs with enhanced metabolic flows in nature.

All this said, ecological economists are opening up the positivist hegemony in many ways; and artificially imposed divisions of men versus women, and humans versus nature, are being challenged. Consider the progressive moves made over the years by the celebrated ecological economist Herman Daly. Alongside the canon of economic efficiency, he has introduced 'environmental sustainability and social justice' as key objectives of the discipline.[14] Alongside GNP, he has advocated the Genuine Progress Indicator (GPI). Alongside, chrematistics, he has reminded us that the origin of the word economics is *oikos*, the study of households, with the ecosystem being like a human household writ large. Beyond short-term productivism, Daly knows that biological time and reproduction is slower than economic time or production, and that intergenerational equity will call for thinking with a long time horizon. Beyond economic reductionism, Daly endorses transdisciplinarity, methodological triangulation, and the democratic principle of subsidiarity.[15]

Yet in other respects, the conservative functionalist heritage of neoclassical economics is still active beneath Daly's approach, and these elements may sometimes cancel out its more progressive implications. The mandatory mathematical modelling is there. And the focus on 'sustainable scale', 'just distribution', and 'efficient allocation' as core processes resonates all too easily with the happy consciousness of green business and its 'triple bottom line'.[16] The three core variables – scale, distribution, allocation – operate within an *ad hoc* system, whose imaginary boundaries are never justified by the economist. Using the abstract language of systems theory and cybernetic analogies, this ecological economics reifies 'the economy' much as the old 'hidden hand' of market liberalism has done. And while scale, distribution, and allocation, are discussed within the rationalist framework of bureaucratic instrumentalism, the objective of top-down manageability looks all too similar to 'a god's eye view' in secular guise. A major defect of systems analysis is that economic functions are described in the passive voice, so creating a sense of anonymity and inevitability. The approach hides differences of power between classes, races, genders, and deflects people's belief in their own capacity for taking responsibility.

A related problem is the idealism that characterises Daly's treatment of value as 'psychic benefit'. Moreover, the discussion tends to proceed in an essentialist way, as if these benefits would be the same for executives and indigenes, or for mothers and fathers.[17] Decision-making parameters like 'marginal benefit' versus 'marginal opportunity cost' also operate in an ahistorical vacuum without a socially specified subject. This ostensibly neutral methodology inadvertently sanitises patterns of distribution and allocation as objective mechanisms. In reality, distribution and allocation are the outcome of decisions made by specific kinds of subject (usually white middle class men) over the life circumstances of apparently lesser humans, the de facto objects of the global North (women everywhere, peasants and indigenes in the South). When the social subject of an analysis is omitted, it reads as if an ideal typical and intrinsic 'human nature' is involved.

By contrast, the transdisciplinary economist might discuss scale, distribution, and allocation, in a way that is more finely attuned to class, ethnicity, gender, and species differences. The key questions would be: Who is it that decides on scale? Who distributes to whom? Who is entitled to make allocations? And: Why? Criticism aside, Daly is a leader among those ecological economists who define 'human capital' and 'natural capital' as interlinked. By destabilising the conventional dualism of humanity and nature as separate spheres of reality, this work begins to shift an assumption traditionally used by a eurocentric civilisation to justify political domination in all its forms. But the transformative potential of ecological economics remains latent as long as sociological bias in its analytic tools passes unnoticed. True, at academic conferences, it is now mandatory to include sections on peasant and indigenous societies, and to host a feminist symposium. But are these treated merely as 'add-ons' to round out the pluralism of an enlightened hegemony? Are these marginal strands basically seen as 'problem areas', examples of distributional conflicts, or 'externalities' waiting to be assimilated to the master-map of ecological economics?

Reproductive labour as leverage

What if the suggestion were made that in building an alternative and truly global political ecology, ecological economics, or environmental ethics, it is just these problematic marginals – house workers, peasants, indigenes – who can model social justice and sustainability for the twenty-first century?[18] Where would such a claim fall in the discourse of ecological economics? Would it entail a move too far beyond the comfort zone of its nascent knowledge base? Are mothers or hunter-gatherers too 'negatively constructed', 'dependent' or 'deviant', as Daly et al. might explain, in relation to the exercise of power, 'the power to name' and the power to theorise? Guha and Martinez-Alier have provided ecological economics with a magisterial review of environmental politics among peasant communities. And John Gowdy, a student of Georgescu-Roegen, defends the rationality of indigenous provisioning practices.[19] But will it be up to ecological feminists, largely outside of the discipline, to flag the significance of an embodied materialist epistemology and women's practical leadership in sustainability science?

This task certainly calls for a deconstruction of conventional wisdom. For instance: if 'scarcity' is a pivotal notion in capitalist patriarchal economics, so 'incapacity' is pivotal to its psychology of domination. As the standard line goes, too many women, the majority of the world's poor, are hopeless victims of masculine violence and exploitation; while peoples of the global South must soon fall under the 'inexorable' wheel of 'modernisation and progress'. This is why neoliberal criteria of success, such as individualistic emancipation and market participation for women, export-led development for peasants, and eco-tourism for First Nation Peoples, are promoted as attractive deals. The UN, WB, G8, and WTO, and quite a few ecological economists, are concerned to see the so-called poor grasp 'the first rung of the development ladder'; but the other side of this coin is entrapment by failing capitalist institutions, with decimation of meta-industrial labour and livelihood resources. George Caffentzis writes that in development discourse, 'extreme poverty' has two contradictory meanings; either (1) 'that households cannot meet basic needs' or (2) they cannot achieve 'an income of $1 per day per person'. Thus, the hypothetical pauper would live on 'the "goods and services" that can be bought for $1 a day in the US'. But, Caffentzis reminds us, there are also viable non-monetary economies out there.

> There are many villages where 'basic needs' of their residents as they conceive them are satisfied, but whose collective income is less than $365 a year per person ... in many villages in Africa adults (including, in certain areas, women) have *access to* (although *not ownership of*) land that they can use for subsistence. This is an enormous wealth ('use value') that cannot be alienated and hence does not have an 'exchange value.' ... Similar points can be made about children. In many parts of Africa, children are 'shared' by villages or extended families and their actual income is below $1 a day per person. These children often have their 'basic needs' satisfied in a collective manner.[20]

Under the UN development model, common land, water, biodiversity, labour, and loving relationships, are pulled away from an ecologically sustainable and culturally autonomous web of self-sufficiency. By the North versus South, 1/0 logic, modernisation means that people must be turned into 'human capital' and their life resources turned into 'natural capital' (primarily to benefit an international minority class of entrepreneurs and its governmental hangers-on).[21] For centuries, communities from Africa to Oceania to South America and beyond, have confronted this appropriation in struggles to control their own local resources. Are ecological economists on their side? Or does the discipline unwittingly, by default, support the colonising mindset with its effects in ecological and *embodied debt*?

Today, there is alarm in international sustainable development circles about rising consumption and emission levels as India and China develop to 'the standard of living' of the global North. But turning the sociological spotlight around, a Swedish government report for instance, concedes that in the year 2000 each Swede ate almost 40 kg of food more than ten years ago and 30 kg more than the European average. The EU consumed more than the whole of Asia put together.[22] Meanwhile, the industrial states, with an ecological footprint that spans 80 per cent of world resources, continue to blame populations at the periphery for environmental degradation introduced by the export of their own 'metabolic rift'. Given this context, the proposition that care-giving women, small farmers or gatherers, are skilled ecological economic managers may prove hard to get across. The suggestion may threaten privileges enjoyed by global business and academic elites. Furthermore, the notion of meta-industrial competence is intellectually demanding, because it involves two apparently competing political principles – 'equality and difference'. As things stand, Daly's objectives of 'environmental sustainability, social justice, and economic efficiency' are extrapolated from the principle of equality within the given economic order. But is this kind of nip and tuck enough, if the social relations of production on which this order rests are fundamentally insecure and unjust relations?

Applying the principles of equality and difference calls for a socio-cultural awareness that is unevenly developed in the transdiscipline of ecological economics. The principle of 'difference' may seem counter-intuitive in a closed hegemonic system, because it signals the incapable 'other' of the capitalist patriarchal mindset. Additionally, in dealing with 'otherness', political ecologists and ecological economists may encounter what seem like conflicting positions within the feminist and postcolonial literature. But here, the scholar needs to bear in mind just who is speaking. Liberal feminist and uncritically productivist Left analyses will reason in favour of emancipation through the industrial paradigm based on an equitable re-distribution of the social product. But as far as political ecology goes, neither of these standpoints makes sense in terms of protecting metabolic value. The problem is '... most theorists of development have attempted to extend models derived from systems of industrial production to nonindustrial systems for which they have only limited relevance ... [but] exchange value is produced [only] in the relation between capital and labor'.[23] That is why ecological feminists maintain that the eco-sufficient sphere of regenerative labour and use value is more important for economics than the sphere of production for exchange. Ecofeminists who adopt this approach include Maria Mies, Vandana Shiva, Mary Mellor, and myself.[24] It is a standpoint grounded in labour – not for instance, an ideological or sociobiological argument about women being 'closer to nature' or 'better than men'. Nor as a historical thesis, is ecofeminism a celebration of idealisms like 'the essential feminine' or 'the noble savage', as defensive development studies academics might assert.[25] An embodied materialist epistemology is based on the day to day experience of negotiating humanity–nature relations. So too, it refutes the self-comforting liberal contention that affluence and post-materialist values are what give rise to environmental consciousness.[26]

An embodied materialism

An embodied materialism encapsulates interactions between habitat, sex, race, governance, science, ethics – an uneasy complexity for stochastic processing! Economists are comfortable measuring what they call 'productivity' but have a hard time accounting for 'reproductivity'. Yet if Georgescu-Roegen's insights were to be honoured consistently, his hybrid practitioners would go straight to the energetics of regenerative cycles. Thus, ecological economists who study material flows recognise that 'The productivity of labor can only be increased by simultaneously increasing the appropriation and transformation of energy stored in material forms produced in nature ...'[27] However, what is missing from that value equation is the role of reproductive or meta-industrial labour in mediating matter/energy transformations and minimising metabolic depletion. The question is: Who in ecological economics has such knowledge to bring to the table?

This is where the ethos of a 'post-normal science' is salient, for the condition of post-normalcy is that domain assumptions must be permanently under consensual review.[28] With such an exercise in mind, Meadows was well ahead of her time in claiming that ecological economics needs a conceptual 'leverage point'. My own response is to suggest that the notions of meta-industrial labour as regenerative and *metabolic fit* as eco-sufficiency, can provide this conceptual leverage.[29]

What follows is an analysis of how meta-industrial provisioning achieves eco-sufficiency based on a phenomenological reading of three exemplars.[30] The first is Vandana Shiva's case study of Indian forest dwellers, a statement of co-evolution and regenerative agency in conditions of scientific complexity. As she writes:

> It is in managing the integrity of ecological cycles in forestry and agriculture that women's [re]productivity has been most developed and evolved. Women transfer fertility from the forests to the field and to animals. They transfer animal waste as fertilizer for crops and crop by-products to animals as fodder. This partnership between women's work and nature's work ensures the sustainability of sustenance.[31]

Similarly, Australian Aboriginal and South East Asian hunter-gatherers, in their deliberative manual work, practise a kind of 'systemic holding', nurturing sustainability as they move through country.[32] In this most efficient and eco-sufficient of bioregional economies, the seasonal walk through country is made in the knowledge that with insightful harvesting, each habitat will replenish and provide again on the return. As Gowdy has noted: the efficiency of the hunter-gatherer is marked in the fact that he or she rarely uses up more matter/energy in resources than is needed for bodily provisioning.

Turning to meta-industrial labour in urban economies, German ecology activist Ulla Terlinden spells out the tacit epistemology behind household reproduction.

> Housework requires of women [or men] a broad range of knowledge and ability. The nature of the work itself determines its organization. The work

at hand must be dealt with in its entirety ... The worker must possess a high degree of personal synthesis, initiative, intuition and flexibility.[33]

Contrast this close empirical engagement with the fragmented industrial division of labour – the numb inconsequential mindset of the investor or assembly line operative. In the context of parental skills, US philosopher Sara Ruddick discusses 'holding' labour, as a manifestation of principles that clearly parallel good ecological reasoning, if not governance.

To hold means to minimize risk and to reconcile differences rather than to sharply accentuate them. Holding [by a man or woman] is a way of seeing with an eye toward maintaining the minimal harmony, material resources, and skills necessary for sustaining a child in safety. It is the attitude elicited by world protection, world-preservation, world-repair ... [34]

While minimising risk in the face of material uncertainty, meta-industrial holding is the ultimate expression of adaptability. And while science as usual is marred by the positivist separation of fact and value, space and time, a cautious awareness of interconnection is commonsense in this embodied materialism. Ironically perhaps, the exacting empiricism of meta-industrial labour, its inbuilt 'reality testing', compares favourably with the most stringent standards of scientific falsificationism.

The regenerative labour of indigenes, mothers, and subsistence workers has many methodological features which facilitate metabolic fit.

- The consumption footprint is small because local resources are used and monitored with daily care by the provisioner.
- Scale is intimate and hands-on, maximising responsiveness to matter/energy transformations so minimising entropy.
- Judgements are built up over time by trial and error, a cradle to grave assessment over an intergenerational time horizon.
- Meta-industrial labour is intrinsically precautionary.

- Lines of responsibility are transparent and accountable – far from the tyranny of small decisions that impairs bureaucratised economies.
- As local social structures are less convoluted than modern industrial ones, there is opportunity for synergistic problem solving.[35]
- In domestic and farm settings, multi-criteria decision-making is essential.
- Regenerative work patiently reconciles human time with unpredictable, non-linear timings in nature.[36]
- This is an economic rationality that knows the difference between stocks and flows.
- It is an autonomous and empowering work process, without a division between the worker's mental and manual skills.
- The labour product is not alienated but immediately enjoyed or shared.
- Meta-industrial provisioning is eco-sufficient because it does not externalise costs through debt.

A number of these observations converge with Daly's interest in economic scale.[37] However, while Daly conceptualises economics and ecology as essentially about 'household functions', and while he will impute monetary value to 'ecological services provided by nature', women's domestic work remains un-valued. Similarly, in the context of the Two Thirds World, Daly's tri-partite functions of scale, distribution, and allocation, also beg a second look. Distribution and allocation either become irrelevant or take a very different form where eco-sufficient provisioning is practised among communities who own land, water, and biodiversity in common, and where an ethic of cooperative labour has survived the onslaught of individualistic 'development'. Martinez-Alier has also argued this point in order to underscore the parochial origins of ecological economics in eurocentric modernity. On the other hand, as the study of political economy is transformed into political ecology, the concept of a meta-industrial class is both integrating and politically inclusive. Women and men from all societies undertake reproductive labour – economic, cultural, and biological – at some stage in their lives. Increasingly though, with modernisation, reproduction as an economically invisible, non-valued, non-monetised, process is avoided – at least by most men, and the handful of women who get to feel like winners for a while under the capitalist patriarchal regime.

Capacity building for the global North

Ecological economists who are not so introspective about the cultural context of their discipline, may find the present critique counter-intuitive. But the idea of 'human capital' can too readily become a sex/gender blind notion – just as the idea of 'the worker' was in early twentieth century Marxism. Productivist terminology papers over the complex of reproductive 'services' provided by women. Without a tool of leverage like 'meta-industrial labour', the intricate thermodynamic contribution of household caregivers can be passed over. Racialised blindness around the work of forest dwellers is a related problem. When labour is ideologically 'naturalised' by gender or race, it becomes non-human, a free resource, an instance of embodied debt. The old humanity versus nature dualism is still a pervasive myth in the dominant culture and in its academic disciplines.

Thus it is one thing to acknowledge, as Georgescu-Roegen did, that ecological economics must be rooted in the materiality of ecology and its matter/energy flows. It is another thing to see how ecological economics itself, is a practice fuelled in a subjectively bioenergetic or psychological sense. That is to say, a scholar's own class, race, or gender will to some extent determine what is plausible as a construct or method. Knowledge is always situated. And of course, if one is not personally disempowered by race or gender, it is easy to miss their significance. This could possibly explain why a massive study of global consumption undertaken in 2004 by the World Watch Institute failed to break down sex/gender differences in patterns of consumer behaviour. It may also help explain why some people keep saying that 'there are no alternatives' when so many others in the world already practise eco-sufficiency. As Nick Faraclas says: 'the alternatives are everywhere'.[38] And as Caffentzis adds:

... there is no automatic reason why people who have 'escaped the poverty trap' through decommodification of basic needs and the development of their commons will necessarily rush to sell their labor-power to the first capitalist offering a wage.[39]

To realise eco-sufficiency and global justice, the most effective 'millennial goal' will be to give back the land taken away from people in the name of 'development'.

The call for conceptual leverage in ecological economics is highlighted by Julie Nelson's brief observations on the self-referential tendency of the professional mainstream. This shows up as a

Preoccupation with status quo – Operating with a chronic assumption that the future will be much like the past.

Dedication to simplified interpretations – Relying on highly simplified characterization of human behaviour and highly aggregate analysis.

Sensitivity to disciplinary boundaries – Staying within rational choice modeling boundaries, neglecting most information from other disciplines.

Commitment to rigidity – Encouraging loyalty to accepted models, no matter how dysfunctional they become.

Deference to established hierarchy – Maintaining image of mainstream economists, whose work is peer reviewed by like-minded economists, as sole rational policy advisors.[40]

Nelson contrasts this closed in-house knowledge making with what she calls 'high reliability organisations' where decision-making power is always given to those with most expertise – regardless of rank. Nevertheless, the frequency of citations to post-normal science in the ecological economics literature indicates that many practitioners are indeed beginning to examine the social construction of their basic assumptions. And they are asking: Who speaks this analysis? What is my interest in formulating problems in the way I do? What entitles me to theorise? This kind of reflexivity can help open the paradigm of economics to voices and values of the global majority. But whereas the dialogic of post-normalcy seems to adopt a liberal-pluralist standpoint, with all positions equivalent to all others, an embodied materialism is not relativist but anchored in what works to protect metabolic value – the ecological bottom line.

As global capitalism begins to unravel, people will be forced to ask: What is the value of 'value'? And they may get to see how self contradictory an economic system is, when it is premised on the denial of human embodiment in nature.[41] So too, exchange value, and even use value in part, will be exposed as narrow anthropocentric notions, arbitrarily constructed through the actions of powerful men. The real 'bottom line' is ecological integrity – a complex of processes signified by metabolic value. One small pioneering nation, Ecuador, now anticipates this conceptual shift in its new Constitution, a document that dissolves the eurocentric humanity versus nature dualism by giving juridical rights to nature. As Article 1 of this Constitution reads:

> Nature or Pachamama, where life is reproduced and exists, has the right to exist, persist, maintain and regenerate its vital cycles, structure, functions and its processes in evolution ... Every person, people, community or nationality, will be able to demand the recognition of rights for nature before the public institutions.[42]

This legal breakthrough opens the way for the further articulation of metabolic value, and then, its institutional endorsement at the heart of community governance and economic reasoning.

At the 2002 World Summit on Sustainable Development in Johannesburg, the 'other' experience of care givers, small farmers, and First Nation Peoples, was presented as 'cultural not economic'. It was located outside the white middle class masculine government and UN agency discourse of sustainability science. At Davos, the World Economic Forum of global capitalist leaders continues this subterfuge. But the WEF is now dual powered by World Social Forum meetings at Porto Alegre, Mumbai, Nairobi. Additionally, the losers under capitalist patriarchal globalisation have been in the streets from Cochabamba to Budapest, and setting up conferences and websites to contest WTO and G8 policies. This historical turning point began at the 1999 Seattle

Peoples' Caucus, when a meeting convened by the Indigenous Environmental Network USA/Canada, Seventh Generation Fund USA, and others, told the world:

> ... we believe that it is also us who can offer viable alternatives to the dominant economic growth, export-oriented development model. Our sustainable lifestyles and cultures, traditional knowledge, cosmologies, spirituality, values of collectivity, reciprocity, respect and reverence for Mother Earth, are crucial in the search for a transformed society where justice, equity, and sustainability will prevail.[43]

The impending meltdown of international capital brings the *alter-mondiale* movement to the front line. And in order to support what these activists are saying, political ecologists, green thinkers, ecological economists, feminists, and other caring people, might focus on three interweaving goals:

- *Ecological Sustainability*: protecting the material/energetic interdependency of species, sex/genders, and generations.
- *Socio-Economic Justice*: protecting metabolic value and the sovereignty of common livelihood.
- *Cultural Autonomy*: protecting 'difference' and the diversity of economic and social practices.

The more complex and technologically developed a society becomes, the harder such political objectives are to reconcile. But an autonomous reproductive labour class, marginal to the neoliberal economy, is well equipped to teach this synergy. In many postcolonial contexts, meta-industrial models remain intact; and already women and men in the global North are setting up their own alternative economies in bioregional networks, spiritual farming communes, local community gardens, and organic markets.[44] As ecological economists reflect on Daly's formula for 'environmental sustainability, social justice, and economic efficiency', some may see sense in replacing his category of efficiency by 'cultural autonomy'. For 'efficiency' is meaningless if the international economic system itself is internally contradictory. It is surely a good time now, for professionals and global justice activists to sit down and talk together, and for both to talk with people who have a developed capacity for eco-sufficiency. But in this, there is a respectful caveat to observe too; as Australian Aboriginal activist Lilla Watson put it:[45]

> If you have come to help me, you are wasting your time. But if you have come because your liberation is bound up with mine, then let us work together.

Notes

1. Martin O'Connor (ed.), *Is Capitalism Sustainable?*, New York: Guilford, 1994; Ramachandra Guha and Joan Martinez-Alier, *Varieties of Environmentalism*, London: Earthscan, 1997, pp. 33–4; Bina Agarwal, 'The Gender and Environment Debate: Lessons from India', *Feminist Studies*, 1992, Vol. 18, No. 1, 119–58; Richard Norgaard, *Development Betrayed*, New York: Routledge, 1994.
2. For the universality of women's exploitation, see: Marilyn Waring, *Counting for Nothing*, Sydney: Allen and Unwin, 1988, a thoroughgoing gender critique of the UN System of National Accounts (UNSNA).
3. Veronika Bennholdt-Thomsen and Maria Mies, *The Subsistence Perspective*, London: Zed Books, 1999, p. 93.
4. Peter Dickens, *Reconstructing Nature*, London: Routledge, 1995; and for an extended account of metabolic rift: John Bellamy Foster, *Marx's Ecology*, New York: Monthly Review, 2000. The humanity–nature metabolism is the harmonious process by which humans take what they need from nature, digest, and give back in return. Marx observed that industrialisation and the rise of cities created a 'metabolic rift' in this thermodynamic reciprocity, with environmental degradation an inevitable result. See also Pat Devine and Ted Benton, 'On the Metabolism between Society and Nature in the UK', *Capitalism Nature Socialism*, 2007, Vol. 18, No. 3, a symposium by members of the UK Red-Green Study Group; and refer again to my chapter 'Ecological Debt: Embodied Debt' in this anthology.
5. Silvia Federici, 'Women, Land-Struggles and the Valorization of Labor', *The Commoner*, 2005, No. 10, Available Online: <www.thecommoner.org> (accessed 5 October 2006); Silvia Federici, *Caliban and the Witch*, New York: Autonomedia, 2004; Ariel Salleh, 'Body Logic: 1/0 Culture' in *Ecofeminism as Politics: Nature, Marx, and the Postmodern*, London: Zed Books, 1997.

6. Nicholas Georgescu-Roegen, *The Entropy Law and the Economic Process*, Harvard University Press, 1971.

7. Stephen Bunker, 'Natural Values and the Physical Inevitability of Uneven Development under Capitalism' in Alf Hornborg, J.R. McNiell, and Joan Martinez-Alier (eds), *Rethinking Environmental History*, Lanham, MD: Altamira, 2007, pp. 251, 254–5.

8. Clive Spash, 'The Development of Ecological Thinking in Economics', *Environmental Values*, 1999, Vol. 8, No. 3, 413–35.

9. On ecofeminist energetics: Salleh, 'As Energy / Labour Flows' in *Ecofeminism as Politics*, pp. 150–69; Vandana Shiva, *Staying Alive: Women, Ecology and Development*, London: Zed Books, 1989; Teresa Brennan, *Exhausting Modernity*, London: Routledge, 1997.

10. Donella Meadows, 'Places to Intervene in a System', *Whole Earth Magazine*, 1997, Winter, Online Available HTTP: <www. wholeearthmag.com/ArticleBin/109.html> (accessed 31 October 2006).

11. Wikipedia, 'Ecological Economics', *Wikipedia: The Free Encyclopedia*, Online Available HTTP: <www.wikipedia> (accessed 30 October 2006).

12. Robert Costanza et al., 'Quality of Life: An Approach Integrating Opportunities, Human Needs, and Subjective Well Being', *Ecological Economics*, 2006, Vol. 61, No. 2, 267–76. 'Quality of Life' is defined as: 'the interaction of human needs and the subjective perception of their fulfillment, as mediated by the opportunities available to meet the needs', p. 270.

13. Ibid., p. 271. Compare Manfred Max-Neef et al., *Human Scale Development*, New York: Apex, 1991.

14. For a recent contribution: Herman Daly, Jon Erickson, and Joshua Farley, *Ecological Economics: A Workbook for Problem Based Learning*, Washington: Island Press, 2005.

15. On subsidiarity: ibid., p. 202.

16. On the tri-partite model: ibid., pp. 6, 26.

17. On psychic benefits: ibid., p. 38. Compare Linda Kaloff and Terre Satterfield (eds), *The Earthscan Reader in Environmental Values*, London: Earthscan, 2005; Peter Soderbaum, *Ecological Economics*, London: Earthscan, 2000.

18. On 'meta-industrial' provisioning and 'embodied materialism': Salleh, 'As Energy / Labour Flows' and 'Agents of Complexity' in *Ecofeminism as Politics*, pp. 164–6 and 175–8; Ariel Salleh, 'Globalisation and the Meta-Industrial Alternative' in Robert Albritton et al. (eds), *New Socialisms: Futures Beyond Globalization*, London: Routledge, 2004. From an embodied materialist perspective, the unique rationality of meta-industrial labour – by peasants,

indigenes, and household caregivers – is a capacity to provision eco-sufficiently, without causing ecological and embodied debt.

19. Guha and Martinez-Alier, *Varieties of Environmentalism*; John Gowdy (ed.), *Limited Wants, Unlimited Means: A Reader in Hunter-Gatherer Economics and the Environment*, Washington: Island Press, 1998; Serge Latouche, *In the Wake of the Affluent Society: An Exploration in Post-development*, M. O'Connor and R. Arnoux (trans.), London: Zed Books, 1993.

20. George Caffentzis, 'Dr. Jeffrey Sachs' *The End of Poverty*: A Political Review', *The Commoner*, 2005, No. 10, Online Available HTTP: <www.thecommoner.org.uk> (accessed 31 October 2006). See also Tony Waters, *The Persistence of Subsistence Agriculture*, Lanham, MD: Lexington, 2007, and Wolfgang Sachs, 'Environment and Human Rights', *Wuppertal Papers*, 2003, No. 137 where an argument is made for the recognition of 'subsistence rights' in international law.

21. Rosa Luxemburg's insight into how capitalism cannot maintain its profits without colonisation and subsumption of the periphery has influenced several materialist ecofeminists, particularly Maria Mies, *Patriarchy and Accumulation on a World Scale*, London: Zed Books, 1986.

22. Gerd Johnsson-Latham, *Initial Study of Lifestyles, Consumption Patterns, Sustainable Development and Gender*, Stockholm: Swedish Ministry of Sustainable Development, 2006, p. 6.

23. Bunker in Hornborg et al., *Rethinking Environmental History*, p. 247, p. 252.

24. For materialist ecofeminism, see: Maria Mies et al., *Women: The Last Colony*, London: Zed Books, 1988; Mary Mellor, *Breaking the Boundaries*, London: Virago, 1992; Shiva, *Staying Alive*; Salleh, *Ecofeminism as Politics*; Federici, *Caliban and the Witch*.

25. For an exchange over ecofeminism versus 'equality' developmentalism: Ariel Salleh, 'An Ecofeminist Bioethic: And What Post-humanism Really Means', *New Left Review*, 1996, No. 217, 138–47. Recently, the ecofeminist case for cultural autonomy appears as a liberal appeal for 'cognitive justice', see: Shiv Visvanathan, 'Knowledge, Justice and Democracy' in M. Leach et al. (eds), *Science and Citizens*, London: Zed Books, 2005.

26. Ronald Ingelhart, *The Silent Revolution*, Princeton University Press, 1977. Likewise, when a notion like 'intrinsic value' is introduced into ecological economics, it is important that it should be a materially grounded construct: see John Proops, 'Ecological Economics: Rationale and Problem Areas', *Ecological Economics*, 1989, Vol. 1, No. 1, 59–76.

27. Bunker in Hornborg et al. (eds), *Rethinking Environmental History*, p. 239.

28. Silvio Funtowicz and Jerome Ravetz, 'Post-Normal Science: Environmental Policy Under Conditions of Complexity', 2004, Online Available HTTP: <www.nusap.net> (accessed 12 November 2004). This in turn, builds on Thomas Kuhn, *The Structure of Scientific Revolutions*, University of Chicago Press, 1962.

29. In using the word 'fit', I am inspired by Jessie Wirrpa, one of the Australian Aboriginal mentors of anthropologist Deborah Bird Rose, author of 'Fitting into Country', *Capitalism Nature Socialism*, 2008, Vol. 19, No. 3, 117–21. At the same time, the idea speaks to Marx's 'metabolic rift', Bellamy Foster, *Marx's Ecology*.

30. The present discussion adapts and builds on work by Salleh, cited in note 18. This seemingly everyday analysis of labour takes validation from Marx, see: Paul Paolucci, 'Assumptions of the Dialectical Method: The Centrality of Labor for the Human Species, Its History, and Individuals', *Critical Sociology*, 2005, Vol. 31, No. 4, 559–81.

31. Shiva, *Staying Alive*, p. 45. See also the subsistence perspective in Bennholdt-Thomsen and Mies, *The Subsistence Perspective*, and Hilkka Pietila, 'Cultivation and Households: The Basics of Nurturing Human Life', *Encyclopedia of Life Support Systems*, Oxford: UNESCO / EOLSS, 2004. The standpoint is supported by contemporary science, for example: Catherine Badgley et al., 'Organic Agriculture and the Global Food Supply', *Renewable Agriculture and Food Systems*, 2007, Vol. 22, No. 1, 86–108. The authors note that: 'Model estimates indicate that organic methods could produce enough food on a global per capita basis to sustain the current human population, and potentially an even larger population ... while reducing the detrimental environmental impacts of conventional agriculture', p. 86.

32. Deborah Rose, *Nourishing Terrains: Australian Aboriginal Views of Landscape and Wilderness*, Canberra: Australian Heritage Commission, 1996.

33. Ulla Terlinden, 'Women in the Ecology Movement' in E. Altbach et al. (eds), *German Feminism*, Albany: SUNY Press, 1984, p. 320.

34. Sara Ruddick, *Maternal Thinking: Toward a Politics of Peace*, Boston: Beacon, 1989, p. 75.

35. On the term 'synergistic', see Max-Neef et al., *Human Scale Development*, and to paraphrase his thesis: Self-managed indigenous economies may synergistically satisfy many needs at once. They are not only environmentally benign, but creatively social. Besides subsistence, they foster learning, participation, innovation, ritual, identity, and belonging. A high quality of life can be enjoyed on

three hours work a day. By contrast, the engineered satisfiers of industrial societies like bureaucracies or cars, cost much energy and time, sabotaging the convenience they were designed for.

36. Barbara Adam, *Timescapes of Modernity: The Environment and Invisible Hazards*, London: Routledge, 1998.

37. On scale: Daly et al., *Ecological Economics*, pp. 19, 124.

38. Nicholas Faraclas, 'Melanesia, the Banks, and the BINGOs: Real Alternatives are Everywhere (Except in the Consultants' Briefcases)' in Veronika Bennholdt-Thomsen, Nicholas Faraclas, and Claudia von Werlhof (eds), *There Is An Alternative: Subsistence and Worldwide Resistance to Corporate Globalization*, London: Zed Books, 2001.

39. Caffentzis, 'Dr. Jeffrey Sachs' *The End of Poverty*'.

40. Julie Nelson, 'Economists, Value Judgements, and Climate Change', Global Development and Environment Institute, Working Paper 2007, No: 07-03, Tufts University, Medford, MA, p. 10.

41. See also Salleh, 'The Deepest Contradiction' in *Ecofeminism as Politics*, pp. 86–99.

42. 'Ecuador: Nature Has Rights', *Green Left Weekly*, 10 September 2008, reprinted from Online Available HTTP: <www.climateand-capitalism.com> (accessed 5 September 2008).

43. Tebtebba Foundation, 'Indigenous Peoples' Seattle Declaration on the Third Ministerial Meeting of the World Trade Organization', Seattle, 8 December 1999, Online Posting <tebtebba@skyinet.net>. Further to the alternative globalisation movement and its use of the World Social Forum process: Jackie Smith et al., *Global Democracy and the World Social Forums*, Boulder: Paradigm, 2008.

44. The literature on meta-industrial alternatives is extensive. An important recent addition to the literature is James Arvanitakis, *The Cultural Commons of Hope*, Berlin: Verlag, 2007. See among others, essays by Gustavo Esteva, Farida Akhter, Helena Norberg Hodge, Christa Muller, and Elisabeth Meyer-Renschhausen in Bennholdt-Thomsen et al., *There Is An Alternative*; the North American Left Biocentrism site, Online Available HTTP: <www. home.ca.inter. net/~greenweb/> (accessed 1 September 2007); experimental projects reported in Liam Leonard (ed.) Special Issue on Utopias, *Ecopolitics*, 2008, Vol. 1, No. 1, Online Available HTTP: <www. ecopoliticsonline.com> (accessed 7 February 2008); and Rachel Stein (ed.), *New Perspectives on Environmental Justice: Gender, Sexuality and Activism*, Rutgers University Press, 2004; Ted Trainer, *Abandon Affluence!*, London: Zed Books, 1987.

45. This often quoted remark by Lilla Watson is widely believed to have been first made at the World Conference to Review and Appraise the Achievements of the UN Decade for Women in Nairobi, 1985.

NOTES ON CONTRIBUTORS

Editor

Ariel Salleh is a researcher in Political Economy at the University of Sydney; longtime activist and Associate Professor in Social Ecology at the University of Western Sydney; author of *Ecofeminism as Politics* (1997) and many widely debated articles on ecopolitical thought.

Chapter authors

Peggy Antrobus is Caribbean co-founder of DAWN, and International Gender and Trade Network; author of *The Global Women's Movement* (2004).

Leigh Brownhill is a co-founder of First Woman: East and Southern African Women's Oral History and Indigenous Knowledge Network; co-editor of *Canadian Development Studies* (2002) special issue.

Ewa Charkiewicz is a gender consultant based in Poland and the Netherlands; co-author of *Transitions to Sustainable Production and Consumption* (2002).

Zohl dé Ishtar is an activist and researcher at the Centre for Peace and Conflict Studies, University of Queensland; author of *Daughters of the Pacific* (1994).

Silvia Federici is Emeritus Professor in International Relations, Hofstra University, US; activist; author of *Caliban and the Witch* (2004).

Gigi Francisco is South East Asia Regional Coordinator for DAWN, based in the Philippines; member of the International Gender and Trade Network.

Susan Hawthorne is the manager of Spinifex Press, Melbourne; activist, poet, and circus performer; author of *Wild Politics* (2002).

Ana Isla is a Peruvian feminist; teaching Sociology and Women's Studies at Brock University, Canada.

Mary Mellor is Professor of Sociology and Chair of the Institute for Sustainable Cities, Northumbria University; author of *Feminism and Ecology* (1997).

Andrea Moraes is a coordinator of Sister Watersheds, Canada/Brazil; lecturer at Ryerson and York University; PhD candidate at the University of Missouri.

Nalini Nayak is a Director of the Self Employed Women's Association, India; sociologist and advocate for fishing communities; co-author of *Conversations* (1999).

Sabine U. O'Hara is Executive Director, Council for International Exchange of Scholars, IIE, Washington DC; specialist in innovative community development; co-author of *Economic Theory for Environmentalists* (1995).

Patricia E. Perkins is Associate Professor in Environmental Studies at York University, Canada; co-editor of *Ecological Economics* (1997), feminist issue.

Leo Podlashuc is an activist with Shack/slum Dwellers International in Africa and Asia; author of *Voices from the Slums* (2007).

Meike Spitzner is Senior Researcher in Gender and Energy Policy at the Wuppertal Institute, Germany; transport adviser to the European Union.

Terisa E. Turner is Associate Professor in Sociology, University of Guelph, Canada; co-director of International Oil Working Group; co-editor of *Canadian Development Studies* (2002) special issue.

Marilyn Waring is a former Member of the New Zealand Parliament; Professor in Public Policy, Auckland University of Technology; author of *If Women Counted* (1987).

Section quotes

Veronika Bennholdt-Thomsen was formerly at University of Bielefeld and is now teaching ecofeminism in Mexico; co-author of *The Subsistence Perspective* (1999).

Teresa Brennan (d. 2003) was an Australian born, Distinguished Professor at Florida Atlantic University; author of *Globalization and its Terrors* (2003).

Carolyn Merchant is Professor of Environmental History, Philosophy and Ethics at UC Berkeley; pioneering ecofeminist, and author of *The Death of Nature* (1980).

Maria Mies is an activist; Emeritus Professor in Social Sciences, Institute for Development Studies, The Hague; author of *Patriarchy and Accumulation on a World Scale* (1986).

Hilkka Pietila is a former Secretary General of the United Nations in Finland; author of *Making Women Matter: The History of Women in the UN* (1993).

Vandana Shiva is Director of the Research Foundation for Science, Technology and Ecology in New Delhi; author of *Staying Alive: Women, Ecology, and Development* (1989).

INDEX